ADVANCE REVIEWS FOR *RECLAIMING DEVELOPMENT IN THE WORLD TRADING SYSTEM*

"Y. S. Lee has written on one of the most intriguing and topical questions facing the current WTO regulatory framework: the adequacy of the existing regime to account for all asymmetries across players. The first part of his book is a diagnosis: the existing regime is ill-equipped to deal with the situation before it. One might of course ask the question, how much can an international regime do to this effect? Development after all, is a wider ballgame, trade liberalization being one of its components (and of varying importance across players). This is where the second part of the book kicks in: when drafting his recipe, the author is well aware that he should be using instruments from the realm of trade policy. He does not prejudge in any way other forms of regulatory intervention. His focus though is trade: his Development-Facilitation Tariff is a tool in this perspective, although the author underscores his awareness that the possibility of abuse should not be underestimated. In the same manner, he goes on to propose a Development-Facilitation Subsidy that would account for the relative poverty of any given country. It is true that economists have often raised a brow when reading the existing WTO Subsidies agreement, and Lee's proposals in this context will find supporters in various corners. Lee explicitly recognizes that the WTO cannot by itself (by virtue of its narrow mandate) address all development policy issues faced by developing countries. His proposals are there to, first, ensure that the current international trade regime be an obstacle to development and, second, provide the necessary flexibility for countries faced with hard choices. His book is a contribution to an ongoing discussion and will provide a welcome addition to the existing literature."

Petros C. Mavroidis
Edwin B. Parker Professor of Law at Columbia Law School, New
York
University of Neuchâtel and CEPR.

"Professor Lee's well-written, well-researched book raises the challenging question of whether the current WTO rules might retard at least some developing countries' further economic improvement by 'kicking away the ladder' – prohibiting or limiting such tools as infant industry protection, which were used by Western countries during earlier stages of their development (and are still used even without that justification!). He makes innovative recommendations, such as a Development-Facilitation Tariff, but is aware of the possibilities of abuse (for example, he suggests public hearings to ensure more transparency than is typically the case with developed country protectionism). Similarly, his Development-Facilitation Subsidy would be limited by caps based on the relative poverty of the country. Even facially neutral trade defense measures such as anti-dumping and safeguards, which are permitted by the WTO as exceptions to free trade rules, can have perverse developmental effects. Local producers in a large market, such as Europe or the United States, can use these tools to protect a home market large enough to provide a viable production base for world scale production. By contrast, flower producers in Colombia or salmon producers in Chile – both nontraditional exports from countries with a history of monoculture – can lose their key markets (which of necessity are overseas) as a result of those measures. The possibility of reversing those measures prospectively after a three-year WTO litigation process, with no repayment of legally collected duties, is illusory for a industry that would be destroyed in the meantime. Supporters of current rules in the WTO, including proponents of adding Competition Law and Investment, will have to deal with Lee's arguments. Lee recognizes that trade rules alone are not the source of development. The challenge for developing *and* developed countries is to make sure that trade rules do not get in the way."

Gary Horlick
Partner, Wilmer Cutler Pickering Hale and Dorr LLP
Former Deputy Secretary of Commerce, Head of U.S. Department
   of Commerce Import Administration

RECLAIMING DEVELOPMENT IN THE WORLD TRADING SYSTEM

Prevalent poverty in less-developed countries is one of the most pressing issues of our time, and economic development in these countries is necessary to bring them out of poverty. As seen in the successful development cases of East Asian countries, international trade is closely relevant to economic development, and export facilitation and effective industrial policies have been the key to the successful development. Current GATT/WTO provisions facilitating development are insufficient and some of WTO provisions prevent developing countries from adopting effective development policies. This book is the first attempt to propose a comprehensive modification of the current GATT/WTO disciplines to better facilitate development in the trading system. The book also examines the need to elevate the level of regulatory treatment of development issues by the WTO and proposes the Agreement on Development Facilitation and the Council for Trade and Development within the WTO.

Yong-Shik Lee (Y. S. Lee) is an academician, lawyer, and former government counsel. An expert in trade law, Lee has pioneered legal analysis in safeguard measures in world trade, leading to the first comprehensive treatise on this subject, *Safeguard Measure in World Trade: The Legal Analysis* (2nd ed. 2005). Currently an associate editor of the *Journal of World Trade*, he has taught international trade law, public international law, trade and development, business law, and arbitration at law schools and business schools internationally.

Reclaiming Development in the World Trading System

YONG-SHIK LEE

CAMBRIDGE
UNIVERSITY PRESS

CAMBRIDGE UNIVERSITY PRESS
Cambridge, New York, Melbourne, Madrid, Cape Town, Singapore, São Paulo

Cambridge University Press
40 West 20th Street, New York, NY 10011-4211, USA

www.cambridge.org
Information on this title: www.cambridge.org/9780521852968

First published 2006

Printed in the United States of America

A catalog record for this publication is available from the British Library.

Library of Congress Cataloging in Publication Data

Lee, Yong-Shik (Lee, Y. S.), 1968–
Reclaiming development in the world trading system / Yong-Shik Lee.
    p.   cm.
Includes bibliographical references and index.
ISBN-13: 978-0-521-85296-8 (hardback)
ISBN-10: 0-521-85296-x (hardback)
1. Free trade – Developing countries.   2. Foreign trade regulation – Developing countries.
3. Developing countries – Commercial policy.   4. Developing countries – Economic policy.
5. World Trade Organization – Developing countries.   6. International trade – Social aspects –
Developing countries.   7. Poverty – Developing countries.   I. Title.
HF2580.9.L44   2005
382′.6′091724 – dc22   2005011912

ISBN-13   978-0-521-85296-8 hardback
ISBN-10   0-521-85296-x hardback

To the late Professor Robert Hudec, whose heart went out to the people of developing countries and whose academism sought a way to meet their interest in the international trading system.

To Park Jung Hee, the late president of Korea, revered for his economic achievement and criticized for his authoritarian rule, and to my fellow Koreans whose leadership, determination, and sacrifice saved my mother country from poverty and paved a way to today's prosperity.

Imagine all the people
Living life in peace . . .
No need for greed or hunger

From John Lennon (1940–1980), "**Imagine**"

Contents

List of Abbreviations . . . . *page* xi

Acknowledgments xv

1   **Poverty, Economic Development, and International Trade** 1

    1.1   The Question of Poverty   1

    1.2   International Trade and Development   6

    1.3   Kicking Away the Ladder?   9

2   **Current Regulatory Framework for International Trade:**
    The WTO System 14

    2.1   Introduction   14

    2.2   Facilitation of Development in WTO Provisions   25

    2.3   Need for Changes   39

3   **Reclaiming Development: Tariff Bindings and Subsidies** 49

    3.1   Two Principal Components of Industrial Promotion
         Policies   49

    3.2   Tariff Bindings   62

    3.3   Subsidies   74

4 **Anti-Dumping and Safeguards** 82

  4.1 Administered Protection   82

  4.2 Anti-Dumping   87

  4.3 Safeguards   96

5 **"Expansion" of Trade Disciplines and Development** 107

  5.1 Agriculture and Textile   107

  5.2 Trade-Related Investment Measures   114

  5.3 Trade-Related Aspects of Intellectual Property Rights   123

  5.4 Trade in Services   132

6 **Foreign Direct Investment and Regional Trade
  Liberalization** 141

  6.1 Regionalism in International Trade and Investment   141

  6.2 Proliferation of Foreign Direct Investment and Free
      Trade Areas   145

  6.3 Foreign Direct Investment and Free Trade: The Answer
      for Economic Development?   151

7 **Conclusion: Putting Back the Ladder** 156

  Epilogue 166

Bibliography 169

Index 177

List of Abbreviations

AD	Anti-dumping
ADF	Agreement on Development Facilitation
ADP Agreement	The Anti-dumping Practices Agreement (Agreement on Implementation of Article VI of the General Agreement on Tariffs and Trade 1994)
AFTA	ASEAN (Association of Southeast Asian Nations) Free Trade Area
AMS	Aggregate Measurement of Support (in Agreement on Agriculture)
APEC	Asia-Pacific Economic Cooperation
ATC	Agreement on Textiles and Clothing
B.I.S.D.	Basic Instruments and Selected Documents (published by GATT)
BIT	Bilateral Investment Treaty
BOP	Balance-of-Payment
CTD	Committee on Trade and Development
CTE	Committee on Trade and Environment
CVD	Countervailing Duty
DDA	Doha Development Agenda
DFS	Development-Facilitation Subsidy
DFT	Development-Facilitation Tariff

DSU	Understanding on Rules and Procedures Governing the Settlement of Disputes
EBA Initiative	"Everything But Arms" Initiative (an initiative of the European Union providing preferential treatment to the trade of least-developed countries)
ESG	Emergency Safeguard Measure
EU	European Union
FTA	Free Trade Agreement
FDI	Foreign Direct Investment
GATS	General Agreement on Trade in Services
GATT	General Agreement on Tariffs and Trade
GDP	Gross Domestic Product
GNI	Gross National Income
GNP	Gross National Product
GSP	Generalized System of Preferences
ILO	International Labour Organisation
IMF	International Monetary Fund
IPR	Intellectual Property Right
ITO	International Trade Organization
LDC	Least-Developed Country
MAI	Multilateral Agreement on Investment
MERCOSUR	Mercado Comun der Sur (the Southern Common Market in Latin America)
Member	Member of the World Trade Organization
MFA	The Multifiber Arrangement
MFN Treatment	Most-Favored-Nation Treatment
NAFTA	North America Free Trade Agreement
NICs	Newly Industrializing Countries
ODA	Official Development Assistance
OECD	Organisation for Economic Co-operation and Development
R&D	Research and Development
RTA	Regional Trade Agreement

SA	Agreement on Safeguards
SCM Agreement	Agreement on Subsidies and Countervailing Measures
S&D Treatment	Special and Differential Treatment
SSG	Special Safeguard (in Agreement on Agriculture)
TRIMs	Trade-Related Investment Measures
TRIPS	Trade-Related Aspects of Intellectual Property Rights
UBOP	Understanding on the Balance-of-Payments Provisions of the General Agreement on Tariffs and Trade 1994
U.N.	United Nations
UNCTAD	United Nations Conference on Trade and Development
UNEP	United Nations Environment Programme
UNIDO	United Nations Industrial Development Organisation
UR	Uruguay Round
U.S.	United States
USD	U.S. Dollar
WIPO	World Intellectual Property Organization
World Bank	International Bank for Reconstruction and Development
WTO	World Trade Organization
WTO Agreement	Marrakesh Agreement Establishing the World Trade Organization

Acknowledgments

As I wrote this book, I was inspired by the work of Dr. Ha-Joon Chang, Cambridge economist and author of *Kicking Away the Ladder* (2002). This historical analysis of economic development has convinced me that there are substantial inconsistencies between the provisions of the current regulatory framework for international trade and the development needs of developing countries. This conviction has motivated me to write this book in an effort to identify those inconsistencies and propose alternative provisions that would allow developing countries to adopt effective development policies.

I am indebted to many excellent scholars and professionals for invaluable advice and guidance: Dr. Ha-Joon Chang, assistant director of Development Studies at the University of Cambridge; Don Wallace, professor of law at Georgetown University Law Center and president of the International Law Institute; Gary Horlick, former deputy secretary of commerce; Don Mayer, professor of management at Oakland University School of Business Administration and the editor-in-chief of the International Business Law Review; Petros Mavroidis, professor of law at Columbia University and associate editor of the *Journal of World Trade*; Mitsuo Matsushita, professor emeritus of law at the University of Tokyo and former member of the World Trade Organization Appellate Body; Jai S. Mah, professor of economics at Dankook University; and Junji Nakagawa, professor of international economic law at the University of Tokyo Institute of Social Science and associate editor of the *Journal of World Trade*. I also thank the late Professor Robert E. Hudec for his insightful work on trade and development that has given immeasurable benefit to so many scholars, including me. Unfortunately, I did not have a chance to meet him. Professor Hudec taught at the University of Minnesota, but when I began to teach at a law school in the Minneapolis/St. Paul area, he had already passed away. Nonetheless, because of his great intellect and generosity toward others, he has become a great example to follow, even after his premature death. This book is in tribute to Professor Hudec.

I express my gratitude to Professor Dani Rodrik of Harvard University for kindly sending me his excellent paper on industrial policy, which is cited extensively in this book. I am also thankful to Cambridge University Press and its staff for their efforts in bringing this book to the light of the day. I would like to thank all other individuals who could not be listed in this limited space but whose kind assistance has been nevertheless essential for completing this book. I remember them in my heart with much gratitude.

ONE

Poverty, Economic Development, and International Trade

1.1 The Question of Poverty[1]

In today's world of unprecedented technological and economic advances, the majority of the world population has not been able to share in this prosperity.[2] Persistent poverty still remains in many parts of the world, and this human tragedy is one of the most pressing problems in our

[1] Most of us understand what poverty means and no elaborate definition would seem necessary. The World Bank describes the nature of poverty as the following: "Poverty is hunger. Poverty is lack of shelter. Poverty is being sick and not being able to see a doctor. Poverty is not being able to go to school and not knowing how to read. Poverty is not having a job, is fear for the future, living one day at a time. Poverty is losing a child to illness brought about by unclean water. Poverty is powerlessness, lack of representation and freedom." <http://www.worldbank.org//poverty>. The World Bank also uses the reference lines set at one dollar and two dollars per day in 1993 Purchasing Power Parity (PPP) terms as "poverty lines." Id.

Although poverty does exist among the population of developed countries, this book focuses on the need to improve the general economic conditions of developing countries where a larger portion of population suffers from poverty.

[2] In 2000, the United Nations estimated that more than half the world's 6 billion people live under substantial deprivation, surviving on incomes equivalent to two dollars or less per day. Only 20 percent of the world population living in the highest-income countries accounts for 86 percent of the world's GDP. <http://www.un.org/events/poverty2000/backpp.htm>.

time. Nevertheless, despite some efforts by international organizations,[3] poverty does not seem to receive priority consideration from leading nations that could provide key political and economic support toward resolving this problem.[4] Consider this issue from another perspective: not only is the relief of persistent poverty our moral obligation[5] but it is also consistent with our long-term security interest because societies with adequate economic resources are less likely to foster violence and terrorism that has torn our world apart throughout history.[6]

How can this problem of poverty be resolved? Poor countries cannot indefinitely depend on donations from outside, even if such donations

[3] In 2000, the United Nations set the Millennium Development Goals with several development objectives. <http://www.un.org//millenniumgoals>. The 2004 report on the implementation of the U.N. Millennium Declaration emphasized the responsibility of developed countries, as well as that of developing countries, to meet the development goals, stating that developed countries must fulfill their responsibilities "by increasing and improving development assistance, concluding a new development-oriented trade round, embracing wider and deeper debt relief and fostering technology transfer." U.N. doc. A/59/282 (Aug. 27, 2004), para. 43.

[4] Although the assistance of developed countries alone may never resolve poverty issues in developing countries without developing countries' significant effort to achieve economic development themselves, developed countries can nevertheless provide essential support by, among other things, helping to create a development-friendly international environment, such as a trading system that facilitates the economic development of developing countries.

[5] For a discussion of the moral grounds to help the poor, see Peter Singer, "Famine, Affluence, and Morality," (1972) 1 *Philosophy & Public Affairs* 229–243.

[6] Although considerable resources have been put forth to "fight" terrorism, relatively little effort and attention has been given to addressing its economic and social causes. Some may argue that the primary causes of worldwide terrorism are religious conflicts and political struggles, rather than economic problems. Nonetheless, economic difficulties and instabilities remain an important cause of this problem: poverty is commonplace in countries viewed as bases for terrorist activities. For instance, Afghanistan, which was accused of providing home for Al Qaeda, and Palestine, which has been the base for terrorist attacks against Israelis, are also characterized by poverty. History has shown that economic problems often lead to violence and war. In the 1930s, serious economic problems in Germany were a primary cause of the fall of the democratic regime and the subsequent rise of Adolf Hitler's Nazi party and the beginning of the Second World War. For the economic causes of the Second World War, see Andrew J. Crozier, *The Causes of the Second World War* (Blackwell Publishers, Oxford, 1997).

could be provided; the only lasting solution would be to create an economy in these countries through economic development[7] that would provide inhabitants with adequate resources and sustain their living standard beyond subsistence. How can poor nations build such an economy? It has been suggested that poverty is not simply a result of bad economic policy; various political, social, and even cultural problems have also been cited as causes of poverty.[8] Because these causes are rather various and complex, many believe that no simple solution to poverty is universally applicable.[9] In each individual case, political, social, economic, and cultural practices and institutions that hamper economic development should first be identified; then specific remedies for each of these problems would have to be applied.[10] In many cases, these problems are simply too difficult and complex to solve, therefore poverty remains.

Certain developing[11] economies have combated these problems successfully and have achieved impressive economic development in the past

[7] Economic development or, simply, development, is the process of a structural transformation of an economy from one based primarily on the production of primary products (i.e., a product consumed in its primary [unprocessed] state) generating low levels of income to another based on modern industries that provides higher levels of income. Many also believe that development is an international human right, as recognized by, *inter alia*, the U.N. Declaration on the Right to Development by the General Assembly in 1986.

[8] See A. F. Petrone (ed.), *Causes and Alleviation of Poverty* (Nova Science Publishers, Inc., 2002). For the effect of culture on development, see Amartya Sen, "Culture and Development," World Bank Paper (December 13, 2000), available at <http://www.worldbank.org/poverty/culture/book/CADNew.pdf>.

[9] Professor Thomas J. Shoenbaum suggests that on a governmental level there are three categories of actions that may be taken: (1) foreign aid and technical assistance; (2) debt forgiveness; and (3) amelioration of conditions for trade and investment. See Shoenbaum, "The WTO and Developing Countries" (paper prepared for the University of Tokyo International Law Study Group, Sep. 24, 2004).

[10] *Id.*

[11] This book concerns the economic development of "developing" countries. Although the term *developing* is generally used as opposed to *developed*, which represents the status of an industrialized economy generating high levels of income, there is no clear definition of "developing" status that is universally applicable. In the World Trade Organization (WTO), a developing status is self-declared, and there is no clear cutoff

decades.[12] For these economies, international trade has been an important vehicle for successful economic development. The legal framework for international trade controls which development policies can be implemented in conjunction with international trade and the way in which they are implemented. Therefore, trade disciplines are quite relevant to poverty and development. The specific regulatory requirements of trade disciplines affect the ability of developing countries to adopt effective development policies. I discuss throughout this book why this is the case and what changes should be made in the current trade disciplines to better facilitate development.

Yet I do not presume that neither a development-friendly international trading system nor any other international support alone will facilitate development and relieve poverty. Economic development efforts by developing countries should proceed, and the following factors would also be essentially important for development: a stable and efficient government, a working institutional arrangement between the public and private sectors,[13] a consistent economic policy, social peace, an educated

standard. The World Bank uses gross national income (GNI) per capita to classify countries into different groups. As of November 2004, the World Bank made this classification according to its 2003 statistics: low-income group ($765 or less per capita), lower-middle-income group (between $766 and $3,035 per capita), upper-middle-income group (between $3,036 and $9,385), and high-income group ($9,386 or above). Information available online at <www.worldbank.org>. Industrialized countries in the high-income group are often considered developed countries, while the others, which in fact include a wide range of economies in terms of development status, are considered developing.

[12] These countries/economies in the East Asian region include South Korea, Taiwan, Singapore, and Hong Kong. The process of economic development in these countries/economies is introduced later in this chapter.

[13] A recent work by Dani Rodrik illustrates an ideal institutional arrangement between the public and private sectors to be in place in order to facilitate development. Rodrik (2004), *infra* note 189. On a different note, another commentator considers that the development of "democratic" institutions is not a prerequisite to development, but such development is rather a result of economic development (as seen in the cases of South Korea and Taiwan). Chang, *infra* note 41, Chapter 3. Thus, the working institutional arrangement is not necessarily determined by the existence of democracy but

population, access to capital, entrepreneurship, and a cultural environment that fosters working ethics and can accommodate changes associated with development. It is true that these conditions are not present in many developing nations.[14] Despite various proposals for development strategies, policies, and international initiatives for decades,[15] the majority of countries that were underdeveloped fifty years ago still remain poor. For many underdeveloped nations, the situation has worsened over the past ten years.[16]

Although a development-friendly trading system alone may not be sufficient to facilitate economic development, it is nevertheless essential. The success story of the East Asian economies, including South Korea, Taiwan, Singapore, and Hong Kong, introduced in the next section, shows why. One argument is that a change of the current trading system would not bring about the economic development of developing countries because most of them do not even meet other necessary conditions for development.[17] In particular, there is a prevalent sentiment that governments of developing countries cannot be trusted with the implementation of state-led development policies for lack of efficient administrative capacity and corruption. It is maintained, therefore, that changing the international

by one of effective cooperation and communications between the public and private sectors, as described by Rodrik. Nonetheless, some measure of transparency and accountability should be imposed to prevent the moral hazard associated with government support. Rodrik (2004), *infra* note 189, pp. 20–21.

[14] For instance, government corruption, lack of internal security and peace, inadequate education, cultural bias, and the reluctance to accept changes associated with industrialization or opposition to industrialization itself are still apparent in many developing countries.

[15] After the Second World War, the World Bank was organized to assist with economic development projects, and other international organizations, such as the United Nations Conference on Trade and Development (UNCTAD) and the United Nations Industrial Development Organisation (UNIDO), aim to improve the economic status of developing countries.

[16] *Supra* note 2. According to the U.N. Human Development Report (2003), fifty-four countries have become poorer than in 1990, as measured by per capita GDP.

[17] *Supra* note 14.

trading system will not result in economic development for these developing countries, will cause inefficiency in the system, and therefore, is not necessary.

This is a logical fallacy, even if claims about the problems with developing countries were to be true. Certainly, it is not difficult to find cases of prevalent corruption and lack of competence on the part of the governments of developing countries. Nonetheless, if we believe that the relief of poverty through economic development is a priority, the trading system should facilitate, rather than hamper, the economic development of those developing countries that are ready to implement development policies, just as the East Asian countries have done in the past decades. Their successful economic development would not have been possible had some of the current requirements of the international trading system been in place because these requirements would not have allowed them to adopt key development policies, particularly those based on trade-related subsidies.[18]

1.2 International Trade and Development

While many developing countries failed to improve their economic conditions in any significant way,[19] some East Asian economies, such as South Korea, Taiwan, Hong Kong, and Singapore, have achieved remarkable economic success during the past four decades.[20] What distinguishes

---

[18] Dani Rodrik commented in his recent work that the current trade rules have made "a significant dent in the abilities of developing countries to employ intelligently-designed industrial policies." Rodrik (2004), *infra* note 189, pp. 34–35. Chapter 3 provides more discussion on this point.

[19] The World Bank underscores the lagging progress in its 1999 poverty estimates: "These (poverty) figures are lower than earlier estimates, indicating that some progress has taken place, but they still remain too high in terms of human suffering, and much more remains to be done."

[20] Those four economies have undergone rapid industrialization since the 1960s and acquired the title of "newly industrializing countries" ("NICs"). All of them have passed the threshold for the high-income country status as classified by the World Bank (GNI

these countries from other developing countries that have failed to achieve economic development? Can development strategies that have a degree of general applicability be drawn from this Asian experience? To answer these queries, the development process of these East Asian countries needs to be examined. I introduce the development case of South Korea to show the success of "outward development strategy."[21] The other East Asian newly industrializing countries (NICs) also implemented this strategy, although the details of each country's policy were different.[22]

South Korea was one of the poorest nations in the world four decades ago, lacking both natural and technological resources.[23] To overcome poverty and develop its economy, South Korea adopted a set of aggressive export strategies. The resources acquired through international trade, as well as the capital influx from abroad, which was encouraged by its success in exports, have enabled South Korea to modernize its industries and

per capita of 9,076 USD or more) as of 2003. Four decades ago, those countries were considered poor, with economies dependent on the production of cheap primary products. Between 1961 and 1996, South Korea increased its GDP by an average of 9.80 percent per annum, Hong Kong by 9.58 percent, Taiwan by 10.21 percent and Singapore by 9.95 percent. Alan Heston, Robert Summers, and Bettina Aten, Penn World Table Version 6.1, Center for International Comparisons at the University of Pennsylvania (CICUP), October 2002. <http://pwt.econ.upenn.edu/php_site/pwt_index.php>.

[21] The development strategies of NICs were often characterized to be "export-oriented" as opposed to the import-substitution policies employed by many other developing countries, including India and Brazil. There is a tendency to believe that this outward development policy was successful because it promoted trade, whereas import-substitution policies restricted trade. *Infra* note 559. However, it was not always the case. For instance, South Korea and Taiwan employed extensive tariff protection while promoting export industries.

[22] For an evolution of industrial policies of the NICs, see Mari Pangestu, "Industrial Policy and Developing Countries," *in* Bernard Hoekman, Aaditya Mattoo, and Philip English (eds.), *Development, Trade, and the WTO: A Handbook, infra* note 225, p. 153, Table 17.1.

[23] The per capita GNP of South Korea was a mere USD 239 in 1963 in 1975 constant prices, and the South Korean economy depended heavily on primary products. Kwang-suk Kim and Joon-kyung Park, *Sources of Economic Growth in Korea: 1963–1981* (Korea Development Institute, 1985), pp. 6–7.

achieve rapid economic growth.[24] This economic development, fueled by the continued success in exports, established South Korea as one of the leading industrial nations with higher living standards.[25] This economic success is also attributed to factors other than the success in export and export industries.[26] Nevertheless, few would dispute that the successful exports have been an engine for Korea's economic achievement.[27] In fact, this export-driven development has become a well-known model and has been studied widely.[28]

[24] Since the early 1960s, when Korea adopted export-oriented development policies, the real value of exports, discounted for the rise of export prices, increased at an average annual rate of 27 percent for the first two decades. Kim and Park (1985), *supra* note 23, pp. 6–7. This export growth was led primarily by the growth of export in manufactured products (its total share in export rose from 27.0 percent in 1962 to 93.7 percent in 1982). *Id.*, Table 2-1, Major Indicators of Korean Economic Growth, 1954–1982, pp. 9. Accordingly, the share of GNP by manufacturing sectors rose from 9.1 percent in 1962 to 34.2 percent in 1982, and that by primary sectors fell from 45.3 percent in 1962 to 19.2 percent in 1982, indicating rapid industrialization of South Korea during this period. *Id.*, Table 2-1, Major Indicators of Korean Economic Growth, 1954–1982, p. 8. The total GNP increased from USD 6.3 billion in 1962 to USD 32 billion in 1982 in 1975 constant prices. GNP per capita also tripled during the same period. *Id.* By any standard, South Korea escaped from poverty within two decades after the initiation of the export-oriented economic development policies in the early 1960s.

[25] Korea's export industries continued to grow rapidly in the 1980s and 1990s. The total value of Korea's exports grew from USD 24.4 billion in 1983 to USD 193.8 billion in 2003, and during the same periods, its GDP grew from USD 85.1 billion to USD 605.3 billion, becoming the eleventh largest economy in 2003. World Bank, *Korea, Rep. at a Glance* (Sep. 16, 2004) and World Bank, World Development Indicator Database (Sep. 2004). <www.worldbank.org>.

[26] Kim and Park (1985), *supra* note 23, p. 6. Factors such as political and social stabilities, effective technocratic bureaucracies, strong political leadership, high level of education, strict work ethics, and higher ratio of savings have been noted as important factors for the successful economic development of South Korea and the other NICs.

[27] Kim and Park (1985), *supra* note 23, p. 6.

[28] See A. O. Krueger, "Trade Policies in Developing Countries" *in* R. W. Jones and P. B. Kenen (eds.), *Handbook of International Economics*, Vol. 1 (North-Holland, N.Y., 1984), pp. 519–569; R. Findlay, "Growth and Development in Trade Models," *id.*, pp. 185–236; T. N. Srinivasan, "Trade, Development, and Growth," *Princeton Essays in International Economics No. 225* (December 2001); G. K. Helleiner (ed.), *Trade Policy, Industrialization, and Development* (Oxford University Press, Oxford, 1992); World Bank, *The East Asian Miracle* (Oxford University Press, New York, 1993).

If international trade can help poor nations to develop their economies and bring them out of poverty, as it did for South Korea and for the other East Asian countries, what are the necessary conditions for export-driven economic development? In this outward development model, export becomes the engine for development by creating demands for domestically produced products otherwise not consumed in their small domestic markets. Export revenues can be reinvested to expand export industries further, and therefore, the output of the economy improves over time with the expansion of the share of manufacturing sectors in the economy.[29] This is the common element observed in the development process of the NICs. In those East Asian countries, a series of economic factors preferable for industrial expansion, such as lower labor costs and a high rate of savings, helped export industries, but governments also played an important role by promoting those industries with various subsidies and tariff protection.[30]

1.3 Kicking Away the Ladder?

I have initially posed two questions about the successful development of the East Asian countries, that is, (i) what distinguishes them from other developing countries that have failed in economic development? and (ii) what effective development strategy can be drawn from their experience? They all have achieved rapid economic growth through expansion of their exports, and this outward development strategy is an effective

---

[29] *Supra* note 24.

[30] Subsidies included the provision of direct financial grants, low-interest loans, social infrastructures, tax rebates and exemptions, technological supports, and implicit bailout guarantees for producers engaging in new, risky ventures. Extensive tariff protections were also offered to protect and facilitate domestic productions. For a discussion of the government role in economic development of the East Asian countries, see Larry E. Westphal, "Industrial Policy in an Export Propelled Economy: Lessons from South Korea's Experience" (in Symposia: The State and Economic Development) (1990) 4(3) *Journal of Economic Perspectives* 41–59; John Brohman, "Postwar Development in the Asian NICs: Does the Neoliberal Model Fit Reality?" (1996) 72(2) *Economic Geography*, 107–130.

development model that can be adopted by other developing countries, assuming that the necessary political, social, and economic conditions are present.[31] The success of this development strategy would depend largely on the government's ability to promote exports.[32] Yet governments of developing countries would not be able to adopt some of the trade-related development policies of the NICs because the current regulatory framework for international trade, represented by the World Trade Organization (WTO), does not allow them to do so.[33]

In his recent book, *Kicking Away the Ladder*, Cambridge economist Ha-Joon Chang notes that almost every developed country today, including those strongly advocating liberal market economies and open trade, employed state-led industrial promotion policies during their own development process, which often included trade protection. Yet after achieving economic development, they have been "kicking away the ladder" and preventing developing countries from adopting effective development policies by imposing regulations of international trade and policy recommendations against these development policies. If correct, his argument raises moral questions and concerns for all of us genuinely interested in relieving poverty through successful economic development.

My premise is that the economic development of developing countries should be considered one of the important priorities of our time. It is possible that some who are not persuaded that this is our moral quest may question why the economic development of developing countries should be a priority. It is worth repeating that supporting the economic

---

[31] Those conditions include a stable and efficient government, working institutional arrangement between the public and private sectors, consistent economic policy, social peace, educated population, access to capital, entrepreneurship, and a cultural environment that fosters working ethics and can accommodate changes associated with development.

[32] *Id.*

[33] Most notably, restrictions on trade-related subsidies. *Supra* note 18. See Chapter 3 *infra*. Many neoclassical economists tend to discount the importance of the government role in economic development. See Chapter 3.1 *infra* for a discussion of the government role in development.

development of developing countries not only addresses our moral concern about the economic tragedy of poor nations[34] but also serves our security interest in this closely interconnected world. In addition, there is an economic reason for supporting the development of developing countries: the successful economic development of developing countries today would also provide the industries of developed countries with new affluent markets and therefore new sources for their own future wealth. Newly developed countries such as South Korea have become important export markets for many developed countries.[35] Therefore, assisting development would create a win-win situation for everyone.

Often policy decisions of modern democracies tend to be swayed by powerful economic constituencies whose concerns may not necessarily embrace social justice or economic equality at home or abroad. Nevertheless, political leadership in developed countries should persuade their constituencies to understand the long-term interest and the significant economic benefit to be gained by promoting economic development throughout the world. The only lasting solution to the current poverty problem is facilitating economic development to create sustainable economies in poor nations.[36] Thus, it is necessary to provide an

---

[34] *Supra* note 5.

[35] The total value of Korea's imports in 1962 was a mere USD 422 million. In 2003, Korea imported the total of USD 178.8 billion (including USD 24.8 billion from the United States and 19.8 billion from the European Union), becoming the thirteenth largest import market for merchandises and the fourteenth largest for services. World Bank (2004), *supra* note 25, and Ministry of Foreign Affairs and Trade of the Republic of Korea, *The Import and Export Status per Major Regional Categories* (2004), available online at <www.mofat.go.kr>.

[36] A substantial amount of aid has been provided to poor countries by governments of wealthy nations, private citizens, and organizations. For instance, the official development assistance (ODA) from developed OECD countries totaled USD 68.48 billion in 2003; ODA statistics available online at <www.oecd.org>. Although this sort of aid would be helpful to the people of many developing countries, the aid alone is not sufficient to root out the problems of poverty throughout the world. An obvious solution to poverty will be to create a sustainable economy by facilitating economic development in poor nations.

international regulatory environment that is consistent with this development interest. Many share this idea.[37] I note that the opinions and voices raised by distinguished experts in the 1999 WTO high-level symposium on trade and development address important development issues with the current trade regime, and I cite them throughout this book.[38] In addition, a recent work of Professor Dani Rodrik at Harvard University John F. Kennedy School of Government, entitled "Industrial Policy for the Twenty-First Century" provides insightful guidance to many of the issues addressed in this book and is also cited extensively.[39]

This book examines the current trade regime and the consistency of its legal framework with the development needs of currently developing countries. It does not attempt to suggest a comprehensive answer to economic development. That would be beyond the scope of this book. What this book aims to achieve is rather modest – the current system has, perhaps inadvertently, put roadblocks on the path of development for many, if not all, developing countries. This book attempts to identify these roadblocks and suggest their removal with a proposal of alternative provisions.[40] The removal of roadblocks does not guarantee the success of a country's journey or even the beginning of one, but this journey would be made much more difficult without their removal.

Chapter 2 introduces the current regulatory framework for international trade, the WTO system, and specific provisions pertaining to the

---

[37] The 2004 Report on the implementation of the U.N. Millennium Declaration stated that developed countries should fulfill their responsibilities to meet the new millennium development goals by, among other things, concluding a new development-oriented trade round. *Supra* note 3.

[38] World Trade Organization, *Report of the WTO High-Level Symposium on Trade and Development* (1999), available online at <www.wto.org>.

[39] Rodrik (2004), *infra* note 189.

[40] Of course, it would take a lot more than removing those roadblocks to enable developing countries to walk on the road of development. A working proposal for development, therefore, would inherently be country specific, although some general principles may be drawn from economic studies, taking into consideration the specific economic, political, social, and cultural endowments and conditions of a given developing country.

facilitation of development. The subsequent chapters provide discussions of specific subject areas of international trade and examine the consistency of the current rules with development needs. I also offer proposals to modify the current rules where such modifications are deemed necessary to facilitate development. If there is indeed a gap between the requirements of the current regulatory framework and the development needs, as Chang has presented,[41] it is time to consider bridging the gap. In the end, this effort will serve not only the economic interest of developing countries but will benefit all of us living today.

[41] Chang argues that today's developed countries adopted state-led development policies during their development process, including state subsidization and trade protections. Ha-Joon Chang, *Kicking Away the Ladder: Development Strategy in Historical Perspective* (Anthem Press, London, 2002). As I discuss in the subsequent chapters, these development policies could still be made effective today, and the international regulatory framework for international trade should allow developing countries to adopt these development policies.

TWO

Current Regulatory Framework for International Trade: The WTO System

2.1 Introduction

2.1.1 Historical Background

As discussed in Chapter 1, the regulatory framework for international trade should allow developing countries to adopt effective development policies. This chapter introduces the current regulatory framework for international trade, represented by the WTO,[42] with a brief account of its historical development. The current trading system includes provisions to facilitate development, and these provisions are also discussed in this chapter. Later chapters analyze the current provisions and conclude that they are not adequate to facilitate development of developing economies. This inadequacy leads us to consider alternative provisions that would better serve the development needs of developing countries.

A multilateral regulatory framework for international trade was first contemplated at the Bretton Woods Conference during the Second World War.[43] Trade protectionism that was prevalent during the 1930s led to

[42] The World Trade Organization, established by the Marrakesh Agreement of 1994 at the end of the Uruguay Round (1986–1994), represents the regulatory framework for international trade today.

[43] John H. Jackson, *The World Trading System* (2nd ed., MIT Press, Cambridge, Mass. 1997), Chapter 2.1.

exclusive trade blocs and was an important cause of this tragic war.[44] Lessons were learned from this experience, and efforts were made to create a new trading system that would promote open trade so that arbitrary trade restrictions and exclusions would not cause yet another major conflict. The Charter for the International Trade Organization (ITO) was drawn up after the war with an objective of establishing a new trading system. However, political support for the creation of the new trading system began to quickly wane after the war, and the United States failed to ratify the ITO because of congressional objection.[45] Without the participation of the United States, the ITO could not come into existence. Instead, the General Agreement on Tariffs and Trade (GATT), a set of rather brief disciplines on the trade in goods that was initially intended to be part of the ITO system, was adopted and began to function as a *de facto* international organization of international trade.[46]

The GATT system lasted for five decades and achieved significant success in lowering both tariff and non-tariff barriers to trade, particularly among industrialized nations, despite its initial lack of status and structure as a formal trade organization.[47] Over the years, however, the limited applicability of GATT disciplines and its incompleteness as a trade institution caused problems. For instance, as international trade expanded rapidly during the postwar periods,[48] some of the new trade issues that were not governed by GATT disciplines, such as trade in services and

---

[44] For the economic causes of the Second World War, refer to Crozier, *The Causes of the Second World War* (Blackwell Publishers, Oxford, 1997).

[45] For the political issues regarding the United States' failure to ratify ITO charters, see Jackson (1997), *supra* note 43, Chapters. 2.1 and 2.2.

[46] *Id.*

[47] There were eight multilateral trade negotiations (rounds) during the GATT era (1947–1994). The first round (the "Doha Round") in the WTO regime began in November 2001. During the previous GATT rounds, tariffs were reduced by an average of 35 percent at each round. As a result, the tariff rates of non-primary products of industrial countries fell to a mere 3.9 percent after the Uruguay Round in 1994. Jackson (1997), *supra* note 43, p. 74.

[48] Merchandise trade volume increased by more than forty-five times between 1950 and 2003. World Trade Organization, International Trade Statistics 2004, chart II.2,

trade-related aspects of intellectual property rights (TRIPS), became significantly important and needed to be addressed under the multilateral trade framework. In addition, exporters of agricultural products demanded that the rules of international trade should also be applied to agricultural products, which had been largely excluded from the application of GATT disciplines.[49] The dispute settlement system also needed to be reinforced.

All these needs called for extensive reforms of the GATT and, eventually, the creation of a new international institutional apparatus to address the new trade issues and to incorporate newly evolving areas of trade, such as services, in the multilateral trading system.[50] A series of efforts had been made to augment the existing GATT provisions, providing new rules for international trade, particularly in the areas of dumping and subsidies.[51] Yet the initial constraint of the GATT system with its application limited to the trade in goods made it difficult to expand the regulatory apparatus of international trade into those new areas. In the Uruguay Round (UR) (1986–1994), the final round of trade negotiations in the GATT regime, discussions began to address the need for a new, comprehensive trade organization to replace the GATT regime.

The UR began in 1986 and continued for eight years. Long and complicated negotiations finally gave birth to the WTO. The institutional apparatus of the GATT was replaced with the WTO, but GATT rules were preserved and absorbed as part of WTO disciplines.[52] The provisions of the GATT still constitute the disciplines of the trade in goods, augmented

World Merchandise Trade by Major Product Group, 1950–03, available online at <www.wto.org>.

[49] *Infra* note 391.

[50] Jackson (1997), *supra* note 43, Chapter 2.3.

[51] Additional rules and regulations were added to GATT disciplines. For instance, new "codes" on anti-dumping measures and countervailing measures were adopted at the end of Tokyo Round negotiations (1973–1979).

[52] "GATT 1994" composed of GATT provisions dated October 30, 1947, as subsequently amended or modified protocols, decisions, and understandings with respect to the GATT provisions as well as the Marrakesh Protocol to GATT 1994. GATT 1994 is part

by the new "agreements" settled during the UR.[53] For this reason, the current WTO system is also called the "GATT/WTO system."[54] As the socialist bloc dismantled in the 1980s, membership in the WTO has been extended to include former communist countries that did not originally participate in the GATT, making the WTO truly the "United Nations of international trade."[55] By the end of the twentieth century, only China and Russia had been left out of this world trade club, among all the major economies in the world; China obtained WTO membership in 2001, and Russia has also submitted an application for WTO membership and is currently going through negotiation for its accession to the WTO.

Unlike its predecessor, GATT, the WTO requires member countries (Members[56]) to comply with *all* provisions in WTO disciplines, except for a small number of plurilateral trade agreements.[57] WTO provisions are extensive and cover a variety of subject areas that are relevant to international trade. These areas include tariffs, quantitative trade restrictions (quotas), sanitary and phytosanitary measures, subsidies, anti-dumping (AD), customs valuations, rules of origin, import licensing, intellectual

of Annex 1 of the Marrakesh Agreement Establishing the World Trade Organization (WTO Agreement) titled "Multilateral Agreements on Trade in Goods."

[53] The text of the WTO provisions has been reprinted in various sources, including WTO, *The Results of the Uruguay Round of Multilateral Trade Negotiations: The Legal Texts* (Cambridge University Press, reprint 2003). The text is also available at the WTO official Web site, <www.wto.org>.

[54] Throughout this book, the terms "WTO system" or "WTO rules" are understood to include GATT disciplines as incorporated in the WTO Agreement.

[55] As of October 13, 2004, membership in the WTO reached 148 nations. Developing countries constitute two-thirds of WTO membership.

[56] The member states of the previous GATT ("contracting members") have become WTO Members after the implementation of the WTO in 1995. WTO Agreement Article XI:1.

[57] This principle of mandatory compliance with all WTO provisions is called "single undertaking." In contrast, the Protocol of Provisional Application of the GATT allowed its members to block the application of GATT provisions to their trade that is not consistent with the existing legislation at the time of their entry into the GATT ("grandfather" rights). Such grandfather rights are not granted to WTO members. Members must comply with all provisions included in the WTO Agreement except Annex 4, Plurilateral Trade Agreements, which are applied only to the Members specifically agreed to these agreements.

property issues, and investment rules. This means that WTO rules would not only affect the conduct of trade but also the ability of Members to adopt and implement a wide range of economic policies that may affect trade, including those concerning economic development. For instance, a use of government subsidy for the promotion of exports would be directly subject to the relevant WTO subsidy rules.[58] Because these WTO rules are mandatory and binding on all Members, Members cannot apply development policies that are inconsistent with these provisions.

WTO rules are considered more effective than the previous GATT disciplines thanks to improved enforceability: the WTO monitors Members' compliance with WTO provisions and acts on suspect violations;[59] Members may also bring a complaint to the WTO for adjudication if a violation of WTO rules by any other Member results in damage to their trade, and the decision by the dispute settlement panel or the Appellate Body will be adopted absent reverse consensus;[60] a material violation of WTO rules may also entail sanctions in the form of trade retaliations as authorized by the WTO.[61] A commentator has observed that the WTO's pursuit of global harmonization of an extensive range of national rules has brought considerable strain among Members, contributing to the failure of the Seattle and Cancun Ministerial Conferences[62] and this failure called for

---

[58] Chapter 3 *infra* provides a further discussion on this subject.

[59] The WTO imposes a number of reporting requirements on Members concerning their compliance with relevant WTO provisions. Various committees and councils established under the WTO oversee the functioning of WTO rules and monitor Members' compliance with WTO requirements. They may investigate suspect violations and authorize sanctions.

[60] The WTO Dispute Settlement Understanding provides the rules for the settlement of disputes among WTO Members (Annex 2, Marrakesh Agreement, *id.*); as of October 2004, more than 85 percent of all WTO decisions on trade disputes had been followed without any compliance issues. In the remaining cases, Members either followed decisions of subsequent compliance panels or were made subject to retaliatory measures approved by the WTO. WTO doc. WT/DS/OV/22 (October 14, 2004).

[61] By October 2004, the WTO authorized seven retaliatory measures. *Id.*

[62] John S. Odell, "The Seattle Impasse and Its Implications for the World Trade Organization," *in* Daniel L. M. Kennedy and James D. Southwick (eds.), *The Political Economy*

a balance between the need for globalization and local interests by recognizing and preserving local regulatory autonomies.[63] At any rate, that WTO rules are mandatory and enforceable on all Members[64] makes them crucial to a developing nation's potential for economic development. It is, therefore, to the core principles that comprise WTO rules that we now turn.

2.1.2 Major Principles of WTO Rules

The core principles of the international trading system were set forth in the original GATT provisions and subsequently succeeded by the WTO. The GATT disciplines consist of thirty-eight articles in three parts that stipulate various requirements concerning the conduct of international trade.[65] The main provisions include the requirement of most-favored-nation (MFN) treatment, the Schedule of Concessions, national treatment, anti-dumping and countervailing duties (CVDs), valuation for customs purposes, rules of origin, general elimination of quantitative restrictions, rules on the balance-of-payment (BOP) measures, government assistance to economic development, safeguards (Article XIX measures), general exceptions and security exceptions, and procedural matters concerning the application of the GATT. These GATT articles

of International Trade Law: Essays in Honor of Robert E. Hudec (Cambridge University Press, Cambridge, 2002); Sungjoon Cho, "A Bridge Too Far: The Fall of the Fifth WTO Ministerial Conference in Cancun and the Future of Trade Constitution" (2004) 7 *Journal of International Economic Law* 219–244.

[63] For a more detailed discussion of this issue, see Veijo Heiskanen, "The Regulatory Philosophy of International Trade Law" (2004) 38 *Journal of World Trade* 1–36.

[64] The mandatory implementation requirement of the WTO has imposed substantial regulatory and administrative burdens on developing countries with limited resources. It has been pointed out that the implementation should have been linked to national capacity and international assistance in areas requiring minimum levels of institutional capacity such as customs valuation. Bernard Hoekman, "Strengthening the Global Trade Architecture for Development" (2002) 1 *World Trade Review* 23–46.

[65] WTO rules are applied to Members and not directly to private parties such as individuals and companies.

have been modified and augmented by various other agreements and understandings settled in the UR.[66] With membership of 148 nations, WTO rules apply to the vast majority of trading nations, and their core principles are becoming the "common law" of world trade.[67] The major principles comprising GATT/WTO disciplines are as follows.

a. Tariff Bindings

Members of the WTO must observe maximum tariff rates on individual products and services as stipulated in the "Schedule of Concessions" (GATT Article II).[68] Members negotiate these maximum tariff rates in the multilateral trade negotiations (rounds).[69] Once those tariff rates are agreed on, Members are not allowed to apply higher tariffs than those negotiated maximum rates stipulated in their Schedule of Concessions, except in the exceptional circumstances as provided by WTO rules.[70] This principle of binding tariff rates provides important stability to the international trading system by preventing tariffs from being "hiked" in times of economic difficulties, which would cause severe damage to international trade.[71]

b. Most-Favored-Nation Principle

Members must accord one another the MFN treatment with respect to imports. Article I of the GATT provides that "any advantage, favour, privilege or immunity granted by any contracting party to any product originating in or destined for any other country shall be accorded immediately and unconditionally to the like product originating in or

---

[66] *Supra* note 53.

[67] Joseph Weiler (ed.), *The EU, the WTO and the NAFTA: Towards a Common Law of International Trade* (Oxford University Press, Oxford, 2000).

[68] WTO, *The Results of the Uruguay Round of Multilateral Trade Negotiations, supra* note 53, pp. 425–427.

[69] Such as the rounds conducted during the GATT era. *Supra* note 47.

[70] For example, safeguard measures, discussed in Chapter 4 *infra*, are such exceptions.

[71] For instance, sharp increases in tariff rates in the 1930s crippled international trade and worsened the worldwide depression.

destined for the territories of all other contracting parties."[72] This rule prohibits Members from discriminating against imports according to their source.[73] Some scholars argue that this MFN principle is deeply entrenched in the international trading system and "has been a central pillar of trade policy for centuries."[74] The MFN principle prevents the formation of protective trading blocs that favor imports from a certain group of nations and discriminates against those from others.[75] This prevention of arbitrary discrimination in international trade also provides important stability to the international trading system.[76]

c. National Treatment

Another core principle of the international trading system is the principle of national treatment. Article III.1 of the GATT provides:

> "The contracting parties recognize that internal taxes and other internal charges, and laws, regulations and requirements affecting the internal sale, offering for sale, purchase, transportation, distribution or use of products, and internal quantitative regulations requiring the mixture, processing or use of products in specified amounts or proportions,

---

[72] WTO, *The Results of the Uruguay Round of Multilateral Trade Negotiations, supra* note 53, p. 424.

[73] The WTO's Generalized System of Preferences (GSP) that provides more favorable tariff treatment to imports from developing countries operates as a major exception to the MFN principle. The authorization of preferential treatment among members of a customs union under GATT Article XXIV is another important exception to the MFN principle. Renato Ruggiero, the former director-general of the WTO, warned against the proliferation of preferential trading groups under this exception, stating that "with the proliferation of regional groupings, the exception could become the rule, and this would risk changing completely the nature of the system." WTO press release (April 24, 1996).

[74] Jackson (1997), *supra* note 43, p. 157.

[75] Article XXIV of the GATT authorizes the creation of a customs union where its establishment does not raise trade barriers against imports from non-member countries. WTO, *The Results of the Uruguay Round of Multilateral Trade Negotiations, supra* note 53, pp. 457–460.

[76] Trade discriminations and restrictions were an important cause of the Second World War to "capture markets and resources" from the competing nations. *Supra* note 44.

should not be applied to imported or domestic products so as to afford protection to domestic production."[77]

This national treatment provision requires Members to accord non-discriminatory treatment to imports *vis-à-vis* domestic products once they have passed through the customs. It allows imports to compete with domestic products on a level playing field and limits trade barriers to the tariffs under the Schedule of Concessions and only to other measures, if any, authorized by WTO rules. Both the MFN and the national treatment principles are also provided in the General Agreement on Trade in Services (GATS) negotiated during the UR, but substantial leeway is allowed for the application of these principles in the service area.[78]

In addition, GATT Article XI also generally prohibits quantitative restrictions on trade unless authorized by exceptional rules.[79] These principles, as well as the objectives specified in the provisions of the Agreement Establishing the World Trade Organization (WTO Agreement),[80] make it clear that the present international trading system aims for "open" or "liberal" trade that is conducted primarily by market forces and not by arbitrary government interventions.[81] Eight rounds of trade negotiations

---

[77] WTO, *The Results of the Uruguay Round of Multilateral Trade Negotiations*, supra note 53, p. 427.

[78] For instance, Article II.2 of the General Agreement on Trade in Services (GATS) allows a modification of the MFN treatment on the basis of the Annex on Article II Exemptions. *Id.*, p. 287. Article XVIII of the GATS also requires the application of national treatment only in the sectors inscribed in the Member's schedule, subject to any conditions and qualifications set out therein. *Id.*, pp. 293–294.

[79] WTO, *The Results of the Uruguay Round of Multilateral Trade Negotiations*, supra note 53, p. 437.

[80] See the preamble of the WTO Agreement." *Id.*, p. 6.

[81] A prominent classical economist, David Ricardo, explained that international trade takes place because of the differences in the *relative advantages* of producing products, as defined by the relative cost of producing given products. David Ricardo, *Principles of Political Economy and Taxation* (1817). According to Ricardo's theory, all parties participating in international trade improve their economic welfare, and government interventions with international trade are not necessary; such interventions reduce the economic welfare to be gained by trade. Ricardo's theory and the subsequent

during the GATT era reduced both tariff and non-tariff barriers substantially,[82] and the effort to reduce trade barriers is continuing. Many hope that this effort will bring international trade closer to free trade.[83] An essential motivation for the GATT after the Second World War was the preservation of peace by providing every nation with access to markets and resources.[84] This objective has been largely fulfilled, and we did not have any major conflict due to any exclusion from trade.

Free trade has been promoted in the context of "fair trade," a phrase that seems to have different meanings depending on *who* uses it in *which* circumstance. The advocates of fair trade from the perspective of domestic producers competing with imports emphasize a "level playing field" and criticize the protection and promotion of industries by foreign governments using means to support industries such as subsidies. However, those who are critical of "globalization" and "free trade" emphasize

Hecksher-Ohlin model that explains the *causes* of the difference in relative advantages formed the cornerstone of modern trade theories. The Hecksher-Ohlin model explains that a country has relative advantage in a product produced by making the most use of a production factor that is relatively abundant in that country. For instance, countries richly endowed with capital export capital-intensive products, while those with labor export labor-intensive products. This theory was presented in Ohlin's master work, *Interregional and International Trade* (1933).

[82] *Supra* note 47.

[83] Many commentators prefer the terms such as "liberal trade," "open trade," and "freer trade" to the term "free trade" in the sense that trade can never be completely "free": many believe that certain government regulations of trade are inevitable; particularly those rules to ensure "fair" trade. In today's world where the functions of government are considered rather essential in many areas of our economic lives, few would argue that government can be (or should be) completely left out of international trade, and my notion of free trade does not preclude all government trade regulations – although I do not support every government regulation enforced in the name of "fair" trade (e.g., anti-dumping actions as applied today). Free trade in today's world may be considered the practice of trade with *minimal* government control and may not necessarily mean the *complete* absence of government regulation of trade. In this sense, I treat the terms such as free trade, liberal trade, open trade, and any other similar terms as synonymous and use them interchangeably throughout this book.

[84] The trade blocs limiting access to markets and resources provided a cause of the Second World War. *Supra* note 44.

poor nations' disadvantages in the global competition and stress that "fair" trade should not work to widen the gap between wealthy and poor nations.[85] The WTO authorizes Members to apply counter measures to "unfair" trade practices in the former sense, such as trade-related government subsidies and dumping practices.[86] In particular, government subsidies promoting exports or discouraging imports came under direct scrutiny by the WTO. The WTO subsidy rules[87] prohibit subsidies directly promoting exports or substituting imports. Some other trade-related subsidies may be also subject to CVDs.[88]

Many believe that free trade will provide us with a real chance to improve living standards for all, both developing and developed nations. This belief is well reflected in a statement of former WTO Director-General Renato Ruggiero: "Achieving a genuine world free trade area would make a tremendous contribution to promoting growth and ensuring a safer world in the century to come."[89] Clear directions and initiatives, including systematic reductions in tariff and non-tariff barriers, were taken under the GATT regime as well as the subsequent WTO to reach this goal. Trade-related government subsidies are either outlawed or made subject to countervailing actions. Would these steps toward "free trade" be truly positive for development? Answering this question will require a historical and empirical examination of development policies as well as a consideration of relevant economic theories. The long debate

---

[85] For a discussion of the idea of "fair trade," see James Bovard, *The Fair Trade Fraud* (St. Martin's Press, 1991) and Steven M. Suranovic, "A Positive Analysis of Fairness with Applications to International Trade" (2000) 23(3) *World Economy* 283–307.

[86] GATT Article VI provides the rules for AD measures and CVDs. WTO, *The Results of the Uruguay Round of Multilateral Trade Negotiations, supra* note 53, pp. 430–432. The ADP Agreement and the Agreement on Subsidies and Countervailing Measures elaborate the GATT rules on AD measures, subsidies, and CVDs. *Id.*, pp. 147–171, 231–274.

[87] *Id.*

[88] The effects of these WTO subsidy rules and AD rules are discussed in more detail in Chapters 3 and 4 *infra*.

[89] WTO press release (24 June 1996). <http://www.wto.org/english/news_e/pres96_e/pro46_e.htm>.

about the effectiveness of infant industry promotion is relevant to this issue, and controversies surrounding the viability of infant industry promotion are examined in Chapter 3.

2.2 Facilitation of Development in WTO Provisions

2.2.1 Introduction

How have GATT/WTO disciplines treated the issue of development?[90] In the early period of the GATT, not much progress was made in meeting development objectives, but attention to the importance of development grew over time as the participation of developing countries increased.[91] With the majority of membership composed of developing countries, development has become a major issue in the WTO. The WTO Agreement (i.e., the Marrakesh Agreement Establishing the WTO) includes the facilitation of development among its major objectives. Its preamble provides in relevant part: "*Recognizing* further that there is need for positive efforts designed to ensure that developing countries, and especially the least developed among them, secure a share in the growth in international trade commensurate with the needs of their economic development."[92]

As shown in this preamble, the WTO recognizes the role of international trade in development and the need to ensure that developing

[90] The late Professor Robert Hudec's insightful work, *Developing Countries in the GATT Legal System*, Thames Essays (Trade Policy Research Centre, London, 1987), provides an excellent account of how the GATT as an institution came to accommodate the increasing involvement of developing countries in the world trading system.

[91] A GATT ministerial decision in November 1957 cited "the failure of the trade of less developed countries to develop as rapidly as that of industrialized countries" as a major problem. Trends in International Trade, 29 November 1957, GATT B.I.S.D (6th Supp.), p. 18 (1958). This decision produced the "Haberler Report," which supported the perception that the export earnings of developing countries were not satisfactory. Gottfried Haberler et al., *Contracting Parties to the GATT, Trends in International Trade* (1958) *cited in*, Shoenbaum (2004), *supra* note 9.

[92] WTO, *The Results of the Uruguay Round of Multilateral Trade Negotiations*, *supra* note 53, p. 4.

countries share in the growth of international trade. The first WTO Ministerial Conference also addressed the importance of integrating developing countries in the multilateral trading system for their economic development.[93] To facilitate this integration, it recalled "that the WTO Agreement embodies provisions conferring differential and more favourable treatment for developing countries, including special attention to the particular situation of least-developed countries."[94] Trade facilitation is an important part of development strategy and needs to be supported by the WTO. The successful development of the NICs was fostered by the rapid increases in their exports.[95] It is thus necessary to examine what specific provisions are in place to facilitate development.

2.2.2 GATT Article XVIII

In order to determine whether the WTO system effectively facilitates development, we need to examine specific WTO provisions designed to meet the objective of facilitating development. Article XVIII of the GATT, "Government Assistance to Economic Development"[96] is one of the primary provisions assisting with development. This provision is to facilitate the establishment of industries by authorizing relevant trade measures. Paragraph 2 provides:

"The contracting parties recognize further that it may be necessary for those contracting parties (contracting parties the economies of which

---

[93] WTO, *Singapore Ministerial Declaration*, WTO doc. WT/MIN(96)/DEC, para. 13 (December 18, 1996).

[94] *Id.* The WTO recognizes least-developed countries (LDCs) as designated by the United Nations based on multiple criteria such as a low-income criterion (under $750 for inclusion, above $900 for graduation), a human resource weakness criterion, and an economic vulnerability criterion. Fifty LDC are on the U.N. list, and thirty of these countries became WTO members as of November 2004. Eight additional LDCs were in the process of accession to the WTO.

[95] See the relevant discussions in Chapter 1.2 *supra*.

[96] WTO, *The Results of the Uruguay Round of Multilateral Trade Negotiations*, *supra* note 53, pp. 447–453.

can only support low standards of living and are in the early stages of development), in order to implement programmes and policies of economic development designed to raise the general standard of living of their people, to take protective or other measures affecting imports, and that such measures are justified in so far as they facilitate the attainment of the objectives of this Agreement. They agree, therefore, that those contracting parties should enjoy additional facilities to enable them (a) to maintain sufficient flexibility in their tariff structure to be able to grant the tariff protection *required for the establishment of a particular industry* and (b) to apply quantitative restrictions for balance of payment purposes in a manner which takes full account of the continued high level of demand for imports likely to be generated by their programmes of economic development." (Explanation and emphasis added.)

This article supports the infant industry promotion policy forwarded by Friedrich List (1789–1846).[97] This policy uses tariff protections to promote domestic industries in the early stages of development. This GATT article allows developing countries to establish a particular industry by authorizing them to maintain a flexible tariff structure. This flexibility would enable developing countries to grant tariff protection for infant industries. Article XVIII also acknowledges the need for trade measures for BOP purposes.[98]

---

[97] Friedrich List is widely known as the father of infant industry promotion, although he was not the first who made this argument. *Infra* note 193. His famous work, *The National System of Political Economy* (1841), sets out his infant industry argument. See Chapter 3.1.2 *infra* for a further discussion of List's argument in favor of infant industry promotion.

[98] Section B of Article XXVIII authorizes balance-of-payment (BOP) measures for development purposes. Paragraph 8 of the article provides, "The contracting parties recognize that contracting parties coming within the scope of paragraph 4(a) of this Article [i.e., developing countries in the early stages of development] tend, when they are in rapid process of development, to experience balance of payment difficulties arising mainly from efforts to expand their internal markets as well as from the instability in their terms of trade." (Explanation added) WTO, *The Results of the Uruguay Round of Multilateral Trade Negotiations, supra* note 53, p. 449.

The provisions of this article facilitating the establishment of an industry apply to Members whose economy (i) can only support low standards of living and (ii) are in the early stages of development (para. 4[a]).[99] How are these two categories, "low standards of living" and "the early stages of development," defined? The GATT does not provide cutoff guidelines to determine them but nevertheless provides some direction: in Annex I of the GATT, "Notes and Supplementary Provisions," Ad Article XVIII clarifies that the former should be determined on the basis of the normal position of that economy and not on "exceptional circumstances such as those which may result from the temporary existence of exceptionally favourable conditions for the staple export product or products of such contracting party."[100] As to the latter category, the application of Article XVIII is not limited to Members in the initial stages of economic development but is also open to other Members whose economies are undergoing a process of industrialization to correct an excessive dependence on primary production.[101]

Other than these, there is no other standard to determine which developing economies are qualified for the preferential treatment of Article XVIII. Nevertheless, the provision of Annex I seems to indicate that these classifications include a wide range of developing economies in transition from a heavy dependence on the production of primary goods to a more manufacturing-oriented economy. Annex I further clarifies:

> "The reference to the establishment of particular industries shall apply not only to the establishment of a new industry, but also to the establishment of a new branch of production in an existing industry and to the substantial transformation of an existing industry, and to the substantial expansion of an existing industry supplying a relatively small proportion of the domestic demand. It shall also cover the reconstruction of

---

[99] WTO, *The Results of the Uruguay Round of Multilateral Trade Negotiations, supra* note 53, p. 447.
[100] GATT Ad Article XVIII, para. 1. *Id.*, p. 486.
[101] GATT Ad Article XVIII, para. 2. *Id.*

an industry destroyed or substantially damaged as a result of hostilities or natural disasters."[102]

This provision authorizes the use of Article XVIII measures for various industrialization efforts relevant to economic development other than the establishment of a new industry, such as the expansion of the existing industries.

Once a developing country qualifies for the application of Article XVIII, what specific accommodations are made under this article? Section A of Article XVIII authorizes a modification of the Schedule of Concessions (i.e., modification of the maximum binding tariff rates) to promote the establishment of a particular industry.[103] This provision requires the modifying Member to negotiate with other Members with which the relevant concession was initially negotiated or having a substantial interest (para. 7[a] of Section A). Therefore, this modification under Article XVIII would require a compensatory measure by the modifying Member, normally in the form of a tariff reduction, to reach agreement with the other Members on the modification.

If no agreement is reached within sixty days after the WTO[104] is notified of the modification, the Member may still modify the concession in question, provided that the WTO finds that the compensatory adjustment offered by the modifying Member is adequate and that every effort was made to reach an agreement.[105] In addition, the modifying Member must give effect to the compensatory adjustment at the same time as the modification.[106] If, however, the WTO finds that the compensatory adjustment

---

[102] *Id.*, p. 486.

[103] *Id.*, p. 448.

[104] The original GATT article uses the term, "CONTRACTING PARTIES." The Explanatory Notes of the General Agreement on Tariffs and Trade 1994 stipulates that the references to the term "contracting party" used in the GATT shall be deemed to read "Member" and those to "CONTRACTING PARTIES" acting jointly in the various articles of the GATT shall be deemed to be references to the WTO. *Id.*, p. 14.

[105] Paragraph 7(b) of Article XVIII. *Id.*, p. 448.

[106] *Id.*

offer is not adequate, other Members with a substantial interest are free to modify or withdraw substantially equivalent concessions (i.e., may apply retaliatory measures by raising tariffs or applying non-tariff measures) against the modifying Member.[107]

Section B of Article XVIII authorizes import restrictions to redress BOP measures, which may occur in rapid process of development, arising from the efforts to expand their internal markets as well as from the instability in their terms of trade.[108] A developing country Member may apply a BOP measure "in such a way as to give priority to the importation of those products which are more essential in the light of its policy of economic development." (para. 10)[109] These measures must be notified to the Committee on Balance-of-Payments Restrictions (Committee),[110] and they are also subject to consultations with the Committee,[111] which periodically reviews these BOP measures.[112] The Committee may make a recommendation to correct any inconsistency between the BOP measure and the relevant provisions of Article XVIII.[113] If the Member applying a BOP measure does not comply with a Committee recommendation to correct a serious inconsistency, any Member whose trade is adversely affected may be authorized to retaliate against the Member applying the BOP measure.[114]

Section C authorizes import restrictions to promote the establishment of a particular industry, other than the tariff modifications under Section A, where no measure consistent with the other provisions of the

---

[107] Id.

[108] Article XVIII, para. 8. Id., pp. 449–451.

[109] Id., p. 449.

[110] The Understanding on the Balance-of-Payments Provisions of the GATT 1994 (UBOP) establishes the Committee on Balance-of-Payment Restrictions to carry out consultations in order to review all BOP measures. The UBOP clarifies BOP provisions in the GATT mostly relating to the procedural matters. Id., pp. 22–25.

[111] Id., para. 12, pp. 449–450.

[112] Id.

[113] Id.

[114] Id.

GATT is practicable to achieve that objective.[115] The measure must be approved by the WTO; otherwise, any other Member whose trade is substantially affected by this measure may apply retaliatory measures against the Member applying the measure.[116] Section D authorizes a Member whose economy is in the process of development but does not come within the categories described in paragraph 4(a) to apply import restrictions to promote the establishment of an industry.[117] The Member must apply to the WTO for approval of such measure.[118]

In summary, Article XVIII addresses the need of developing countries to establish and promote industries for the purpose of economic development by authorizing import restrictions. However, the provisions of this article also require developing countries to conduct negotiations and to offer reciprocal concessions. This requirement of consultations and negotiations may cause considerable delays in implementing necessary trade measures for development purposes, and the reciprocal concessions may also burden their economy and prove counter-effective to their development interests. Although it is desirable to allow developing countries additional facilities to have a more flexible tariff structure, as Article XVIII attempts to do, this type of multilateral scrutiny diminishes their effectiveness in assisting with development.

If the relief of poverty through economic development is a priority, these negotiations and reciprocal concessions, which may cause delays and may also impose substantial economic burden on developing countries, should not be required as a precondition to modify the Schedule of Concessions for development purpose. The authorization of unilateral tariff modifications without the requirement of negotiations and compensatory adjustments would not be inherently unfair when it is done for the purpose of development. In fact, many developed countries today

---

[115] *Id.*, p. 451.
[116] *Id.*, paras. 17 and 21, pp. 452–453.
[117] *Id.*, para. 22, p. 453.
[118] *Id.*

seldom offered reciprocal trade concessions when they applied high tariffs and other trade measures to facilitate their own industries in the past.[119] A question of abuse may arise when developing countries are allowed to modify tariffs unilaterally for the purpose of development. I discuss a specific proposal in the next chapter that would allow unilateral modifications of binding tariff rates but, at the same time, would reduce potential abuse.

2.2.3 GATT Articles XXXVI–XXXVIII

Another set of the GATT provisions attempting to facilitate development is Part IV of the GATT (Articles XXXVI–XXXVIII) entitled "Trade and Development." The complaints of Uruguay in 1961 made against 576 restrictions maintained by developed countries that allegedly nullified and impaired Uruguayan exports and the subsequent formation of the United Nations Conference on Trade and Development (UNCTAD) spurred initiatives in the GATT to facilitate development, which included the adoption of Part VI of the GATT.[120] These provisions lay out the principles, objectives, and commitments to be made by developed country Members and joint action for aiding development.[121] Although largely declaratory, these provisions address important aspects of the trade and development issues.

Article XXXVI[122] emphasizes the vital role of export earnings in economic development and provides for the possible authorization of special

---

[119] Chang illustrates the trade and industrial policies of today's major developed economies adopted during their own development periods. H.-J. Chang, *Kicking Away the Ladder*, *supra* note 41, Chapter 2, pp. 13–68.

[120] Shoenbaum (2004), *supra* note 104.

[121] The original GATT provisions use the term "less-developed country." It is to be understood as "developing country (Member)" in the context of the WTO. *Supra* note 104.

[122] WTO, *The Results of the Uruguay Round of Multilateral Trade Negotiations*, *supra* note 53, pp. 468–469.

measures to promote trade and development. It also addresses the need for more favorable and acceptable conditions of access to world markets for primary products on which many developing countries depend. The article acknowledges the need to diversify the economic structure and to avoid an excessive dependence on the export of primary products. It also addresses an important relationship between trade and financial assistance to development.[123] Finally, the article clarifies that there should be no expectation of reciprocity on the part of developed countries for commitments made by them in trade negotiations to reduce or remove tariffs and other barriers to the trade of developing country Members.[124] It is interesting to note that the article expressly stipulates that the principle of reciprocity is not applied between developed and developing countries when it comes to tariff reductions because, by allowing non-reciprocity, it seems to acknowledge the need of developing countries to maintain some tariff protections for their domestic industries.

Article XXXVII[125] elaborates commitments on the part of developed country Members to assist with economic development of developing countries. The provisions of this article obligate developed country Members to accord high priority to the reduction and elimination of import barriers to products of particular export interest to developing Members and to refrain from introducing or increasing import barriers to such products.[126] They are also obligated to refrain from introducing new fiscal measures that are applicable specifically to primary products wholly or mainly produced in developing countries and hamper the growth of

---

[123] *Id.*

[124] *Id.*, para. 8, pp. 469.

[125] *Id.*, pp. 469–471.

[126] *Id.*, p. 469. With respect to this commitment, paragraph 1 of Article XXXVII provides in relevant part, "The developed contacting parties shall to the fullest extent possible – that is, except when compelling reasons, which may include legal reasons, make it impossible – give effect to the following provisions." *Id.* This provision allows developed countries to avoid this commitment by, for instance, legislating for restraints on imports from developing countries.

consumption of those products and accord high priority to the reduction and elimination of these measures.[127]

An interested Member may report a violation of this commitment to the WTO, and the WTO will consult with the relevant developed country Member for the resolution of the matter.[128] Developed country Members are also required to make efforts to maintain trade margins at equitable levels for developing countries where a government directly or indirectly determines the resale price of products wholly or mainly produced in developing country Members.[129] They are also obligated to adopt measures to provide a greater scope for the development of imports from those developing countries.[130] Special regard is to be given to the trade interests of developing countries in the application of trade measures against imports (para. 3).[131]

Article XXXVIII[132] provides for joint action to assist with the development of developing countries. In addition to the commitments of developed countries to facilitate economic development provided in the preceding articles, Article XXXVIII calls for institutional effort by the WTO to provide assistance to development. Specifically, the WTO is obligated to take action to provide improved and acceptable conditions of access to world markets for primary goods of particular interest to developing country Members. It is also obligated to take action to devise measures designed to stabilize and improve conditions of world markets in those products, including measures designed to attain stable, equitable, and remunerative prices for exports of such products.[133]

The article also obligates the WTO to engage in certain activities for the purpose of aiding developing country Members. These activities include

---

[127] *Id.*, pp. 469–470.
[128] *Id.*, p. 470.
[129] *Id.*
[130] *Id.*
[131] *Id.*
[132] *Id.*, pp. 471–472.
[133] *Id.*

collaboration with other relevant U.N. organizations in the matters of trade and development. The WTO is also required to collaborate with governments and international organizations in the following areas: analyzing the development plans and policies of individual developing country Members; seeking feasible methods to expand trade for the purpose of economic development; and examining trade and aid relationships with a view to devise measures to promote the development of export potential and to facilitate access to export markets for the products of the industries thus developed. It also requires monitoring of the development of world trade with special reference to the growth rate of the trade of developing country Members as well as the establishment of institutional arrangements as may be necessary to implement these provisions.[134]

The provisions in GATT Articles XXXVI–XXXVIII include an impressive array of measures, commitments, and collaborations on the part of developed countries and the WTO in support of economic development. However, those provisions are largely declaratory and are not really obligatory in the sense that a violation of these provisions does not entail any effective sanction. In addition, Article XXXVII excuses developed country Members from the various commitments laid down in the article to assist developing country Members by invoking "compelling" reasons.[135] These compelling reasons may include domestic legal obligations and, therefore, developed countries may escape from those so-called commitments by legislating against them. It is doubtful that the commitments under Articles XXXVI–XXXVIII have actually affected the policies of developed countries in any significant way to accord more favorable treatment to developing countries. For instance, the instances of tariff peaks[136] and tariff escalations[137] by developed countries show that those commitments,

---

[134] *Id.*

[135] *Supra* note 123.

[136] Tariff peaks impose higher tariff rates on selected imports mostly from developing countries such as textile, clothing, fish and fish products.

[137] Tariff escalations impose higher tariff rates on finished products and lower rates on raw materials.

which should have prevented tariff peaks and tariff escalations that target exports from developing countries, are not quite enforceable in reality. Tariff peaks and tariff escalations have been reduced after the UR but still exist, hampering exports from developing countries.

Therefore, Articles XXXVI–XXXVIII will not likely have any serious effect on the conduct of developed countries in their trade relations *vis-à-vis* developing countries. The declaratory nature of these provisions has remained unchanged since no additional rules were agreed on during the UR in order to improve the enforceability of these commitments.[138] It is not surprising because the UR was primarily directed toward strengthening trade disciplines for "free" and "fair" trade,[139] and it was not so much about facilitating development in favor of developing countries. Perhaps what we can draw from these GATT articles that purport to facilitate development is not the enforceable requirements imposed on developed countries but an important principle expressed in Article XXXVI, that reciprocity should not be imposed on developing countries in consideration of their development needs for the concessions provided by developed countries.

2.2.4 "Enabling Clause"

A set of policy statements was made in the form of the GATT Decision on November 28, 1979, in favor of developing country Members.[140] It is referred to as the "enabling clause." This enabling clause permanently approved the General System of Preferences (GSP) and the exchange of preferences among developing country members (para. 2a). It also provided a differential and preferential treatment for developing countries

---

[138] In fact, it may be difficult to devise development-assistance provisions that have practical enforceability; i.e.,what sanctions can be applied to a violation of such obligations?

[139] Refer to the concepts of free trade and fair trade discussed in Chapter 2.1.2 *supra*.

[140] GATT Contracting Parties, Decision of November 28, 1979, on Differential and More Favourable Treatment, Reciprocity and Fuller Participation of Developing Countries, GATT B.I.S.D. (26th Supp., 1980), p. 203.

with respect to non-tariff measures (para. 2d) and special treatment of the least-developed countries (LDCs) (para. 2b). The enabling clause also states that developed countries should not expect reciprocity for the commitments made by them in trade concessions (para. 5) and that developed countries should exercise utmost restraint in seeking concessions from LDCs (para. 6).

This enabling clause is considered to have settled debate within the GATT and established the policy of special and preferential treatment for developing countries.[141] Nonetheless, it is doubtful that this clause has actually made any real difference in the policy decisions of developed countries regarding their trade relations with developing countries; the effectiveness of this clause is simply questionable. With respect to the GSP, its beneficial effect on the trade of developing countries has been diminishing as overall tariff rates imposed by developed countries have dropped significantly over the years,[142] and "sensitive products" such as agricultural products, textiles, and clothing, which are the major export products of developing countries, have been either excluded or received less preference.[143] In addition, it has been observed that political conditions (e.g., labor standard requirements) have been imposed on developing countries to receive preferential treatment,[144] and stringent rules of origin have diminished the use of the preferential system.[145]

---

[141] Shoenbaum (2004), *supra* note 9.

[142] For instance, under the U.S.'s GSP scheme, imports from GSP beneficiaries were subject to an average tariff of 4 percent in 2000, only 1.5 percentage points below the average MFN tariff rate. The European Union (EU) imposed 4.9 percent on the beneficiaries in 2000, 2 percent lower than MFN rate. WTO doc. WT/COMTD/W/77/Rev.1/Add.4 (Feb. 2, 2002).

[143] *Id.*

[144] *Id.* The legality of these conditionalities has been questioned since the enabling clause requires that preferences are being "generalized, non-reciprocal and non-discriminatory." Lorand Bartels, "The WTO Enabling Clause and Positive Conditionality in the European Community's GSP Program" (2003) 6 *Journal of International Economic Law* 507–532.

[145] For more discussion, see Stefano Inama, "Market Access for LDCs: Issues to Be Addressed" (2002) 36 *Journal of World Trade* 101–113.

The enabling clause does not seem to provide any effective sanction against a violation of these commitments therein, just as in the case of Part IV of the GATT. The enabling clause *enables* developed countries to provide preference for developing countries, but it does not *obligate* them to do so or regulate the manner in which such preference should be provided (e.g., whether developed countries are allowed to attach political conditions to the preference). Despite a series of noble expressions of policy preference for developing countries enumerated in the enabling clause, developing countries still believe that developed countries have not lived up to their commitments to provide special and preferential treatment to developing countries.[146]

Some developed countries have offered preferential treatment to LDCs greater than that provided under the existing GSP scheme. For instance, the European Union (EU) has recently introduced the "Everything But Arms" (EBA) initiative, offering duty-free and quota-free treatment to products currently exported by LDCs.[147] Other countries, such as the United States and Canada, have offered similar preferential treatment to LDCs, although less comprehensive and more limited in scope than the EBA initiative.[148] In consideration of the dire economic need of LDCs, an EBA type of duty-free and quota-free treatment to the trade of LDCs needs to be implemented on the WTO level, except, perhaps, that those less-affluent developing countries that cannot afford to provide this treatment should be allowed to suspend the application of this treatment until they achieve a developed economic status. Just like the EBA initiative, a transitional period can be set for the complete removal of trade barriers

---

[146] Shoenbaum (2004), *supra* note 9.

[147] For an initial evaluation of the EBA initiative, see Paul Brenton, "Integrating the Least Developed Countries into the World Trading System: The Current Impact of European Union Preferences Under 'Everything But Arms'" (2003) 37 *Journal of World Trade* 623–646.

[148] For instance, the United States has recently implemented the Africa Growth and Opportunity Act, which offers improved access to certain African, but not Asian, LDCs. *Id.*, pp. 644–645.

to sensitive products.[149] While applying preference to LDCs, Members should also ensure that non-tariff measures do not undermine the trade benefit of these preferences.[150]

2.3 Need for Changes

2.3.1 Inadequacies of Current "Special and Differential" Treatment and the Need for Rule Modifications

The inadequacies of development-assistance provisions in WTO disciplines suggest that more needs to be done. Provisions according preference for developing countries, other than the articles previously discussed, exist in WTO disciplines, with the majority of them found in the subsequent UR agreements that give "special and differential (S&D) treatment" to developing countries.[151] With respect to the application of WTO requirements, these provisions relax the requirements of the current disciplines for the benefit of developing countries, require protection of the interests of developing countries, or give more compliance time (transition period) for developing countries. However, this S&D treatment, as currently provided, is not sufficient to meet the development needs of developing countries for the following reasons.

[149] In the EBA initiative, trade liberalization is complete except for three products – fresh bananas, rice, and sugar – where tariffs will be gradually reduced to zero (in 2006 for bananas and 2009 for rice and sugar). Duty-free tariff quotas for rice and sugar will be increased annually. *Id.*, p. 625.

[150] It has been observed that non-tariff measures, as well as stringent rules of origin, continue to limit exports from LDCs significantly. Inama (2002), *supra* note 145, p. 115. Applications of administered protection, such as AD measures, CVDs, and safeguards, can also diminish the beneficial effect of preference for LDCs.

[151] 145 such provisions are scattered throughout several WTO agreements, understandings, and GATT articles. Twenty-two are applied exclusively to LDCs. For a review of the special and differential treatment (S&D) provisions in the WTO, see WTO, *Implementation of Special and Differential Treatment Provisions in WTO Agreements and Decisions – Note by Secretariat*, WTO doc. WT/COMTD/W/77 (Oct. 25, 2000).

First, the relaxation of current requirements in favor of developing countries and the protection of their interests are insufficient. For instance, Article 9.1 of the Agreement on Safeguards (SA) requires the exemption of imports originating in a developing country Member from safeguards where the portion of such imports does not exceed 3 percent, provided that the collective share of imports from all such developing country Members (under 3 percent) accounts for not more than 9 percent.[152] Article 9.2 of the SA also allows developing country Members to apply safeguards for a period up to two years beyond the maximum duration and to reapply safeguards to the same product after shortened intervals.[153] These provisions are designed to offer preference to developing country Members applying a safeguard measure or subject to one, but this preference has been too limiting because of the tight ceilings (individual 3 percent and collective 9 percent) and criticized as being not very helpful for developing countries.[154] Not much leeway has been provided to developing countries in other core trade regulations closely relevant to their trade, such as tariff bindings, subsidies, and AD rules, as further discussed in the subsequent chapters.

Where the transition period is provided as a preference, the S&D treatment will expire after a stipulated period for transition. Such expiration is not commensurate with the development interests of developing countries because the development need of a particular developing country may require a continuation of the S&D treatment after the expiration of the transition period.[155] Where exemptions from WTO obligations are given on a permanent basis as in subsidy rules, only a small number

---

[152] WTO, *The Results of the Uruguay Round of Multilateral Trade Negotiations, supra* note 53, pp. 279–280.

[153] *Id.*

[154] Jai S. Mah, "Injury and Causation in the Agreement on Safeguards" (2001) 4 *Journal of World Intellectual Property* 380–382.

[155] The subsequent chapters introduce economic grounds to advocate more general and comprehensive preferential treatment than currently existing and also discuss specifically what preference should be given in each area, including tariff bindings, subsidies, AD practices, and safeguards.

of developing countries (such as LDCs) benefit from this exemption.[156] Some of the advanced developing countries may not require a continued application of this type of S&D treatment after its expiration, but many may do. The current S&D treatment does not provide differentiated treatment to developing countries of widely different development status, except preferential treatment to LDCs in limited areas. It has been pointed out that the need for greater differentiation in S&D treatment has become obvious.[157]

During the UR, developed countries were generally reluctant to agree on S&D treatment to developing countries on a permanent basis and tried to limit the extent and the duration of this treatment. The limitations of the current S&D treatment reflect the prevalent attitude that a same set of rules should eventually be applied to *all* nations, both developed and developing countries, and that the S&D treatment should be limited and not to be renewed or expanded. In line with this sentiment, a prominent speaker in the 1999 WTO high-level symposium on trade and development advised developing countries to "avoid a push for renewed S&D treatment."[158] This "one rule for all nations" is not consistent with the development needs of developing countries and may actually hamper development efforts significantly.[159]

Furthermore, many current requirements in WTO disciplines are not consistent with the development interests of developing countries. For

---

[156] For instance, only LDCs are exempted from the prohibition of export subsidies. See Chapter 3.3, *infra* for a relevant discussion.

[157] Michael Hart and Bill Dymond, "Special and Differential Treatment and the Doha 'Development' Round" (2003) 37 *Journal of World Trade* 409.

[158] Per C. Fred Bergsten. WTO, *Report of the WTO High-Level Symposium on Trade and Development* (1999), *supra* note 38.

[159] The subsequent discussions in Chapters 3.1 and 4.1, *infra* explain why this is the case. See also *infra* note 451. In addition, most developing countries have already experienced considerable difficulties in complying with the stringent requirements of the WTO provisions. It was observed that as of January 1, 2000, 80 or 90 of 109 developing and transition economy members of the WTO were in violation of the agreements on sanitary and phytosanitary (SPS) measures, customs valuation, as well as on trade-related aspects of intellectual property rights. J. Michael Finger, "The WTO's Special Burden on Less Developed Countries" (2000) 19(3) *Cato Journal* 435.

instance, the principle of binding tariff rates makes it difficult for developing countries to raise tariffs to protect their infant industries. Article XVIII authorizes trade measures necessary for the promotion of an infant industry, including tariff increases. Nonetheless, the multilateral control placed in Article XVIII requiring time-consuming negotiations and burdensome compensations may not allow developing countries to adjust their tariff bindings for the purpose of economic development in time.[160] Alternative treatment should be provided to meet the development need of developing countries, as further discussed in Chapter 3.2.

In addition, the prohibition of export subsidies under the Agreement on Subsidies and Countervailing Measures (SCM Agreement) prevents developing countries from applying measures to promote export industries for a development purpose.[161] Chapter 3.3 introduces a possible mechanism to enable developing countries to adopt these measures without dismantling the current structure of the SCM Agreement. It also has been observed that compliance with some of the WTO requirements (e.g., setting up an IPR regime under the requirement of the TRIPS Agreement) is costly and puts considerable burden on developing countries by requiring developing countries to divert scarce resources that should be invested elsewhere to meet more immediate economic needs.[162] This problem raises doubt about the wisdom of imposing an extensive regulatory scheme on developing countries as some of the WTO provisions attempt to do. This issue will be further discussed in the subsequent chapters.

I have discussed the legal framework for international trade and examined the current provisions facilitating development. This examination has revealed significant inadequacies in the current provisions. Modification of these provisions alone will not be sufficient because there are other

---

[160] Section A of Article XVIII has not been invoked since the WTO entered into force, and Section C has been invoked on only a few occasions. WTO doc. WT/COMTD/39 (July 24, 2002).

[161] *Supra* note 156. See also Rodrik (2004), *infra* note 189, p. 33.

[162] *Infra* note 464. Michael Hart and Bill Dymond (2003), *supra* note 157, p. 408.

specific rules in the WTO that impose barriers to development efforts (e.g., subsidy rules). This requires us to consider making changes in a wide range of rules governing specific areas of trade that have significant effects on development. These areas include the Schedule of Concessions, subsidies, AD measures, safeguards, trade-related investment measures (TRIMs), TRIPS, and trade in services. Foreign direct investment (FDI) and regional trade liberalization by free trade agreements (FTAs) outside the multilateral framework of the WTO are also relevant to our concern and need to be addressed. The subsequent chapters discuss these specific areas, examine the effect of the current rules on development, and propose alternative provisions where necessary.

2.3.2 Proposal for a Council for Trade and Development and Agreement on Development Facilitation

I conclude this chapter with an examination of whether adequate attention has been given to trade and development issues within the WTO organizational apparatus. Criticism was raised that developing country issues, such as technology transfer, financial mechanism, capacity-building, debt relief, and supply-side constraints, had not been addressed adequately.[163] Issues concerning trade and development are complex and require continuous and long-term attention on the institutional level. This means that a permanent body with an appropriate mandate might be necessary within the WTO to address issues pertaining to trade and development. Does the WTO have an adequate organizational structure to address development issues, and does it adequately work on these issues with sufficient resources?

As to the institutional apparatus, the Committee on Trade and Development (CTD) is currently organized in the WTO under the General Council. The CTD has a mandate to address issues concerning developing

---

[163] Per India, WTO, *Report of the WTO High-Level Symposium on Trade and Development* (1999), *supra* note 38.

countries that include implementation of preferential provisions for developing countries, guidelines for technical cooperation, increased participation of developing countries in the trading system, and the position of LDCs.[164] Regional trade arrangements among developing countries also have to be reported to the CTD, and the CTD also handles notifications of GSP programs and preferential arrangements among developing countries such as Mercado Comun der Sur (MERCOSUR), Common Market for Eastern and Southern Africa (COMESA), and Association of Southeast Asian Nations Free Trade Area (AFTA).[165] The Subcommittee on Least-Developed Countries, also established under the CTD, focuses on issues particular to LDCs: integration of LDCs into the multilateral trading system, technical cooperation, and implementation of preferential provisions for LDCs.

With this institutional structure in place, the WTO, through its Training and Technical Cooperation Institute, provides assistance to developing countries, such as regular training sessions on trade policy in Geneva, about 400 technical cooperation activities annually, including seminars and workshops in various countries and courses in Geneva, and legal assistance to developing countries.[166] It also initiated a WTO Reference Center program in 1997 with the objective of creating a network of computerized information centers in developing countries. The International Trade Centre, a joint body with UNCTAD, also helps developing countries to expand export and to improve their import operations.

These activities are undoubtedly helpful to developing countries, particularly in capacity-building aspects, but the scope of assistance is rather

---

[164] The description of the Committee function is found at the WTO Web site at <www.wto.org>.

[165] Id.

[166] For legal assistance, thirty-two WTO governments set up "the Advisory Centre on WTO Law" in 2001. Its members consist of countries contributing to the funding and those receiving legal advice. LDCs are automatically eligible for advice, and other developing countries and transition economies have to be fee-paying members to receive advice. For further information, refer to the WTO Web site at <www.wto.org>.

limited. Other essential development issues, such as technology transfer, financial mechanism, and debt relief have not been covered by these activities because the CTD does not have a mandate to address these issues within the WTO. Developing countries have called for the discussion of these issues in the WTO, and in response to this demand, a working group on Trade, Debt, and Finance and another group on Trade and Technology Transfer have been established under the Doha Development Agenda (DDA).[167] The CTD, as the primary body in the WTO concerning trade and development, meets in special sessions to handle work under the DDA.

There is a question as to the sufficiency of the current organizational apparatus to address complex and long-term development issues, which consists of the CTD and the Subcommittee on LDCs, aided by the Training and Technical Cooperation Institute under the WTO Secretariat. First, this question can be addressed by way of comparison with the treatment of another issue prompted by developed countries: TRIPS. A full council, not a committee, is organized to cover complex and long-term TRIPS issues.[168] If the magnitude of development issues should be considered to be no less important than that of developed country issues such as TRIPS, perhaps we should consider elevating the level of the institutional body on trade and development to the council level as well. This elevation will not only make a symbolic statement recognizing the essential importance of development issues but also meet practical needs as follows.

Some of the development issues currently addressed in WTO working groups, such as trade, debt, and finance and trade and technology transfer have fundamental implications on development. Should these

---

[167] The DDA addresses the issues of trade, debt, and finance; trade and transfer of technology; technical cooperation and capacity building; LDCs; and special and differential treatment. WTO, *Ministerial Declaration*, WT/MIN(01)/DEC/1 (Nov. 20, 2001).

[168] The Council for Trade-Related Aspects of Intellectual Property Rights (TRIPS) has been organized under Article IV of the WTO Agreement. WTO, *The Results of the Uruguay Round of Multilateral Trade Negotiations, supra* note 53, p 5.

issues become a permanent agenda to be covered by the WTO, monitored and addressed on a permanent basis, then the importance of these issues requires the establishment of separate committees replacing the current working groups. A separate Council for Trade and Development can oversee the operations of these committees. In addition, as individual developing countries face unique problems with increasing their participation in the WTO and with securing the full benefit of WTO membership, the creation of a separate committee seems necessary to bring adequate institutional attention to the various problems facing individual developing countries to assist with their needs more effectively and individually. The current Advisory Centre on WTO Law[169] can be expanded and incorporated into this body to render effective legal advice to developing country Members.

The proposed expansion of the current organizational apparatus would mean an expansion of the staff and an increase in resources available to assist with developing countries. The current WTO budget of 1.36 million Swiss francs (roughly 1.18 million U.S. Dollars [USD][170]) for technical cooperation and of 4.29 million Swiss francs (3.72 million USD) for training would be inadequately low to meet this proposal. Some Members have financially assisted trade ministers and representatives of developing countries to participate in WTO meetings and negotiations. This sort of necessary financial aid should not be left to the generosity of individual Members but should be provided systematically on the institutional level as part of assistance to individual developing countries. The WTO Advisory Centre on WTO Law should also be supported with the WTO budget and not out of the pockets of wealthy Members. Logistics need to be improved with the need and financial circumstances of developing countries in mind; WTO meetings and negotiations schedules should also be set in a way to maximize the participation of

---

[169] *Supra* note 166.

[170] This conversion is calculated based on the exchange rate as of December 2004.

developing countries.[171] The WTO budget allocation to the activities and functions of trade and development should be significantly increased to meet these needs.

Finally, the feasibility and desirability of a separate set of rules facilitating development needs to be considered. By this, I propose to consider a separate agreement in WTO disciplines provisionally entitled "Agreement on Development Facilitation" (ADF). Why would a separate agreement be necessary to facilitate development in trade disciplines? The answer is already evident in that development has not been adequately addressed and facilitated in WTO disciplines,[172] and a set of rules focusing on the facilitation of development would set the development agenda in WTO disciplines just as the TRIPS Agreement did for IPR issues. Although the present Doha round entertains a series of development issues,[173] the current WTO disciplines do not adequately facilitate development.

GATT Articles XXXVI–XXXVIII, as well as provisions of the enabling clause, are largely declaratory and do not create enforceable obligations. Perhaps the ADF could develop specific legal obligations to bind at least some of the commitments under Part IV of the GATT on developed country Members, just as other UR agreements expanded and elaborated the provisions of the GATT, turning them into more specific, enforceable obligations. The ADF could also develop the systematic monitoring and surveillance of the implementation of these obligations thus developed.

---

[171] Renato Ruggiero, former general-director of the WTO, acknowledged that some developing and LDCs had difficulty in participating fully in the organization, mainly because of too many meetings, which was an objective problem but not the result of a deliberate policy of exclusion. WTO, *Report of the WTO High-Level Symposium on Trade and Development* (1999), *supra* note 38. The application of the current Web technology should be considered to replace meetings and conferences in Geneva with online conferences so that developing countries may increase their participation without having to commit their limited financial resources and manpower to costly trips to Geneva.

[172] *Supra* note 163, and *infra* note 566.

[173] *Supra* note 167.

The proposed committees could take up monitoring and surveillance functions and report to the Council for Trade and Development.

Provisions offering S&D treatment to developing countries, although insufficient, are scattered throughout various provisions of WTO disciplines without any coherent regulatory structure. Many of them are temporary, expiring after a certain period of time. Some of this temporary S&D treatment, such as the subsidy rules for developing countries,[174] needs to be converted into permanent rules as part of the new agreement. The inclusion of these scattered provisions in a separate and enforceable agreement may also provide a coherent and permanent regulatory structure to S&D treatment that is currently lacking, for instance, by providing clear and objective standards to determine the developing country status.

What else should be included in the ADF? The subsequent chapters propose substantive provisions to facilitate economic development, and these provisions may be included. I do not intend here to suggest an exhaustive list of provisions to be included in the ADF, and the scope and the contents of the ADF need to be further discussed, taking into account the progress made in the current discussion of the DDA. The ADF may require a separate status within Annex 1 of the WTO Agreement as it would affect the operation of GATS and the TRIPS Agreement, as well as the Multilateral Agreements on Trade in Goods. At any rate, the ADF would make a statement that development issues are considered to be as essential as other issues promoted by developed countries such as TRIPS, which has attained a separate regulatory treatment, and is no longer only a subject of elaborate rhetoric, by providing a coherent and permanent regulatory structure on trade and development, which has been missing from the UR.

---

[174] See Chapter 3 *infra.*

THREE

Reclaiming Development: Tariff Bindings and Subsidies

3.1 Two Principal Components of Industrial Promotion Policies

3.1.1 Introduction

I have discussed in the preceding two chapters the idea that the international trading system needs to allow developing countries to adopt effective development policies. What specifically are these policies, and how effective are they for economic development? Throughout history, nations have applied various policies to promote industries. Government policies targeting promotion of domestic industries are called "industrial policy."[175] To promote industries, governments have used a range of policy tools that include direct financial grants, loan guarantees,

---

[175] According to the World Bank, industrial policy is defined as "government efforts to alter industrial structure to promote productivity based growth." World Bank, *The East Asian Miracle: Economic Growth and Public Policy* (New York, Oxford University Press, 1992). A wide range of government policies affect industry directly or indirectly, and therefore, it is not easy to define the precise terms of the industrial policy. In this book, I use the term "industrial policy" or "industrial promotion policy" as referring to a broad range of government policies with a primary objective of promoting industries, including infant industry promotion. See also Dominick Salvatore, *International Economics* (8th ed., John Wiley & Sons, Hoboken, N.J., 2003), pp. 287–295, for a discussion of industrial policy.

tax rebates/reductions, research and development (R&D) support, facilitation of social infrastructure, and various trade measures to protect domestic industries from imports.[176]

In particular, trade measures and subsidies have historically been the two principal components of national industrial policies to promote industries, particularly in the earlier stages of their development ("infant industry promotion"). However, many economists today argue that policies using trade measures and government subsidies to promote industries are not effective and cause a distortion of resource allocation and economic inefficiencies.[177] It is, therefore, necessary to consider the viability of these industrial promotion policies and then discuss how tariffs and subsidies are treated under the WTO. I also propose alternative provisions concerning binding tariff rates and subsidies later in this chapter, which would better facilitate economic development.

3.1.2 "Invisible Hand" versus Infant Industry Promotion

There has long been debate about whether governments should lead economic development or whether they should refrain from doing so because an economy performs most efficiently when it is left to the "invisible hand" of market forces.[178] It is essential to consider historical and empirical evidence as well as relevant economic theories to determine

---

[176] Dani Rodrik believes that industrial policy is concerned with the provisions of public goods for the productive sector, such as public labs and public R&D, health and infrastructure facilities, sanitary and phytosanitary standards, infrastructure, vocational and technical training, and from this perspective, further concludes that "industrial policy is just good economic policy of the type that traditional, orthodox approaches prescribe." Rodrik (2004), *infra* note 189, pp. 38–39.

[177] *Infra* note 199.

[178] Classical economist Adam Smith argued in his masterpiece, *An Inquiry into the Nature and Causes of the Wealth of Nations* (1776), that this "invisible hand" of market forces allows the economy to function most efficiently and that government intervention is necessary only exceptionally where the market fails. This market theory formed the cornerstone of modern economics. Economists have observed market failures in cases of monopoly, monopsony (markets with one buyer and many sellers), externalities, public goods, and asymmetric information.

whether industrial promotion policies are economically sound. Historically, developed economies that support higher living standards today have invariably developed manufacturing industries that yield higher levels of income.[179] Then how are such industries developed? Does the profit-maximizing mechanism of market forces direct resources to those industrial sectors efficiently without state intervention?[180]

The classical economic and trade theories by Adam Smith and David Ricardo do not support a state promotion of industry or an imposition of trade measures because state interventions, according to those theories, will only cause economic inefficiency and a distortion of trade.[181] Adam Smith recognized economic growth, but he believed that it comes from a division of labor[182] rather than a state promotion of industries. In fact, Book IV of his famous *Wealth of Nations*[183] adamantly opposes the mercantile system that favors monopolies at home and abroad. State promotion of industry may necessarily involve some measure of protection for domestic industries that Adam Smith opposed. The currently prevalent

---

[179] In contrast, a heavy dependency on primary products is characteristic of the economies of poor countries. Successful economic development cases have shown increases in the share of manufacturing industries. For instance, the share of GNP by manufacturing sectors in South Korea rose from 9.1 percent in 1962 to 34.2 percent in 1982 as Korea's economic development progressed, and that of primary sectors fell from 45.3 percent in 1962 to 19.2 percent in 1982. Kwang-suk Kim and Joon-kyung Park, *Sources of Economic Growth in Korea: 1963–1981*, Korea Development Institute (1985), Table 2-1, Major Indicators of Korean Economic Growth, 1954–1982, pp. 8.

[180] It has been observed that industrial restructuring rarely takes place without significant government assistance. Rodrik, *infra* note 189, p. 15. For instance, the unknown risk of expanding into new, non-traditional production activities may deter private sectors from engaging in such activities. *Id.*, pp. 7–8. Even if innovative entrepreneurs bear the risk and become successful, they may have to share their gains with latecomers who benefit from their experience but do not pay for the risk. *Id.*, pp. 8–9.

[181] *Supra* notes 81 and 178.

[182] Smith believed that economic efficiency will be maximized and economic growth will be achieved by separation of a manufacturing process into a number of sub-tasks, with each task performed by a separate person or group of persons. This specialization or division of labor is the basis of mass-production techniques. Adam Smith, *supra* note 178.

[183] *Id.*

"neoclassical" or "neoliberal" economic stance,[184] which has largely followed Adam Smith's principal idea, does not favor these "state interventions."[185] A set of neoliberal policies, so-called "Washington Consensus,"[186] is also reflected in the regulatory makeup of the WTO that has set the binding tariff system and outlawed certain trade-related state subsidies.[187]

The debate on the economic viability of state industrial promotion centers around the question of whether state planning and intervention

[184] Neoclassical economics, referring to a grouping of economic schools generally favoring free market approaches, emerged in the late nineteenth century in opposition to Marxism and reaffirmed that the market promotes economic efficiency and fair social distribution. It has become the dominant, mainstream economics in Anglo-American universities after the Second World War and also influenced the positions of the postwar international economic institutions such as International Monetary Fund (IMF) and World Bank. Neoclassical economics forms the core of a political-economic philosophy, widely referred to as "neoliberalism" that discourages positive government interventions in the economy and promotes free market approaches, including privatization and trade liberalization. In this sense, the terms "neoclassical" economic stance and "neoliberal" stance are considered to be synonymous and used interchangeably throughout this book without distinction. IMF conditionalities during the financial crisis in Asia, which caused adverse effects on the economy of the crisis-stricken countries, reflected this stance and imposed restrictions on government trade and industrial policies. Rodrik (2004), *infra* note 189, p. 33. See also Hider A. Khan, *Global Markets and Financial Crises in Asia* (Palgrave Macmillan, New York, 2004). With respect to trade, the pursuit of free trade, an important part of the neoliberal economic stance, has been the objective of the GATT regime and more so of the subsequent WTO.

[185] Criticism has been raised that the market theory of classical economics has been taken to the extreme by neoliberalists to the extent that the belief in the market and in market forces has become an end in itself.

[186] The phrase "Washington Consensus," originated by John Williamson, refers to a set of policies representing the lowest common denominator of policy advice being addressed by Washington-based institutions, such as fiscal discipline, a redirection of public expenditure priorities toward areas offering both high economic returns and the potential to improve income distribution, (such as primary health care, primary education, and infrastructure), tax reform to lower marginal rates and broaden the tax base, interest rate liberalization, a competitive exchange rate, trade liberalization, liberalization of inflows of foreign direct investment, privatization, deregulation (to abolish barriers to entry and exit), and protection of property rights. Global Trade Negotiations, Center for International Development at Harvard University, available at <http://www.cid.harvard.edu/cidtrade/issues/washington.html>.

[187] See the relevant discussions in Chapters 3.2 and 3.3, *infra*.

can work better than the market forces based on the free flow of information and individual economic freedom. Because classical market theory assumes free flow of information,[188] leading to an optimization of individual economic behavior, effective markets must make timely and accurate information available to individual and corporate participants. Therefore, although the efficiency of state intervention may be doubted in developed economies, where there is a greater availability of economic information, the role of government can be naturally emphasized in developing economies, where such information available to individuals and companies is significantly limited. Hence, in developing countries, where information is limited and where there is no adequately functioning financial market, only governments may have the ability to transfer the necessary resources to support industries in the early stages of their development.[189] Ha-Joon Chang's work shows us that governments played an

---

[188] Adam Smith's conviction in the efficiency of a market economy is based on the individual ability to make the best economic choice and making such a choice would not be possible without necessary information and the freedom to do so. He stated, "What is the species of domestic industry which his capital can employ, and of which the produce is likely to be of the greatest value, every individual, it is evident, can, in his local situation, judge much better than any statesman or lawgiver can do for him" Adam Smith, *supra* note 178. Nonetheless, this conventional wisdom has been doubted by many, as expressed by Dani Rodrik, in his recent work, which stated, "Yes, the government has imperfect information ... so does the private sector." Rodrik (2004), *infra* note 189, p. 3.

[189] *Supra* note 180. For the role of the government in economic development, promoting industrial development and facilitating transfer of resources, see Edward S. Mason, "The Role of Government in Economic Development" (1960) 50(2) *American Economic Review* 636–641; Anne O. Krueger and Baran Tuncer, "An Empirical Test of the Infant Industry Argument" (1982) 72(5) *American Economic Review* 1142–1152 (An empirical examination revealed that protection was not warranted in Turkish case.); Larry E. Westphal, "Industrial Policy in an Export Propelled Economy: Lessons From South Korea's Experience" (in Symposia: The State and Economic Development) (1990) 4(3) *Journal of Economic Perspectives* 41–59; John Brohman, "Postwar Development in the Asian NICs: Does the Neoliberal Model Fit Reality?" (1996) 72(2) *Economic Geography*, 107–130; Jacques Poot, "A Synthesis of Empirical Research of the Impact on Long-Run Growth" (2000) 31(4) *Growth & Change* 516–546; Martijn R. E. Brons, Henri L. F. DeGroot, and Peter Nijkamp, "Growth Effects of Governmental Policies: A Comparative Analysis in a Multi-Country Context" (2000) 31(4) *Growth & Change* 547–572. The

important role in promoting manufacturing industries during the development stages of today's developed countries, including the United States and Britain.[190]

Despite the brilliance of the market economy theory developed by Adam Smith and accepted and elaborated by subsequent economists, it is intrinsically difficult to understand *how* economies in the relatively primitive stages, depending heavily on the production of primary products, can build industries that would yield higher income without some deliberate efforts on the part of the government, particularly when the private sectors lack both resources and information to do so.[191] Adam Smith warned the Americans that their industrialization effort would be futile and America would be better off by continuing to produce agricultural products.[192] However, many U.S. leaders at that time believed otherwise

following references provide helpful guidance on the role of governments in facilitating infrastructure and in securing necessary capital for development. Barry Eichengreen, *Financing Infrastructure in Developing Countries: Lessons from the Railway Age* (1994) (prepared as a background paper for the World Bank's *World Development Report* on infrastructure issues in developing countries); Ashella Tshedza Ndhlovu, *Mobilization of Capital Funds by Urban Local Authorities: Zimbabwe* (South African Development Community (SADC) Information Centre on Local Governance, 2001); Dani Rodrik, *Industrial Policy for the Twenty-First Century* (paper prepared for UNIDO, September 2004), available at <http://ksghome.harvard.edu/~drodrik/UNIDOSep.pdf>.

[190] Chang, *supra* note 41, Chapter 3, pp. 13–68. Infant industry promotion policies also included extensive trade protection to shield domestic industries from competitive foreign imports. As shown in Chang's work, today's major advocates of free trade, Britain and United States, also employed extensive trade protections during their own development stages. *Id.,* pp. 19–32.

[191] It has been suggested that information externalities (i.e., problems of the risk not compensated for those who first engage in new ventures) and coordination problems (lack of other support services and infrastructure necessary for the new production activities, associated with high fixed costs) are barriers to private producers initiating new production and the government can render important assistance in this regard. Rodrik (2004), *supra* note 189. In implementing industrial policies, the importance of close cooperation and communication between the government and private sector has also been emphasized: the government should elicit information from the private sector. *Id.,* pp. 16–17, 24–25.

[192] Adam Smith stated in *Wealth of Nations*, "Were the Americans, either by combination or by any other sort of violence, to stop the importation of European manufactures,

and determined that it was important for the United States to embark on industrialization by adopting extensive trade measures against foreign industrial products as necessary.[193] Despite Smith's warning, the United States subsequently adopted high tariff barriers against foreign manufactured goods and protected domestic industries from foreign imports.[194]

The United States emerged as a major industrialized nation at the end of the nineteenth century and enjoyed economic prosperity. Would the United States have achieved the same economic prosperity had it followed Adam Smith's advice and not embarked on industrialization aided by extensive tariff protections? Alternatively, would the United

and, by thus giving a monopoly to such of their own countrymen as could manufacture the like goods, divert any considerable part of their capital into this employment, they would retard instead of accelerating the further increase in the value of their annual produce, and would obstruct instead of promoting the progress of their country towards real wealth and greatness." Cited in Chang, *supra* note 41, p. 5.

[193] Alexander Hamilton argued that, to start new industries in the United States that could soon become internationally competitive, the initial losses of those industries should be guaranteed by government aid, which could take the form of import duties or prohibition of imports altogether. J. Dorfman and R. Tugwell, *Early American Policy – Six Columbia Contributors* (Columbia University Press, New York, 1960), pp. 31–32. Henry Clay, who was Abraham Lincoln's early mentor, advocated the "American System" of trade protection in opposition to what he called the "British System" of free trade, which, he subsequently argued, was part of the British imperialist system that consigned the United States to a role of primary product exporter. P. Conkin, *Prophets of Prosperity: America's First Political Economists* (Indiana University Press, Bloomington, 1980).

[194] The United States gradually increased tariff rates throughout the nineteenth century, reaching an average tariff rate of around 40 percent for manufactured products in 1820 and onward. The victory of the Civil War by the industrial northern states ensured that protectionist policies were maintained until the First World War. Chang (2002), *supra* note 41, pp. 25–28; U.S. intellectuals and politicians in the nineteenth century were concerned that the free trade theory was not suited to the United States, and Thomas Jefferson even tried to stop publication of Ricardo's *Principles of Political Economy and Taxation* in the United States! E. Reinert, "Diminishing Returns and Economic Sustainability: The Dilemma of Resource-based Economies under a Free Trade Regime," *in* H. Stein et al. (eds.), *International Trade Regulation, National Development Strategies and the Environment – Towards Sustainable Development?* (Centre for Development and the Environment, University of Oslo, 1996), p. 5.

States have transformed its largely agricultural-based economy into a major industrial economy in the late nineteenth century and achieved economic prosperity without tariff protections? These hypothetical questions are not easy to answer. There is no conclusive evidence that these trade protections always promote new industries successfully and lead to economic prosperity. Nevertheless, as Hamilton and Clay previously argued,[195] trade protection has been historically one of the important elements, if not solely sufficient, for economic development by facilitating the establishment of industries.[196]

The theory of infant industry promotion was formulated in the 1840s by German economist Friedrich List, who was originally known to be a free trade advocate but began to support the infant industry argument after his exile in the United States (1789–1795), where he learned of the works of American politicians and economists who supported infant industry protection, such as Alexander Hamilton and Daniel Raymond.[197] List argued that while free trade is beneficial among the economies of similar stages of development, trade protection is necessary for developing countries to promote "infant industries" (i.e., industries in the early stages of development).[198] As mentioned, mainstream economists today tend to oppose infant industry promotion policy as economically inefficient.[199]

---

[195] See *supra* note 193.

[196] *Supra* note 190.

[197] W. Handerson, *Friedrich List – Economist and Visionary, 1789–1846* (Frank Cass, London, 1983).

[198] Friedrich List, *The National System of Political Economy* (1841).

[199] For a recent critique, see Michael Porter, *Can Japan Compete?* (Macmillan, Basingstoke, U.K., 2000). Also, Anne O. Krueger and Baran Tuncer's earlier article, "An Empirical Test of the Infant Industry Argument," *supra* note 189, argues that an empirical test did not justify industrial protection in Turkey. In contrast, another line of economists, who pioneered "development economics," including Rosenstein-Rodan, Mandelbaum, Lewis, Rostow, Kuznets, Gerschenkron, Hirschman, and Kindleberger, believed that state-led development policies are key to development. For a discussion of the contribution made by development economists to the study of economics, see Pranab Bardhan, "Economics of Development and the Development of Economics" (1993) 7(2) *Journal*

The opponents of infant industry promotion quickly point out that there is no evidence that the government knows better than the market about which industry would be "essential" for economic development.[200] They argue that without state intervention, resources will flow into the most efficient industries by operation of the "invisible hand" of market forces, just as advocated by Adam Smith, and therefore, the role of the state should be minimized to correct market failures.[201] A historical contradiction with this position has already been discussed; in the earlier stages of development, it is inherently difficult to facilitate new industries without deliberate mobilization of resources, which could only be done by the state.[202] It has been also observed that industrial restructuring rarely takes place without significant government assistance because the unknown risk of expanding into new, non-traditional production activities may deter private sectors from engaging in such activities.[203] It is, therefore, not surprising to see that nearly every major developed country today has adopted deliberate state-led industrial promotion policies during their development, including some measure of trade protection and subsidies.[204]

---

of Economic Perspectives 129–142. Wassily Leontief's famous input-output analysis is also relevant to development policy initiatives because it identifies the required increases in the elements of inputs for certain output increase. Wassily W. Leontief, The Structure of American Economy, 1919–1929: An Empirical Application of Equilibrium Analysis (Harvard University Press, Cambridge, Mass., 1941). Leontief warned against theoretical assumptions not supported by empirical data, which were prevalently used among mainstream economists.

[200] Salvatore (2003), supra note 173, p. 288.

[201] Supra note 181.

[202] There is no efficient capital market, and there is limited availability of information in the primitive private sectors of undeveloped countries. Foreign direct investment (FDI) may supply the needed capital and information, but its availability is also limited. In addition, FDI may not replace the role of state for economic development on other grounds. See Chapter 6 infra for the relevant discussion.

[203] Supra note 180.

[204] H.-J. Chang discusses cases of infant industry protection in Great Britain, United States, Germany, France, Sweden, Belgium, the Netherlands, Switzerland, Japan, and other newly industrializing East Asian countries ("NICs"). Chang, supra note 41, pp. 19–51.

Another concern about state-led industrial policy is that those industries promoted by the government in developing countries may not be sustained without continuing government subsidies due to the lack of domestic market demand for their products.[205] International trade becomes relevant at this point, perhaps somewhat differently from what has been envisaged by Ricardo's theory.[206] Demand from larger overseas markets can create sufficient revenue to sustain promoted industries.[207] Japan and the other newly industrialized economies in Asia, such as South Korea, Taiwan, Singapore, and Hong Kong, all enjoyed the success of export, which fueled their economic development. The infant industry promotion policy provides initial support and protection while the new industry goes through the learning curve. The success of this policy is finally achieved when the industry becomes competitive enough to

---

[205] The lack of domestic demand was considered to be a primary cause of the failure of import-substitution policy adopted by India and elsewhere. For a review of import-substitution policy, see I. Little et al., *Industries and Trade in Some Developing Countries* (Oxford University Press, London, 1970); Anne. O. Krueger, "Alternative Strategies and Employment in LDCs" (1978) 68(2) *American Economic Review* 270–274; H. Bruton, "Import Substitution," *in* H. B. Chenery and T. N. Srinivasan (eds.), *Handbook of Development Economics*, Vol. 2 (North-Holland, Amsterdam, 1989), pp. 1601–1644; H. Bruton, "A Reconsideration of Import Substitution" (1998) 12 *Journal of Economic Perspective* 903–936.

[206] *Supra* note 81. A recent study has revealed that developing economies tend to diversify, rather than concentrate, production patterns in a large cross section, suggesting that the driving force of economic development cannot be the forces of comparative advantage. Jean Imbs and Romain Wacziarg, "Stages of Diversification" (March 2003) 93(1) *American Economic Review* 63–86. It is also supported by the fact that the number of export products tends to increase, rather than decrease, in the process of economic development. Bailey Klinger and Daniel Lederman, "Discovery and Development: An Empirical Exploration of 'New' Products," World Bank, August 2004.

[207] A commentator mentioned that there is nothing in the empirical literature to suggest that exports generate the kind of positive externalities that would justify their subsidization as a general rule. Rodrik (2004), *supra* note 189, p. 34. On the contrary, it is difficult to see how developing countries with small domestic markets could ever generate sufficient revenues, at least initially, without exporting to other countries. As discussed in Chapter 1 *supra*, exports have been an engine for economic development. The success of outward-oriented development policy has been well documented. *Supra* note 28.

sustain itself without government subsidies, justifying initial economic inefficiencies resulting from the protection. The economic achievement by the outward-oriented policies of the East Asian countries, which emphasized both state industrial support and export, is a good example of this success.[208]

3.1.3 Concluding the Infant Industry Promotion Debate

Should this infant industry policy be facilitated by WTO rules? There is no guarantee that infant industry promotion will always successfully lead to the economic development of a developing country.[209] A commentator has also noted that government intervention should target new activities (a new technology, training, a new good or service) that require assistance, rather than sectors per se.[210] In addition, the success of development initiatives would depend on the presence of other political, social, and economic factors, such as those addressed in Chapter 1 (i.e., a stable and efficient government, working institutional arrangement between the public and private sectors,[211] consistent economic policy, social peace, educated population, access to capital, and a cultural environment that fosters working ethics and can accommodate changes associated with

---

[208] *Supra* note 28.

[209] For instance, the import-substitution policy of former Western colonies, such as India, after the Second World War is largely considered a failed economic policy, leading to economic inefficiency and ultimately failing to relieve poverty in that nation. The possibility of a failure is considered to be common and should not deter the implementation of industrial policy. Rodrik (2004), *supra* note 189, p. 25.

[210] *Id.*, pp. 14, 23. The commentator seems to indicate that blanket support for specific sectors is likely to be less productive. However, different sectors have different needs for support, and it might not be possible to respond to all those needs with limited public resources. This limitation may necessitate a sectoral priority/emphasis to maximize the impact of government support on the economy and development. Effective infant industry promotion policies are calibrated to support such activities necessary to promote new industries.

[211] *Supra* note 13.

development). Nonetheless, where these conditions are present,[212] infant industry promotion can provide a working chance to improve developing economies, as demonstrated in the successful development cases of the East Asian economies[213] as well as in many other developed countries today.[214]

[212] It may be difficult to have all these conditions present in a developing country. An insufficiency of one or more of these conditions may create difficulties for the successful implementation of industrial promotion policy, but these difficulties do not necessarily preclude the possibility of success. Thus, a developing country with less-than-perfect conditions may still adopt industrial promotion policy and, at the same time, also try to improve these conditions. Such improvement may also be made part of the policy package (e.g., create a working institutional arrangement to better cooperate and communicate with the private sectors). Economic improvement tends to improve these conditions (e.g., better education) and, in turn, create a better environment for the implementation of industrial policy.

[213] The World Bank noted in its 1993 Report, *The East Asian Miracle, supra* note 28, that the East Asian experience had been a confirmation of its market-friendly approach to policy. On the contrary, it has been argued that a closer examination reveals the weaknesses and questions about some of the critical elements of analysis contained in the report and, consequently, that many of the report's conclusions and recommendations, relating to trade and industrial strategy in particular, need to be "heavily" discounted. Dani Rodrik, "King Kong Meets Godzilla: The World Bank and the East Asian Miracle," CEPR Discussion Paper No. 944 (Centre for Economic Policy Research, London, 1994), available online at <http://www.cepr.org/pubs/dps/DP944.asp>. Perhaps the World Bank Report emphasized one aspect of the East Asian development that did use the market mechanism, but as noted, the East Asian countries also adopted extensive government subsidization and trade protection to facilitate industries, which is not exactly the prescription of neoclassical/neoliberal economics.

[214] A number of historical references also indicate that most of today's developed countries, including the United States and Great Britain, which are often considered to be the champions of free trade, as well as other countries developed in later periods, such as Germany and Japan, also employed infant industry promotion policies extensively while they were in the development stages. *Supra* note 204. Professor Junji Nakagawa of Tokyo University has argued that this is a too simplistic generalization since the United States after the Civil War, Germany under Bismarck, and Japan after the Second World War cannot be "put in a same basket: environments were different; market structures were different; governments, and their policy instruments were different; and economic theories were different." A discussion of these suggested differences is largely irrelevant to the point of the argument unless it is identified *specifically how* these differences actually preclude the argument for infant industry promotion; for instance, economists

I mentioned earlier that today's developed countries established manufacturing industries during their development, which suggests that currently developing countries would also have to establish manufacturing sectors or upgrade their existing manufacturing base to improve their economic output. However, since the economies of developed countries today are predominantly service oriented (around 70 percent of the GDP in 1999),[215] it has been questioned whether developing economies can also be transformed into the same type of sophisticated service economies that yield high levels of income, without establishing or improving manufacturing industries. If this is feasible, infant industry promotion to facilitate manufacturing industries may not be necessary.

An examination of current developing economies does not seem to suggest, at least in a general sense, that services alone have facilitated development or are likely to do so in the future: services also take up more than 50 percent of the GDP in developing countries (more than 40 percent in LDCs);[216] nonetheless, these services do not seem to work as an engine for development as the manufacturing industries did for today's developed countries in the past.[217] Of course, this does not mean that no service industry in a developing country has an economic potential that can contribute to development. If there is a service industry with such potential, it could also be facilitated just as a manufacturing industry; the rationale of infant industry promotion can be applied to promising service industries with development potential as it is to manufacturing industries.[218]

accept the essence of the market theory advocated by Adam Smith more than 200 years ago and consider it to be still applicable, although with some variances, to today's economies which are obviously different from those of Adam Smith's time and from one another.

[215] World Bank, High Income Data Profile, available online at <www.worldbank.com>.

[216] World Bank, Low and Middle Income Data Profile (2004), available online at <www.worldbank.com>.

[217] Service industries in developing countries do not seem to lead productivity increases in the economy.

[218] Nonetheless, manufactured products are typically more exportable than services in developing countries, and therefore, when infant industry promotion is implemented

It should be noted that the provisions of Article XVIII, which are still standing today, clarify that GATT/WTO disciplines authorize and support infant industry promotion policy.[219] Nonetheless, some of the current provisions in the WTO are inconsistent with this and create significant difficulties for developing countries in adopting effective development policies. It is particularly true for some of the key measures of infant industry promotion, such as tariff protection and subsidies. Several UR agreements such as the SCM Agreement substantially reduce the ability of developing countries to apply effective development policies.[220] The remainder of this chapter considers WTO rules on tariffs and subsidies, respectively, and proposes alternative provisions to better facilitate the economic development of developing countries, while seeking to maintain the stability of the international trading system.

3.2 Tariff Bindings[221]

The WTO allows Members to apply negotiated tariffs and prohibits non-tariff measures (e.g., quantitative measures) unless these measures are exceptionally authorized by relevant WTO provisions. The maximum tariff rates on each product are "bound" and could not be arbitrarily adjusted by the importing Member: the WTO system is based on the principle that its Members negotiate import "concessions" with one another and commit themselves not to restrict imports in violation of those concessions (subject to specified exceptions in WTO rules). This principle provides essential stability to the international trading system. The import concessions are made in the form of maximum tariff bindings

in the outward-development scheme, the target of infant industry promotion would more likely be manufacturing industries rather than services.

[219] See Chapter 2.2 *supra*.

[220] *Supra* note 18.

[221] The proposals made in Chapters 3.2 and 3.3 of the book first appeared in the author's article, entitled "Facilitating Development in the World Trading System – A Proposal for Development Facilitation Tariff and Development Facilitating Subsidy" (2004) 38 Journal of World Trade 935–954.

on individual products and stipulated in the Schedule of Concessions. Paragraph 1 of GATT Article II provides:

(a) Each contracting party shall accord to the commerce of the other contracting parties treatment no less favourable than that provided for in the appropriate Part of the appropriate Schedule annexed to this Agreement.

(b) The products described in Part I of the Schedule relating to any contracting party, which are the products of territories of other contracting parties, shall, on their importation into the territory to which the Schedule relates, and subject to the terms, conditions or qualifications set forth in that Schedule, be exempt from ordinary customs duties in excess of those set forth and provided therein. Such products shall also be exempt from all other duties or charges of any kind imposed on or in connection with the importation in excess of those imposed on the date of this Agreement or those directly and mandatorily required to be imposed thereafter by legislation in force in the importing territory on that date.

(c) The products described in Part II of the Schedule relating to any contracting party which are the products of territories entitled under Article I to receive preferential treatment upon importation into the territory to which the Schedule relates shall, on their importation into such territory, and subject to the terms, conditions or qualifications set forth in that Schedule, be exempt from ordinary customs duties in excess of those set forth and provided for in Part II of that Schedule. Such products shall also be exempt from all other duties or charges of any kind imposed on or in connection with importation in excess of those imposed on the date of this Agreement or those directly or mandatorily required to be imposed thereafter by legislation in force in the importing territory on that date. Nothing in this Article shall prevent any contracting party from maintaining its requirements existing on the date of this Agreement as to the eligibility of goods for entry at preferential rates of duty.[222]

---

[222] WTO, *The Results of the Uruguay Round of Multilateral Trade Negotiations, supra* note 53, pp. 425–427.

Since the GATT regime began in 1947, several multilateral trade negotiations were held for the purpose of tariff reductions. This effort led to significant success, and the average tariff rates of industrial countries on industrial products dropped from around 40 percent in the beginning of the GATT era to about 3 percent at the conclusion of the UR.[223] In effect, tariffs are no longer a major barrier to trade among developed countries. Developing countries, as their participation in the world trading system has increased, have also been encouraged and at times demanded to reduce their tariff rates[224] and have done so significantly.[225] Nonetheless, benefit to developing countries from these trade concessions has been rather controversial.[226]

Continuous tariff reduction has been positive for the expansion of trade worldwide,[227] and the requirement of binding concessions (tariff bindings) has been essential in stabilizing the international trading

---

[223] *Supra* note 47.

[224] Many commentators emphasize the benefit to be gained by developing countries for increasing their market access. See Hans Peter Lankes, "Market Access for Developing Countries" (2002) 39(3) *Finance and Development* 8–12.

[225] See World Trade Organization, UR: Market Access for Industrial Products, Table II.2, Developing Economy Tariff Reduction on Industrial Products by Individual Country, available online at <http://www.wto.org/english/thewto_e/whatis_e/eol/e/pdf/urt24.pdf>. Some developing countries made considerable import concessions during the Uruguay Round (UR). For instance, India offered an average tariff reduction of 6.16 percent, while it only received an average reduction of 1.22 percent for its exports. Similarly, Thailand offered 5.93 percent and received only 1.46 percent on average. These concessions were significant, although the pre-UR tariff rates of developing countries were generally higher than those of developed countries. J. Michael Finger and A. Alan Winters, "Reciprocity in the WTO" *in* Bernard Hoekman, Aaditya Mattoo, and Philip English (eds.), *Development, Trade, and the WTO: A Handbook* (World Bank, Washington D.C., 2002), p. 57, Table 7.3.

[226] In the 1999 WTO high-level symposium, the representative of India argued that developing countries had not gained from the UR. In response, C. Fred Bergsten, director of the Institute of International Economics (Washington, D.C.), stated that a World Bank study had indicated a 1.2–2 percent annual benefit in additional GDP growth for developing countries from the UR. WTO, *Report of the WTO High-Level Symposium on Trade and Development* (1999), *supra* note 38.

[227] *Supra* note 48.

system. But is this system of tariff bindings also consistent with the development interests of developing countries? Under the current rule, both developing and developed countries are bound by their concessions and cannot retract these concessions or modify them without an agreement with the other interested parties.[228] The modification requires time-consuming negotiations and possibly burdensome compensation on the part of the modifying developing countries, and a failure to come to an agreement on compensation may lead to costly retaliation.[229] This constraint ties the hands of developing countries in need of trade protection for the promotion of their domestic industries.

As discussed earlier, infant industry promotion policies often include tariff protections in the early stages of development. Therefore, a more flexible treatment should be provided to developing countries with respect to binding concessions.[230] Arguably, the need for tariff protection should have been contemplated by developing countries when they agreed to specific tariff bindings in the multilateral trade negotiations. Nonetheless, their economic needs may change and so do national goals following political shifts (e.g., election of a new government, end of a dictatorship, etc.), and therefore, development initiatives may begin long after the conclusion of trade negotiations. If so, the developing country should not be prohibited from offering trade protection to its infant industry because of its previous import commitments, and it should be allowed to do so without prolonging negotiations and the burden of

---

[228] Article XXVIII provides for a modification of schedules. WTO, *The Results of the Uruguay Round of Multilateral Trade Negotiations, supra* note 53, pp. 462–465. See also the relevant discussions of GATT Article XVIII, Section A, in the preceding chapter. *Id.*, p. 448.

[229] *Id.*

[230] Article XVIII contemplates this treatment. Paragraph 2 of Article XVIII provides in relevant part, "They agree, therefore, that those contracting parties should enjoy additional facilities to enable them (a) to maintain sufficient flexibility in their tariff structure to be able to grant the tariff protection required for the establishment of a particular industry," WTO, *The Results of the Uruguay Round of Multilateral Trade Negotiations, supra* note 53, p. 448.

compensations or threat of retaliations. This additional tariff imposed above the maximum rate in the scheduled commitments for the purpose of infant industry promotion can be called a "Development-Facilitation Tariff" or "DFT."

There might be some objections to this proposal. For example, there will likely be some concern that this liberal treatment may lead to rampant protectionism by developing countries without either a genuine need or a constructive plan for infant industry promotion. Some may also raise doubts about the effectiveness of trade protection for the promotion of a domestic industry, but I have already discussed the debate on the validity of infant industry promotion policies and the potential benefit of infant industry promotion policies earlier in this chapter. Despite the possibility of abuse, a developing country should be allowed to choose policies that are best suited for its own development, fully considering the ramifications of the proposed tariff increases. If it finally determines that its industrial promotion policy demands the adoption of DFT, its previous import commitments should not tie its hands.

To prevent abuse, certain procedures should be implemented for DFT applications. For instance, a developing country should be required to publish a proposed infant industry promotion plan before proposing to apply a DFT, along with a mandatory schedule for the proposed increased tariff rates and the maximum duration for the proposed DFT. The plan should show a schedule for subsequent reductions in the DFT rate in accordance to the progress of the industrial promotion.[231] In addition, public hearings should also be required before the decision to apply a DFT to secure the transparency and to improve the prudence of DFT applications. In addition, a developing country proposing to apply a DFT should be required to make appropriate notice to the WTO in each stage of its applications so that the interested Members are made aware of

---

[231] In addition, there should be a "waiting period" for DFT applications after the publication of an industrial promotion plan to give an appropriate notice to the other interested countries.

its progress.[232] Consultation with the interested Members should also be required before the application of a DFT so that views can be exchanged on the proposed measure and possible accommodations can be made to reduce damage to the trade of these interested Members.

The DFT administrations and implementations should be non-discriminatory, and the MFN principle should be observed for DFT applications (i.e., the proposed DFT should be applied to all imports without discrimination according to their sources). Yet consideration should be given where a specific tariff binding is the result of negotiations with another developing country. Although the application of a DFT may be justified for the purpose of economic development, it should not be done at the expense of the development interests of other developing countries. In this regard, the MFN application should be modified to the extent that a DFT should not be applied to imports from other developing countries that negotiated the specific tariff binding with the modifying developing country unless the former agree to the application of the particular DFT. In the absence of such agreement, the relevant provisions of Article XVIII should be applied.[233]

This proposal lifts the existing multilateral control in Article XVIII[234] that reduces the developing country's ability to adopt an infant industry promotion policy but at the same time the proposal discourages DFT applications without concrete development plans. In addition, this proposal includes some procedural safeguards to enhance transparency

---

[232] These notices can be modeled after the notification requirements in the Agreement on Safeguards. Article 12.1 requires a Member proposing to apply a safeguard measure to notify the Committee on Safeguards immediately after (i) initiating an investigation process for a safeguard measure, (ii) making a finding of serious injury to the domestic industry, (iii) making a decision to apply a safeguard measure. Agreement on Safeguards, art. 12. *The Results of the Uruguay Round of Multilateral Trade Negotiations, supra* note 53, p. 281.

[233] Paragraph 7(b) of Article XVIII allows the exporting Members to apply retaliatory measures where agreement is not reached with the importing Member modifying the Schedule of Concessions. *Id.*, p. 448. The same rule can be applied here.

[234] *Id.*, pp. 447–453.

such as the publication of an infant industry development plan. Procedural requirements, such as this publication and hearings, will help to inform the public of the government's industrial promotion plan. Public knowledge of the plan and the possible public pressure may induce the government to devise responsible and sensible plans for industrial promotion. The prior notice requirement included in my proposal should give the interested countries the needed time to assess the effect of the proposed DFT application and make any necessary preparations to deal with such effect on their own economy.

In applying a DFT, developing countries should be treated differently in accordance with the development stages, measured by per capita gross national income (GNI) of a particular developing country proposing to apply a DFT.[235] For instance, South Korea, with around 12,000 USD per capita GNI as of 2003,[236] is considered to be either "developed" or "developing" according to the particular standards applied.[237] But even those who consider that South Korea is still in developing stages[238] would agree that South Korea has reached an economic status that is substantially higher than most other developing countries, and therefore, it would make little sense to accord the same preferential treatment in DFT applications to a country like South Korea that is given to the other developing countries with much lower per-capita income.

---

[235] GNI refers to "gross national income." Per capita GNI is commonly used as a measure of the individual living standard in a given country. The World Bank uses per capita GNI figures to classify countries into different income levels. *Supra* note 11.

[236] World Bank, Korea Rep. at a Glance (Sep. 16, 2004), available online at <http://www.worldbank.org>.

[237] As of December 2004, the World Bank considered economies with 9,386 USD per capita GNI or above to be in the "high-income" group. *Supra* note 11. According to this classification, it would be sensible to consider South Korea, whose economy is largely based on modern industries, to be a "developed" economy. However, the UNCTAD did not include South Korea among developed countries in its 2004 world investment report.

[238] Although the World Bank included South Korea in the high-income group, its per capita GNI of 12,030 USD (2003) is substantially lower than those of many other developed countries. In 2003, an average per capita GNI of high-income countries as classified by the World Bank was 28,550 USD. *Supra* note 236.

Thus, different DFT rates should be authorized according to the relevant development stage of an individual developing country, measured by per capita GNI. In other words, different "caps" (maximum DFT rates) should be imposed according to the income level of a particular developing country proposing to apply a DFT. How should the DFT cap be decided for a specific developing country? As a DFT should be applicable by a *developing* country that has the need for tariff protection for its infant industry promotion, the first order of business is to set the threshold for a developed economy in terms of per capita GNI. An appropriate maximum DFT rate should then be decided according to the particular income level of the country proposing to apply a DFT. One possible way is to set the possible maximum DFT rates needed for the promotion of an infant industry for the developing countries of the lowest economic status (i.e., with the minimum industrial base) and then determine an appropriate DFT cap for each individual developing country, up to an overall maximum.

For instance, suppose that 15,000 USD per capita GNI is set as the threshold for the developed status. Suppose also that the maximum applicable DFT rate is 100 percent *ad valorem*. The cap DFT rate applicable to an individual developing country can be prescribed according to its per capita GNI level, identified as a percentage of that 15,000 USD threshold level. For example, if Country A's per capita GNI is 15,000 USD, this income level is 100 percent of the threshold, and therefore, no DFT is applicable ((100% − 100%) × 100% = 0%). If, on the other hand, Country B's per capita GNI is 1,500 USD, this income level is 10 percent of the threshold, and 90 percent of the maximum DFT should be allowed as the DFT cap for Country B ((100% − 10%) × 100% = 90%). DFTs should be applied only to those imports that compete or are likely to compete with the domestic industry to be promoted and not to all imports across the board.

I do not intend to stipulate specific figures of the overall maximum DFT rate or specific ways of its imposition (e.g., whether an identical DFT cap for an individual developing country on all imports should be imposed or different DFT caps for individual products should be imposed) because these specific questions should be further considered and debated with due consideration of their effect on development. At this stage, I emphasize that some leeway beyond the binding import concessions under GATT Article II should be allowed for developing countries where a developing country has a concrete plan for the promotion of an industry. I also stress that this leeway should be allowed discriminatorily according to the development stages of individual developing countries as measured by per capita GNI or its equivalent. For the least-developed economies, a cap on the DFT rates should be exempted entirely to allow them maximum tariff flexibility to implement their economic development plans.[239]

Some may argue that the introduction of DFTs in the world trading system will undermine the import concessions made by developing countries and disrupt the balance of concessions achieved through trade negotiations. Although those concessions are important, the need for economic development should be given priority over this concern. The effect of DFTs on world trade will be rather limited as the majority portion of world trade is conducted among developed economies, which would not be subject to DFT applications.[240] Also, developing countries with limited negotiating power often find themselves having to accept the demand of developed countries with more powerful economies and to make concessions beyond the levels that they are ready to offer.[241] Consequently,

---

[239] It would be consistent with the proposition made by Article XI of the WTO Agreement stating, "The Least-developed countries recognized as such by the United Nations will be required to undertake commitments and concessions to the extent consistent with their individual development, financial and trade needs or their administrative and industrial capabilities." WTO, *The Results of the Uruguay Round of Multilateral Trade Negotiations, supra* note 53, p. 11. I also propose later in this chapter not to bind LDCs with their commitments made under their Schedule of Concessions until they graduate from the LDC status. If this should be done, the DFT cap would be irrelevant to LDCs.

[240] According to WTO statistics, the share of imports by developing countries is less than one-third of the total imports in the world (2003). WTO, International Trade Statistics 2004, Table 1.6 Leading Exporters and Importers in Merchandise Trade (excluding intra-EU trade), available online at <http://www.wto.org>.

[241] For developing countries and trade negotiations, see Anne O. Krueger, "The Developing Countries and the Next Round of Multilateral Trade Negotiations" (1999) 22(9) *World Economy* 909–932.

where there are clear development plans that demand import protection, it would be fair to allow import restraints to meet development needs.

The current system already allows trade protection for the purpose of economic development beyond the import commitments already made,[242] but the current provisions require negotiations and compensation and also allow exporting countries to retaliate in the absence of agreement on compensation.[243] My proposal intends to relieve developing countries of this burden and enable them to adopt effective development policies. At the same time, the proposal limits import restraints for the development purpose to additional tariffs, which are generally considered to be less trade restrictive than quantitative restrictions.[244] If more protection is needed beyond what is allowed under the DFT scheme, developing countries may always resort to Article XVIII, which does not impose tariff ceilings. For the application of a DFT, detailed provisions will have to be added to WTO rules with respect to the determination of the applicable DFT rates, the scope of the imports subject to the DFT application, as well as appropriate procedural requirements, such as public hearing and prior notification.

In addition to the DFT proposal, another point should be made with respect to the import concessions under GATT Article II.[245] As paragraph 8 of GATT Article XXXVI indicates,[246] developing countries should be allowed the benefit of membership in the WTO without being required to confer reciprocal trade benefits in return for any concession offered by developed countries.[247] Their accession into the WTO should not be

---

[242] See the relevant discussion in Chapter 2 on GATT Article XVIII.

[243] *Id.*

[244] Trade restrictive effects of tariffs are generally considered less than those of quantitative restrictions. For the trade effects of tariffs and quantitative restrictions, see Salvatore (2003), *supra* note 173, Chapters 8 and 9.

[245] WTO, *The Results of the Uruguay Round of Multilateral Trade Negotiations, supra* note 53, pp. 488–490.

[246] *Id.*, p. 534.

[247] Robert Hudec offered a different but interesting view that developing countries that accept more reciprocity are likely to adopt policies that are more outward-looking,

impeded by stringent demands for market access or any other restrictive demands that are greater than those required of the original WTO members.[248] To avoid delays and dragging negotiations on import concessions for developing countries, some objective guidelines on minimum import concessions may have to be prescribed so that developing countries meeting these threshold requirements would not be delayed from joining the WTO.[249]

In determining those threshold import concessions, the concept of a sliding scale, similar to the determination of DFT caps, can also be applied here with stipulations that developing countries with lower per capita GNIs can only be required to provide relatively lower import concessions to a smaller portion of their imports.[250] In particular, attention should be

rather than inward-looking and more protectionist, and therefore, more beneficial in development terms. Hudec, *Developing Countries in the GATT Legal System, supra* note 90. Nonetheless, developing countries which adopted outward-looking, export-based development policies, such as South Korea, also offered tariff protections to infant domestic industries as part of their development strategies. At any rate, the choice should be left to the developing country and the reciprocity should not be imposed. Although Hudec believed that reciprocity is a virtue at home, he nevertheless concluded that a greater degree of commitment within the WTO by developing countries still offers no necessary promise of improved market access conditions in developed country markets. *Id.*

[248] A commentator has observed, "Countries that are not yet members of the WTO are often hit with more restrictive demands as part of their accession negotiations." Rodrik (2004), *supra* note 189, p. 33.

[249] In addition to import concessions, there may be other considerations with respect to the accession of a particular country into the WTO, such as a transparent legal system affecting trade. These other issues should be considered separately and may be subject to further negotiations. In any case, the entry into the WTO of developing countries that have expressed a desire to join should not be delayed. Carlos Magariños, director-general of UNIDO, has proposed expedited entry of developing countries in the 1999 WTO high-level symposium on trade and development. He also called for careful study of the timing, sequencing, and degree of market liberalization, which would allow developing countries to adapt individually to the consequences of open markets. WTO, *Report on the WTO High-Level Symposium on Trade and Development* (1999), *supra* note 38.

[250] For instance, suppose that the threshold per capita GNI that requires a market access for all non-primary goods is 15,000 USD. If Country A's per capita GNI is 1,500 USD,

given to LDCs [251] with dire economic needs. In recognition of the need of LDCs, the UR participants agreed on the "Decision on Measures in Favour of Least-Developed Countries," which provides that LDCs are only required to "undertake commitments and concessions to the extent consistent with their individual development, financial and trade needs, or their administrative and institutional capabilities."[252]

Nonetheless, more than one-third of LDCs have not yet attained membership in the WTO, with several of them waiting in line.[253] To improve their economy, these countries would need, more than any other country, the trade concessions that WTO membership would provide. A clearer and broader waiver than the one provided under the decision[254] should be granted to LDCs to expedite their accession to the WTO.[255] For instance, consideration should be given to a possible preferential scheme under which LDCs applying for WTO membership are not required to submit their Schedule of Concessions and the existing LDC Members are not

---

equivalent to 10 percent of this threshold per capita GNI, this country may be required to provide import concessions amounting to 10 percent of its total imports.

[251] See *supra* note 93 for the definition of LDCs.

[252] Decision on Measures in Favour of Least-Developed Countries, para. 1. WTO, *The Results of the Uruguay Round of Multilateral Trade Negotiations, supra* note 53, p. 231. Article XI of the WTO Agreement also includes the identical clause. *Supra* note 239.

[253] It has been observed that "the process of WTO accession has been and is likely to continue to be lengthy, complex, and challenging for all countries, especially the LDCs." The observer recommends the improvement of the institutional infrastructure to implement WTO disciplines and the adoption of liberal trade policy to expedite the process. Constantine Michalopoulos, "WTO Accession" *in* Bernard Hoekman, Aaditya Mattoo, and Philip English (eds.), *Development, Trade, and the WTO: A Handbook* (World Bank, Washington D.C., 2002), p. 69. The question is whether an LDC applying for WTO membership can afford such institutional infrastructure and liberal trade policies, and the regulatory preference making it easier for LDCs to acquire WTO membership is, therefore, necessary.

[254] *Id.*

[255] In the 1999 WTO high-level symposium on trade and development, the representative of South Korea proposed to provide more flexible procedures for accession, calling for the adoption of the "umbrella waiver" – a legal basis to provide preferential treatment to LDCs. WTO, *Report on the WTO High-Level Symposium on Trade and Development* (1999), *supra* note 38.

bound by their commitments under their schedule until all these LDCs "graduate" from the LDC status. This sort of preference allows LDCs maximum economic flexibility to facilitate development and to avoid potential delays of their accession to the WTO over their concessions.

3.3 Subsidies[256]

Another essential element of industrial promotion policies is government subsidy. Subsidies include various forms of government support, including financial grants, subsidized loans, loan guarantees, tax exemptions or reductions, and R&D support.[257] Government can also support an industry by building production facilities and infrastructure for them. Article 1 of the SCM Agreement provides that an industry is deemed to have received a subsidy where a *benefit* is conferred on the industry as a result of (i) direct transfer from the government of funds (including grants, loans, or equity infusion) or government guarantees of payment of loans; (ii) government foregoing the revenue that should otherwise have been collected; or (iii) government providing goods or services or purchasing goods.[258]

In the early stages of economic development, where the private sector lacks adequate resources for the establishment and promotion of an industry, government support can play an essential role. In fact, many developed countries today provided a wide range of government subsidies to promote their domestic industries during their own development stages.[259] However, it has also been pointed out that government subsidies

---

[256] *Supra* note 221.

[257] Subsidies may even include implicit government guarantees to bail out domestic producers who bear the risk to engage in new productive pursuits but subsequently fail. See Rodrik (2004), *supra* note 189, p. 14.

[258] WTO, *The Results of the Uruguay Round of Multilateral Trade Negotiations, supra* note 53, p. 231.

[259] See Chang, *supra* note 41, Chapter 2. For instance, the United Kingdom provided extensive export subsidies to textile products in the eighteenth century, the United States offered subsidies to railway companies in the nineteenth century and invested heavily in R&D of new technologies, and Germany also subsidized a number of industries,

may distort international trade where it is provided to promote export and discourage import.[260] For instance, the government, by providing subsidies, may assume part of the production cost and, therefore, enable domestic industries to charge lower prices to their exports than they otherwise can. The government can also provide incentives to purchase domestic products by giving subsidies contingent on a use of domestic products. Critics argue that this practice is economically inefficient.

Under the SCM Agreement, export subsidies (subsidies that are provided contingent on export performance) and import-substitution subsidies (subsidies that are contingent on the use of domestic over imported goods) are prohibited as they have adverse effects on international trade.[261] In addition, a subsidy is "actionable" (i.e., the other country may retaliate against this subsidy with counter measures)[262] when certain conditions are met: (i) the subsidy is specifically limited to an enterprise or group of enterprises, an industrial sector or group of industries, or a designed geographic region within the jurisdiction of the granting authority (*specificity requirement*)[263] and (ii) the subsidy causes adverse effects to the interests of other Members. Adverse effects include (a) injury[264] to the domestic industry of the importing country, (b) nullification or impairment of benefits of bound tariff rates, or (c) serious

including textiles and metals. Other developed countries today, including France, the Netherlands, Sweden, Japan, and the East Asian countries (NICs) all provided subsidies to promote their industries.

[260] See Salvatore (2003), *supra* note 173, pp. 281–286.

[261] WTO, *The Results of the Uruguay Round of Multilateral Trade Negotiations*, *supra* note 53, p. 233. Annex I of the SCM Agreement includes the illustrative list of prohibited export subsidies. *Id.*, pp. 265–267.

[262] A country whose trade is affected by a subsidy may request consultations with the country applying the subsidy in question and, if a mutually agreed solution is not found, may also complain to the WTO Dispute Settlement Body. The WTO may also authorize counter measures (retaliation) if the subsidizing country does not withdraw the subsidy in question pursuant to its decision. The SCM Agreement, art. 7. *Id.*, pp. 237–239.

[263] The SCM Agreement, art. 2. *Id.*, p. 232.

[264] Injury is within the meaning of Article VI of GATT 1994, which is "material injury," The SCM Agreement, art. 11.2. *Id.*, pp. 243–244, and GATT, art. VI, para. 6. *Id.*, pp. 431–432.

prejudice to the domestic industry.[265] Countervailing duties, which are additional tariffs imposed on imports to offset the effect of subsidies,[266] are also applicable as a remedy where subsidization causes or threatens material injury to an established domestic industry or retard materially the establishment of a domestic industry.[267]

As of June 2003, there were as many as 103 CVD actions (including price undertakings, i.e., voluntary commitments to raise prices by the exporter to offset the effect of trade-related subsidies) in force.[268] The majority of CVD actions have targeted developing countries: between July 2002 and June 2003, seven out of thirteen CVD investigations were initiated against imports from developing countries.[269] Current WTO subsidy provisions prohibiting export subsidies and import-substitution subsidies and those authorizing countervailing measures against actionable subsidies[270] are impediments to the industrial promotion effort of developing countries. Those provisions reduce the key ability of developing countries to provide support to promote their industries in the early stages of development.[271]

Infant industries in developing economies often need export markets because of their limited domestic market. Government support is called

---

[265] The SCM Agreement, art. 5, *Id.*, pp. 235. Article 6 of the SCM Agreement lists cases in which the serious prejudice to the domestic industry is deemed to exist. *Id.*, pp. 235–236.

[266] Part V of the SCM Agreement (Articles 10–23) provides for substantive and procedural rules for the application of CVDs. *Id.*, pp. 243–258. Exporters can also avoid CVDs by undertaking to increase their export prices (price undertaking). This price undertaking is voluntary on the part of the exporters, and the importing country may consider the acceptance of the undertaking impractical, for instance, where the number of actual or potential exporters is too great. The SCM Agreement, art. 18. *Id.*, pp. 253–254.

[267] GATT Article VI, para. 6, pp. 431–432.

[268] WTO, *Annual Report* (WTO, Geneva, 2004), p. 45. According to this report, 57 CVD actions were applied by the United States, 20 by European Communities, and 10 by Canada.

[269] *Id.*

[270] *Supra* notes 261–265.

[271] *Supra* note 18. Note that today's developed countries provided extensive subsidies during their development stages, which would have been either prohibited or actionable under the SCM, *supra* note 259, Chang, *supra* note 41, Chapter 2.

on to improve their competitiveness in the foreign market as well as in their own. The SCM Agreement recognizes this and affirms that "subsidies may play an important role in economic development programmes of developing country Members."[272] The SCM Agreement also provides certain S&D treatment to developing countries: LDC Members are not prohibited from applying export subsidies,[273] and the other developing countries are also permitted to apply export subsidies for a period of eight years from the implementation date of the WTO Agreement, which already has expired.[274]

The subsidy rules also authorize LDC Members and the other developing country Members to apply import-substitution subsidies for eight and five years, respectively, after the implementation of the WTO Agreement.[275] These "grace periods" for phase out have expired, and the only remaining preference is applied to a handful of the LDC Members with respect to export subsidies whose per capita gross national product (GNP) is below $1,000.[276] This exemption is far too limiting, and the exemption that is only applied to the LDCs should be extended to other developing countries as well. Subsidies that are essential for the promotion of an infant industry are now either prohibited or made actionable, leaving developing countries with insufficient means to promote domestic industries and to exploit international trade for development.

The following example illustrates the difficulty faced by developing countries today. Suppose that the government of Country A, with a per capita GNI of $1,000, which barely escapes the LDC status entitled to the preference under the SCM Agreement, wants to help domestic industries

---

[272] The SCA Agreement, art. 27.1, WTO, *The Results of the Uruguay Round of Multilateral Trade Negotiations, supra* note 53, p. 261.

[273] The SCA Agreement, art. 27.2(a). *Id.*, p. 261. This preference ceases to apply to any of these LDC Members when it reaches 1,000 USD GNP per capita. Annex VII. *Id.*, p. 274.

[274] The SCA Agreement, art. 27.2(a). *Id.*, p. 261. The WTO Agreement was entered into force as of 1995.

[275] The SCA Agreement, art. 27.3. *Id.*, p. 261.

[276] *Supra* note 273.

building steel mills as part of its industrial promotion plan. Because of the unavailability of domestic financial resources, the government provides the domestic industries with a loan guarantee. Thanks to the strength of this government guarantee, these industrialists can borrow money from abroad and build steel mills. The government also provides them with a tax reduction in an effort to assist with the development of the steel industry and also encourages domestic steel consumers to purchase steel products from these mills by offering some financial incentives (e.g., a tax break on the purchase of domestic steel products). Aided by these policies and favorable economic factors such as lower labor costs, the promoted industry becomes successful, particularly in exports, and contributes to the economic development of Country A. This example illustrates how today's prosperous industries in the NICs were first developed, contributing to their rapid economic growth.[277]

Under the present WTO subsidy rules, however, this success story cannot be repeated. First, CVDs would be applicable to the government subsidy (loan guarantee) as well as subsequent financial incentives (tax reductions) specifically provided to the steel industry.[278] The financial incentives provided to domestic steel consumers will also be prohibited as import-substitution subsidies. If the government of Country A guaranteed the loan and offered tax reductions contingent on export performance, these measures would also be prohibited as export subsidies. Today's regulatory framework for international trade does not allow developing countries to adopt effective development policies that were used by today's developed countries.[279]

This illustration suggests that the current subsidy rules have made "a significant dent in the abilities of developing countries to employ

---

[277] See the relevant discussions in Chapter 1.2 *supra*.

[278] The domestic industry of the importing country needs to sustain material injury for the application of a CVD action (*supra* note 267), but the threshold for material injury is not considered high.

[279] *Supra* note 259. Chang, *supra* note 41, Chapter 3.

intelligently-designed industrial policies"[280] and that the present ban on export subsidies and import-substitution subsidies under Article 3.1 of the SCM Agreement[281] should be lifted in favor of developing countries in consideration of the importance of subsidies in development. In addition, the application of CVD actions against the trade of developing countries should also be limited. This would enable developing countries to provide their domestic industries with trade-related subsidies and to facilitate development without the threat of retaliatory measures on their export. In limiting CVD actions, a wide difference in the development status and income levels existing among developing countries should be considered.

A differentiated treatment, such as the one employed for the application of a DFT, would be necessary to account for a wide difference among developing countries in terms of development, authorizing different subsidy levels to individual developing countries for the purpose of development that are otherwise actionable. These subsidy levels should be set in accordance with their development status measured by their income levels (per capita GNI). A sliding scale approach, which is adopted for the application of a DFT,[282] can also be applied to determine the levels of a "Development-Facilitation Subsidy" (DFS) that are otherwise prohibited or actionable. The DFS is a development tool, as is the DFT, and therefore cannot be applied by developed countries. Therefore, an income threshold for developed economies should first be set. Different DFS caps (maximum DFS levels) for individual developing countries can then be devised in accordance with the income level of a particular developing country. CVD actions can be taken against subsidies imposed beyond these caps. How should these DFS caps for individual developing countries be set? One way is to set a DFS cap against the value of trade,

---

[280] Rodrik (2004), *supra* note 189, pp. 34–35.
[281] *Supra* note 261.
[282] See the relevant discussion in Chapter 3.2 *supra*.

calculated by the impact of subsidies on the prices of traded products as measured by the percentages of the total product value.[283]

For instance, suppose that the per capita GNI threshold for a developed economy is set as 15,000 USD and that the possible highest DFS cap is 100 percent of the value (price) of an individual developing country's trade. Assume that Country A's per capita GNI is 15,000 USD. As its per capita GNI is equal to the threshold, Country A cannot apply any DFS ((100% − 100%) × 25% = 0). Now assume that Country B's per capita GNI is 6,000 USD. It is equal to 40 percent of the threshold for the developed economy. The maximum DFS level (DFS cap) for this developing country is (100% − 40%) × 100% = 60%. The subsidy cap is 60 percent of the value of its trade. Again, this numerical standard is provided as an example, and the adequate percentage for the overall maximum DFS needs to be further studied considering their effect on trade and development.

There would be different ways to administer a DFS. One is to set the DFS cap for all products and not to regulate DFS rates for each product. Alternatively, the DFS caps for individual products or groups of like products can be set. More discussions will be necessary to determine whether the DFS caps on individual products are feasible and necessary, and if so, whether they should be decided identically across the board or differently according to individual products/groups of products. If the latter is appropriate, the international market share of the concerned product or a group of products by the individual developing country, as well as the income levels of that particular individual developing country, should be considered in determining DFS caps.[284]

Procedural safeguards should also be put in place to avoid abuse of the application of a DFS where there is no concrete industrial promotion

---

[283] Subsidies are calculated for the determination of CVD rates. See *supra* note 266.

[284] For instance, S&D treatment to developing countries discontinues under the current subsidy rules when its export product reaches a share of at least 3.25 percent in the world market. The SCM Agreement, art. 27, WTO, *The Results of the Uruguay Round of Multilateral Trade Negotiations*, *supra* note 53, pp. 261–263.

plan. For instance, a developing country proposing to apply a DFS should be required to publish a proposed infant industry promotion plan before the application of the DFS. A mandatory schedule for a DFS application, including its maximum period, and its subsequent reduction in accordance with the progress of the industry promotion should also be required. Additional procedural safeguards, such as public hearings, should also be imposed to improve the transparency and the prudence of DFS applications. Appropriate notices to the WTO should be imposed on a developing country proposing to apply a DFS at appropriate stages of its application.[285] The present notification requirement of specific subsidies should be maintained.[286]

A question may arise as to whether the availability of a DFS would lead to a subsidy race among developing countries, diminishing the effect of the subsidy for the industrial promotion of individual developing countries and only causing a distortion of trade. The answer to this question is that a developing country should be trusted with its own best judgment as to whether it should provide its domestic industries with subsidies. Many economic and political factors would affect a government decision to grant subsidies, and a prudent government will consider the existence and even the possibility of similar subsidies that may be applied by the competing countries in the future. A developing country will subsidize export industries that it believes have the best potential of success, and the possibility of these competing subsidies will be part of that equation.

---

[285] *Supra* note 232.
[286] The SCM Agreement, art. 25. *Id.*, pp. 259–261.

FOUR

Anti-Dumping and Safeguards

4.1 Administered Protection

The WTO system authorizes the application of certain measures on trade, and this chapter discusses the effects of some of the major trade measures on development. Trade measures include a vast array of government measures that affect trade, frequently applied in the form of (increased) tariffs and quotas.[287] Governments apply trade measures for various political and economic reasons. For instance, trade measures are an important instrument of infant industry promotion.[288] Certain trade measures, such as AD measures, CVD measures, and safeguard measures, are called "administered protection" because they are applied for the protection of a specific domestic industry, and this protection is administered by the terms of the relevant WTO rules. Measures of administered protection are frequently applied and have significant ramifications on development. Because subsidy issues and CVD actions are already covered in the preceding chapter, this chapter discusses AD actions and safeguard measures.

---

[287] Relevant WTO provisions regulate the substantive and procedural aspects of trade measures.

[288] See Chapter 3 *supra* for the relevant discussion.

Why do we allow governments to adopt measures of administered protection while the objective of the WTO system is to pursue open trade?[289] The rationale for AD measures and CVD actions is rather different from that for safeguard measures: with respect to the former, the justification is found in the promotion of "fair trade."[290] Here, unfairly low prices (dumping), as well as a trade-related government subsidy, is believed to provide the exporters with an "unfair" advantage; therefore, the importing country has a right to offset this unfair advantage by applying counter-trade measures. The justification for safeguard measures is somewhat different in that safeguards are applicable regardless of the existence of "unfair" trade practices on the part of the exporter. Safeguard measures are applied to protect a domestic industry temporarily when an increase in imports causes or threatens to cause serious injury to a domestic industry. Safeguard measures give the domestic industry some time to adjust to competition with imports through temporary protection and also enable the importing country to avoid acute economic and political problems associated with rapid import increases, such as massive unemployment.[291]

The concept of "fair trade," which provides the underlying justification for AD measures and CVD actions, reveals some problems from the perspective of development. The fair trade argument was first spurred by large increases in exports from Japan and the NICs in the 1970s and 1980s,[292] and these export increases created concern for the competing

---

[289] See Chapter 2.2 *supra* for a discussion of open trade.

[290] For the concept of fair trade, see Chapter 2.2 *supra*.

[291] Y. S. Lee, *Safeguard Measures in World Trade: The Legal Analysis* (2nd ed. Kluwer Law International, The Hague, 2005), Chapter 1.

[292] The growth of exports from the NICs, fueled by their rapid industrial growth, was phenomenal during those periods. For instance, during 1980–1990, the exports from South Korea, Taiwan, Hong Kong, and Singapore grew at the average annual rate of 12.0 percent, 8.9 percent, 14.4 percent, and 10.0 percent, respectively. Japan had also expanded its exports rapidly during the postwar period. World Bank, *World Development Report 1997*.

producers in North America and Europe because their positions were threatened by the increasing competition with imports from these countries. This concern was transformed into significant protectionist pressure to protect domestic industries from imports. Hundreds of trade-restricting measures called "gray-area measures"[293] were applied against exports, particularly those from the East Asian countries. When the trade deficit of the United States mounted during the 1980s, the "unfair" trade practices of those exporting countries were blamed for the trade imbalance.[294]

Those who advocate "fair trade"[295] from the perspective of domestic producers argue that exporters and domestic producers should compete on a "level playing field"; that is, industries supported by trade-related subsidies (e.g., export subsidies) and those benefiting from trade protections have "unfair" advantages over others that do not receive such support. The advocates of "fair trade" often urge their own government to watch out for foreign trade practices and respond to an unfair practice of the trading partner that may have an adverse effect on domestic producers. These unfair trade practices include trade-related subsidies, import barriers, and private practices, such as dumping and restrictive

---

[293] Those measures were called "gray-area measures" because they escaped the control of the GATT that prohibited unilateral restraints on trade. These measures included voluntary export restraints (VERs), orderly marketing arrangements (OMAs) and voluntary restraint agreements (VRAs) and took the form of an agreement to restrain the volume of trade between the exporting and importing countries. Gray-area measures were applied primarily against exports from Japan and the NICs; these countries often accepted gray-area measures to avoid more restrictive trade sanctions by the importing countries. Gray-area measures proliferated in the 1980s and the early 1990s. In early 1991, as many as 284 gray-area measures were known to be in force. The WTO Agreement on Safeguards prohibits all gray-area measures. Lee (2005), *supra* note 291, Chapter 2.3.

[294] On the export side, those "unfair trade practices" include practices of dumping and government subsidies for exports. On the import side, complaints were raised that the domestic markets of Japan and some NICs were not as accessible as the other developed countries.

[295] *Supra* note 85.

business practices that are believed to put the competing domestic producers at a disadvantage.[296]

The argument in favor of fair trade, in the context of trade relations between developed and developing countries, is not consistent with the promotion of development. Infant industries of developing countries are not poised to compete with more efficient counterparts from developed economies. Some measures of protection and promotion may be necessary to enable these infant industries to develop. If it is our priority to promote the economic development of poor nations, our focus should not be so much on how "fair" the competition between the industries of developing and developed nations should be, but how we should help poor countries to promote their industries successfully so that they can have viable economies that would bring them out of poverty.

For this reason, the argument in favor of the "level playing field" is misplaced with respect to trade between developed and developing nations. Measures promoting exports of developing countries, such as subsidies and trade protection, should be tolerated until their economy develops and provides their majority population with appropriate levels of income that would meet their basic needs. The argument in favor of "fair" trade would indeed be fair when it is directed to the trade between the countries of similar development status but not between the developed and developing countries. This type of trade accommodation is envisaged where GATT Article XXXVI emphasizes that developed countries *should not expect* developing countries to provide reciprocal concessions for the concessions made by developed countries.[297]

---

[296] In response to these "unfair practices," the United States adopted a set of statutory provisions (Trade Act 1974, Section 301), which required the U.S. government to monitor foreign trade practices, negotiate with foreign governments on trade issues, and apply a unilateral sanction against imports from a country that is found to exercise an unfair trade practice ("Section 301 actions"). It has been criticized that the existence of an unfair trade practice is determined based on rather vague and dubious grounds. See James Bovard, *The Myth of Fair Trade*, Cato Institute, Policy Analysis No. 264 (Nov. 1. 1991).

[297] *Supra* note 122.

Concerns may be raised that such tolerance and trade accommodation may lead to substantial increases in imports from developing countries and may cause serious damage to the domestic industries of developed countries competing with these imports. Developed countries in North America and Europe experienced rapid increases in imports from the East Asian countries in the 1970s and the 1980s, causing problems to their domestic industries. These import increases and injury to domestic industries caused an outcry for protection. Should developed countries be asked to tolerate increases in imports from developing countries that cause serious injury to their own domestic industries to help with the economic development of developing countries? Perhaps developing countries may not be willing or may not be politically able to do so if their own domestic industries would be put in peril for trade accommodation.

Safeguard measures[298] authorized by WTO rules provide some answer to this concern. The Agreement on Safeguards (SA) authorizes importing countries to apply a temporary import restriction that can be imposed in the form of increased tariffs and quotas when an increase in imports causes or threatens to cause serious injury to a domestic industry.[299] These safeguard measures work as a shock absorber against acute economic and social problems associated with rapid increases in imports, such as massive unemployment. Safeguards facilitate the economic adjustment of the affected domestic industry[300] and provide a shield against serious injury to domestic industries. The existence of this safety net enables developed countries to increase market access to imports from developing countries.[301]

---

[298] For more discussion of safeguard measures, Lee (2005), *supra* note 291 and see also Chapter 4.3 *infra.*

[299] Article 2.1 of the WTO Agreement on Safeguards, reprinted in WTO, *The Results of the Uruguay Round of Multilateral Trade Negotiations, supra* note 53, p. 275.

[300] Lee (2005), *supra* note 291, Chapter 1.

[301] However, frequent applications of safeguards may undermine the economic interests of exporting countries. WTO dispute panels and the Appellate Body have been vigilant against disputed safeguards that do not meet the requirements of the WTO Agreement

Measures of administered protection are counter-effective to the development interests of developing countries when they are applied to imports from developing countries and thus their application should be limited. Therefore, certain limitations on CVD actions targeting exports from developing countries have been proposed in Chapter 3, and similar considerations have to be given to the application of AD measures and safeguards. This accommodation would not only help facilitate the development of poor countries but would also be beneficial to developed countries in the long run: the tolerance of the seemingly "unfair" industrial and trade policies implemented by developing countries today may well be the investment for developed countries themselves for tomorrow because the successful economic development of developing countries will provide the industries of the developed countries with promising new markets and new sources for their wealth, as seen in the development process of the East Asian countries.[302]

4.2 Anti-Dumping

The current WTO rules allow Members to take an AD action in the form of increased tariffs against "dumped" imports. AD actions supposedly offset the trade impact of dumping that is presumably unfair.[303] The WTO Agreement on Implementation of Article VI of the GATT 1994 ("Anti-dumping Practices Agreement" or "ADP Agreement") sets out the concept of "dumping" as the sale under "normal value" (e.g., the

---

on Safeguards (SA). The SA provides S&D treatment to imports from developing countries where the share of imports from developing countries is *de minimis*. Further discussion of this issue is provided in Chapter 4.3 *infra*.

[302] See the relevant discussion in Chapter 1.3 *supra*.

[303] For the specific determination of dumping margins and the imposition and collection of anti-dumping duties, see "The ADP Agreement," arts. 6.10 and 9. WTO, *The Results of the Uruguay Round of Multilateral Trade Negotiations, supra* note 53, pp. 157–158, 160–162. Price undertakings are also allowed as in the application of CVD actions. *Supra* note 266. The ADP Agreement, art. 8. *Id.*, pp. 159–160. For the origin of anti-dumping measures, see Congressional Budget Office, *How the GATT Affects Antidumping and Countervailing-duty Policy* (Sep. 1994), p. 18.

home price of the exported product). Article 2.1 of the ADP Agreement provides:

> [A] product is to be considered as being dumped, i.e. introduced into the commerce of another country at less than its normal value, if the export price of the product exported from one country to another is less than the comparable price, in the ordinary course of trade, for the like product when destined for consumption in the exporting country.[304]

Alternatively, dumping may also be found by comparison to the price of the product sold in a third country or to the full production cost of the product plus reasonable profit where an adequate comparison to the home price is not feasible. Article 2.2 of the ADP Agreement provides:

> When there are no sales of the like product in the ordinary course of trade in the domestic market of the exporting country or when, because of the particular market situation or the low volume of the sales in the domestic market of the exporting country, such sales do not permit a proper comparison, the margin of dumping shall be determined by comparison with a comparable price of the like product when exported to an appropriate third country, provided that this price is representative, or with the cost of production in the country of origin plus a reasonable amount for administrative, selling and general costs and for profits.[305]

AD actions[306] are the most frequently applied import measures in the world today. As of June 2003, there were as many as 1,323 AD actions reported to be in force.[307] Developed countries, notably the United States, European Communities, and Canada, have been the primary users of AD measures,[308] but at a rapidly increasing rate, developing countries also

---

[304] The ADP Agreement, art. 2.1. *Id.*, p. 147.

[305] The ADP Agreement, art. 2.2. *Id.*, p. 147.

[306] Anti-dumping (AD) actions include both AD duties and price undertakings.

[307] WTO, *Annual Report* (WTO, Geneva, 2004), p. 46.

[308] Of the 1,323 AD measures reported to be in force as of June 2003, 21 percent were maintained by the United States, 15 percent by the European Communities, and 7 percent by Canada. *Id.*, p. 83.

have begun to use this device to curtail imports.[309] Exports from developing countries have been the primary target for AD actions. Between July 2002 and June 2003, more than half of the 238 AD investigations targeted imports from developing countries.[310] Considering that the total exports from developing countries are less than half the exports from developed countries,[311] a substantially higher rate of exports from developing countries has been targeted for AD actions.

Because "dumping" is subject to AD actions as an "unfair" trade practice, it would be helpful to understand why exporters "dump" their products in the first place. Explanations often classify dumping into different types, and these classifications help us understand the nature of dumping and its cause.[312] First, "persistent dumping," also called international price discrimination, represents the persistent tendency of domestic monopolists to maximize profit by selling their product at a higher price in the domestic market, where they are insulated by transportation costs and possibly trade barriers, than the price that they can charge in a foreign market, where they have to compete with foreign producers.[313] Second, "sporadic dumping" is the occasional sale of a product at a lower price abroad than domestically to unload an unforeseen and temporary surplus of the product without having to reduce domestic prices.[314]

In cases of persistent dumping and sporadic dumping, the benefit to domestic consumers from low prices may actually exceed the losses of domestic producers, thereby increasing the overall economic welfare.[315]

---

[309] For instance, among those 1,323 AD measures in force, the numbers of AD measures maintained by India and South Africa were 210 and 96, respectively. *Id.*

[310] *Id.*

[311] WTO, International Trade Statistics 2004, available online at <www.wto.org>.

[312] Salvatore (2003), *supra* note 173, p. 280.

[313] *Id.* For instance, where the producer's fixed cost (i.e., production facilities) is covered by the domestic sale and more product can be produced without increasing the fixed cost (e.g., by employing night shifts), the producers can charge less for the same product to be sold abroad because the export price does not need to cover the fixed cost but only the variable cost such as labor.

[314] Salvatore (2003), *supra* note 173, p. 280.

[315] *Id.*

Therefore, reputable economists did not see any problem with this type of price discrimination.[316] Price discrimination is prevalently practiced in domestic businesses, that is, sales of discount air tickets and year-end clearance sales of various products; the sale price is often below cost. These practices are not a violation of domestic anti-competition laws. If this price discrimination is not sanctioned, there is little justification to hold foreign exporters to a higher standard for doing the same thing and regulate them.

Yet another type of dumping has been considered as causing actual economic harm to the importing country, undermining the interests of both domestic producers and consumers in the end. It is "predatory dumping," defined as the temporary sale of a product at a lower price abroad to drive foreign producers out of business, after which prices are raised to take advantage of the newly acquired monopoly power abroad.[317] It is inherently anti-competitive behavior (or "unfair competition"), and trade restrictions to counter predatory dumping are, therefore, justified.[318] However, it is difficult to discern predatory intent on the part of the exporter. Even where the exporter's predatory intent is somehow shown, it is also doubtful that this predation attempt will be successful at all,[319] particularly in today's world where international competition among producers is increasingly intense. Even if predatory dumping is possible, it should be much less of a concern today because of safeguards.

Subject to the provisions of the SA, safeguard measures authorize temporary import restrictions where an increase in imports causes or threatens to cause serious injury to a domestic industry.[320] The duration of a

---

[316] Richard Posner, *The Robinson-Patman Act: Federal Regulation of Price Differences* (American Enterprise Institute, Washington, DC, 1976) and Thomas W. Ross, "Winners and Losers under the Robinson-Patman Act" (1984) 27 *Journal of Law and Economics* 243.

[317] Salvatore (2003), *supra* note 173, p. 280.

[318] *Id.* See also, Greg Mastel, "The U.S. Steel Industry and Antidumping Law" (1999) 42(3) *Challenge* 84–94.

[319] Jacob Viner, *Dumping: A Problem in International Trade* (Kelly, New York, 1966), p. 120.

[320] *Infra* note 341.

safeguard is up to four years and can be extended once.[321] Safeguards can protect the domestic industry from any predation attempt because this sort of attempt, if successful, will cause serious injury to the domestic industry. Therefore, this availability of safeguards should discourage foreign exporters from engaging in predation attempts because it would make little sense for them to undercut prices to drive all competitors out of the market only to find that their exports are then restricted by safeguards.

It was also pointed out that producers might undercut prices not necessarily to drive their competitors out of business but to increase their market share to improve the brand familiarity with customers in hopes to see demand for their brand eventually increased.[322] In any case, if dumping, regardless of whatever its inherent motive may be, leads to an increase in imports that causes or threatens to cause serious injury to the domestic industry, such imports will be subject to safeguards. There is concern in applying a safeguard in place of an AD measure because safeguards are applied to "all" imports irrespective of their source (on the MFN basis);[323] safeguards will also affect all other exporters, those who did not engage in dumping as well as those who did. This indeed may not be fair to the former, and the adverse effect to them should be minimized. Article 5.2(b) of the SA allows the importing country to assign a lesser quota to the exporting country whose exports have disproportionately increased; therefore, a lesser quota may be assigned to the dumping exporters under this rule whose exports are bound to increase disproportionately.[324] Tariff-quotas can also be devised to target dumped imports.

[321] *Infra* note 345.

[322] See Jackson (1997), *supra* note 43, p. 254.

[323] Agreement on Safeguards, art. 2.2. WTO, *The Results of the Uruguay Round of Multilateral Trade Negotiations, supra* note 53, p. 275.

[324] WTO, *The Results of the Uruguay Round of Multilateral Trade Negotiations, supra* note 53, pp. 277–278. Another possibility is to apply safeguards to the products under a certain threshold price to target only dumped imports. However, this treatment may be considered a de facto violation of the MFN application of safeguards under Article 2.2 of the Agreement on Safeguards. See Lee (2005), *supra* note 293, Chapter 4.4.

The justification for AD measures seems rather weak with respect to persistent dumping and sporadic dumping. Predatory dumping, though the likelihood of its success is fairly limited, may justify trade restrictions, but safeguard measures can replace AD measures. In addition, significant arbitrariness inherent in the current AD rules and the prevalent abuse of AD measures raise doubt about the necessity of AD measures in the world trading system today. Although the underlying concept of dumping (i.e., export price below normal value [home price]) is straightforward, the actual determination of dumping is not.[325] It is the inherent arbitrariness and complication in the determination of "normal value" that need to be considered further.

The complexity and arbitrariness in the determination of normal value can be easily seen. For example, there may not be a single home market price to compare, and the complex adjusted average may have to be calculated to come up with a reference home price; the home country may not completely be a market economy (e.g., "transitional economy"), and therefore, the home price may not represent the true market price;[326] or the product in question may not even be sold in the home market or too few of it is sold to be the basis of a valid home price. In all these cases, the price needs to be "constructed" by an evaluation of cost (constructed cost) plus reasonable profit.[327] Finding the "export price" that is necessary to determine the existence of dumping by comparison with the home price can be equally complex because a number of adjustments to the transaction price may be necessary to keep the comparison with the home price fair. These adjustments may include complex calculations involving numerous items such as warranty services and advertising costs.

---

[325] WTO, *The Results of the Uruguay Round of Multilateral Trade Negotiations, supra* note 53, pp. 147–150.

[326] The "socialist market economy" of China is an example of this, although its transformation into a more complete capitalism seems well under way.

[327] The complexity is also added to by extraneous factors, such as different foreign accounting practices that may affect cost calculations, difficulty in understanding the foreign system, and different business practices abroad. See Jackson (1997), *supra* note 43, p. 251.

This complexity and arbitrariness has been a breeding ground for the abuse of AD actions. Depending on a specific methodology adopted to calculate costs and average prices, the result can be vastly different, not to mention that the measure of "reasonable profit" can also vary.[328] National authorities can adopt a methodology that will yield the least desirable result for the exporters[329] and then come up with a finding of dumping that will justify an AD action.[330] The authorities will also be able to find different dumping margins depending on their choice of methodology and calculation.[331] This perhaps explains why numerous AD measures are applied every year.[332] This arbitrariness in the current AD rules and its significant adverse effect on trade have led to the inclusion of the AD rules in the new Doha Round agenda for possible modifications of the rules.[333] Nonetheless, it would seem unlikely that the inherent arbitrariness in the determination of dumping could be reduced to a satisfactory level.[334]

---

[328] A recent study has revealed that in the case of the United States, the vast majority of national AD practices do not even actually identify either price discrimination or sales below cost. Brink Lindsey, "The U.S. Antidumping Law: Rhetoric versus Reality," Cato Institute Trade Policy Analysis No. 7 (August 16, 1999).

[329] Article 2 of the ADP Agreement authorizes such leeway in the determination of dumping. WTO, *The Results of the Uruguay Round of Multilateral Trade Negotiations, supra* note 53, pp. 147–150.

[330] Although the provisions of the ADP Agreement attempt to provide disciplines on AD actions, "in common parlance, it is usual to designate all low-cost imports as dumped imports." International Trade Centre UNCTAD/WTO and Commonwealth Secretariat, *Business Guide to the Uruguay Round* (ITC/CS, Geneva, 1995), p. 181.

[331] *Supra* note 329.

[332] *Supra* note 307.

[333] WTO, *Ministerial Declaration*, WT/MIN(01)/DEC/1 (Nov. 20, 2001), para. 28. Reform proposals have been made to reduce the abuse and arbitrariness in the application of AD measures. See Brink Lindsey and Dan Ikenson, "Reforming the Antidumping Agreement: A Road Map for WTO Negotiations," Cato Institute Trade Policy Analysis No. 21 (Dec. 11, 2002).

[334] It is because the very attempt to determine the "normalcy" of a price in a market economy, in which prices are determined by market forces and not by any normative rules, is inherently arbitrary no matter what standard is applied. It was pointed out that "[t]he primary justification for the antidumping law is really more political than economic. The guiding precept is *legitimacy* rather than *efficiency*." Brink Lindsey, "The U.S. Antidumping Law: Rhetoric versus Reality," *supra* note 328, p. 3.

All these problems with the current AD disciplines suggest that there is indeed little rationale to preserve this archaic system of AD practices.[335] The AD measures are based on a wrong premise that somehow there is a "normal price" to be determined and that a sale at a price less than this normal price is "unfair," and therefore should be sanctioned. The individual market decides the price, and it is not for the government to determine what the "normal" price is. Anti-competitive behavior, such as predation, has been cited as a justification for AD measures. Nonetheless, the likelihood of success of such practices is minimal, and another trade measure, safeguards, whose disciplines are much tighter than AD measures and, therefore, are much less susceptible to abuse, can respond to predation attempts. Therefore, AD measures should be removed from the international trading system altogether,[336] although vested political interests in maintaining AD measures would seem to make their elimination unlikely in the near future.[337]

AD measures are particularly a problem for developing countries. The competitiveness of their products is normally based on low prices,

---

[335] Not surprisingly, the General Agreement on Trade in Services (GATS), the first multilateral disciplines for trade in services, does not provide AD measures while mandating negotiations for the rules for subsidies and safeguards. See the relevant discussions in Chapter 5 *infra*. Many economists have refuted the justification for AD measures. A recent critic described that AD measures are like the "invisible suit" of Hans Christian Anderson's fairy tale about the "Emperor's New Clothes" in that everyone pretends to recognize what does not have any real substance. William A. Kerr and Laura J. Loppacher, "Anti-Dumping in the Doha Negotiation: Fairy Tales at the World Trade Organization" (2004) 38 *Journal of World Trade* 211.

[336] Yale economist T. N. Srinivasan has characterized anti-dumping as the equivalent of a "nuclear weapon in the armory of trade policy" and suggested removing it in the 1999 WTO high-level symposium on Trade and Development. World Trade Organization, *Report on the WTO High-Level Symposium on Trade and Development* (1999), *supra* note 38.

[337] AD measures have been politically favored trade measures because they are relatively easier to apply, in comparison to other trade measures, such as safeguards to protect domestic producers and the interest of their constituencies. Protectionists have strongly argued for the preservation of AD measures in the name of securing a "level playing field." Brink Lindsey and Daniel J. Ikenson, "Coming Home to Roost: Proliferating Antidumping Laws and the Growing Threat to U.S. Exports," Cato Institute Trade Policy Analysis No. 14 (July 30, 2001), pp. 1–2.

primarily due to lower labor costs. If developing countries are to achieve economic development through international trade, they should be allowed to exploit the advantage that they have in lower labor costs and the resulting lower prices. AD measures are a major impediment to the effort of developing countries to achieve development through exports because the lower prices of their export products have easily triggered the application of AD measures for decades.[338] Although a lower price alone is not sufficient for the application of AD measures,[339] the current provisions permitting the "construction" of costs and reference prices make it relatively easy for the national authorities to find dumping and apply AD measures against exports from developing countries.

For this reason, even if the complete removal of AD measures from the international trading system would be difficult at this time,[340] AD measures should not be applied to exports from developing countries. Developed countries may find this limited exemption in favor of developing countries difficult to accept because they have used AD measures primarily against cheaper imports from developing countries. However, if we are to facilitate development through international trade, developing countries should be allowed to take a full advantage of their lower costs and prices. This would be difficult if their exports would easily be targeted by AD measures based on dubious and ambiguous rules with so much room for abuse. Again, safeguard measures can respond to the predatory dumping that results in the displacement of domestic products, which may be the only true justification of the AD rules despite its limited likelihood of success.

With respect to the exemption of AD measures in favor of developing countries, there might be a concern similar to the one that has been raised

---

[338] *Supra* note 330.
[339] Dumping must also *cause* or *threaten* material injury to the domestic industry for the application of an AD measure. GATT Article VI, para. 6, WTO, *The Results of the Uruguay Round of Multilateral Trade Negotiations, supra* note 53, pp. 431–432. Unlike the serious injury required for the application of a safeguard measure, as discussed in Chapter 4.3 *infra*, the threshold for material injury is not considered high.
[340] *Supra* note 337.

in the previous discussion of export subsidies: the absence of AD measures applied to exports from developing countries may encourage exporters from these countries to compete with one another by undercutting prices and reducing profits, thereby diminishing their prospects for economic development through export promotion. Again, developing countries should be trusted with their own best judgment. It is not certain that those exporters would necessarily consider price undercutting a viable and sustainable practice, particularly with the existence of safeguards. At any rate, a possibility of price undercutting between competitors always exists in any business, and it is part of the equation that any prudent exporter would duly consider when they contemplate engaging in such a practice.

4.3 Safeguards

The remaining measures of administered protection are safeguards. "Safeguards" or "safeguard measures" are emergency import restraints applicable where increased imports cause or threaten to cause serious injury to a competing domestic industry of the import country.[341] The GATT provides rules for safeguard measures (Article XIX),[342] and the subsequent WTO Agreement on Safeguards elaborates on these rules and now provides the main disciplines on safeguards.[343] Safeguards relieve the import country of the economic and social problems caused by rapid import increases, such as massive unemployment, by enabling the import

---

[341] Article 2 of the WTO Agreement on Safeguards sets forth general requirements for the application of a safeguard measure. WTO, *The Results of the Uruguay Round of Multilateral Trade Negotiations*, *supra* note 53, pp. 275. For a comprehensive coverage on the subject of safeguards, see Lee (2005), *supra* note 293.

[342] GATT, art. XIX. WTO, *The Results of the Uruguay Round of Multilateral Trade Negotiations*, *supra* note 53, pp. 454–455.

[343] Unlike the provisions of Article XIX comprising only five paragraphs of general rules, the SA provides detailed substantive and procedural rules for the application of a safeguard measure. *Id.*, pp. 275–283. John Jackson called the SA "a substantial achievement, and indeed a heroic statement of principle." Jackson (1997), *supra* note 43, p. 210.

country to maintain the status quo through temporary import restraints. Safeguards are also meant to facilitate the economic adjustment of the importing country to increased competition with imports.[344] The maximum duration of safeguards is four years, extendable only once up to the same period.[345]

Safeguard measures can be considered to be a "safety net" for the problems that market liberalization can incidentally cause. Economic justifications for safeguards are rather controversial (i.e., whether safeguards are the best way to facilitate economic adjustment).[346] Nonetheless, the existence of safeguard measures helps countries increase their market access and also dissolve significant political pressure to protect domestic industries during the times of rapid import increases.[347] The number of safeguards implemented is much less than that of CVD actions or AD actions but has been increasing since the beginning of the WTO. One hundred fifty safeguard measures were reported over the five decades of the GATT, with an average of less than four measures a year; during 2003, the Committee on Safeguards received nineteen notifications concerning decisions to apply safeguard measures, an increase from ten in 2002.[348]

Despite these justifications, safeguards can cause significant problems to the exports of developing countries. In an ideal development scenario, a developing country successfully establishes export industries. Exports from this developing country then compete well with the domestic products of the importing countries and increase market share, possibly causing injury to the competing domestic producers of the importing country. From the perspective of the exporting developing country, this is a success story that has been shown in the development case of the East

---

[344] For the economic and political justifications of safeguards, see Lee (2005), *supra* note 293, Chapter 1.

[345] SA, art. 7. WTO, *The Results of the Uruguay Round of Multilateral Trade Negotiations, supra* note 53, pp. 278–279. Developing countries may extend the duration by an additional two years. SA, art. 9.2. *Id.*, p. 280.

[346] *Supra* note 344.

[347] *Id.*

[348] WTO, Annual Reports 2003 and 2004, p. 24 and p. 43, respectively.

Asian economies.[349] Nevertheless, under the current rule, this developing country can be punished for its success where its exports are competitive enough to cause serious injury to the domestic industry of the importing country. Safeguard measures hamper exports from developing countries and can cause adverse effects on their economic development.

What should then be done to resolve this problem for developing countries? Developed countries may find it difficult, politically and economically, to accept serious injury to their domestic industries: it is one thing to say that developed countries should accept and tolerate the application of a DFT and DFS in consideration of development interests of developing countries,[350] where the impact of these measures on their own economies might be limited, but it would be quite another to argue that developed countries should also tolerate such injury to their domestic industries that may lead to serious economic, social, and political consequences (e.g., massive unemployment). So how do we balance this conflict between the interest to facilitate exports from developing countries for their economic development and the need for trade protection to prevent the acute problems associated with massive increases in imports?

The current rules on safeguards already provide some solution to this problem. Under the SA, the importing country is obligated to apply a safeguard measure *only to the extent necessary to prevent or remedy serious injury,*[351] that is, the extent of the measure should be proportionate to the extent of injury to the domestic industry. If this requirement of proportionate response is observed, the developing country may still continue to export after the application of the safeguard measure, albeit in reduced quantities because of the measure.[352] In addition, the current safeguard

---

[349] See Chapter 1.2 *supra* for a discussion of the relation between international trade and economic development.

[350] See the relevant discussions in Chapters 3.2 and 3.3 *supra*.

[351] SA, art. 5.1. WTO, *The Results of the Uruguay Round of Multilateral Trade Negotiations, supra* note 53, p. 277.

[352] Article 5.1 of the SA specifies the minimum quota level. It provides in relevant part, "if a quantitative restriction is used, such a measure shall not reduce the quantity of

rule requires the exemption of imports from developing countries where the share of imports from developing countries is insignificant.[353]

The participants of the UR discussed the possibility of a total exemption of imports from LDCs, but they failed to agree on this exemption.[354] Imports from LDCs should be exempted in consideration of their particularly dire need for economic development. This complete exemption for imports from LDCs would be feasible and would not be likely to cause any significant harm to the economies of the importing countries because the market share of exports from LDCs is rather insignificant.[355] In applying subsidy rules, LDCs are currently exempted from the requirement prohibiting export subsidies in consideration of their need for development.[356] Parallel consideration should also be given with respect to the application of safeguards by exempting imports originating in LDCs from safeguards.

Should this type of total exemption be also given to developing countries other than LDCs? Developed countries may find this extended exemption difficult to accommodate as the exporting industries of some

imports below the level of a recent period which shall be the average of imports in the last three representative years for which statistics are available unless clear justification is given that a different level is necessary to prevent or remedy serious injury." *Id.* No specific ceiling is imposed where restrictions other than quantitative measures (e.g., added tariffs) are applied.

[353] For instance, under Article 9 of the SA, safeguard measures are not to be applied against a product originating in a developing country Member as long as its share of imports of the product concerned to the importing Member does not exceed three percent, provided that developing country Members with less than a three percent share of imports collectively account for not more than nine percent of the total imports of the product concerned. SA, art. 9.1. WTO, *The Results of the Uruguay Round of Multilateral Trade Negotiations, supra* note 53, pp. 279–280. Critics have argued that these three and nine percent ceilings are too limiting. In addition, the two-year additional extension of a safeguard measure allowed for developing countries and the shortened interval before the re-introduction of a safeguard measure provided in Article 9.2 of the SA are also not particularly helpful. See Mah (2001), *supra* note 152, 380–382.

[354] Lee (2005), *supra* note 293, Chapter 2.4.

[355] The share of merchandise exports by LDCs is less than one percent of total world exports. WTO, *International Trade Statistics 2004.*

[356] *Supra* note 273.

developing countries with considerable manufacturing capacities have threatened the position of the domestic industries of developed countries. For instance, exports from the East Asian developing countries were frequently subject to import restraints by developed countries during the 1970s and 1980s in the form of "voluntary" trade restriction agreements (gray-area measures),[357] including "voluntary export restraints" (VERs), "voluntary restraint agreements" (VRAs) and "orderly marketing arrangements" (OMAs). Gray-area measures escaped the control of the GATT because they were maintained in the form of "agreements" between the exporting and importing countries.[358] In early 1991, there were as many as 284 known gray-area measures in contrast to only twenty-four safeguards.[359] Currently, the SA prohibits all gray-area measures.[360]

If it is not feasible to exempt exports from all developing countries from safeguards, how should these exports be treated in the application of safeguards to better facilitate their development? Could the concept of the sliding scale (the differentiated treatment in accordance with the per capita GNI of the developing country), as discussed in the context of the DFT and DFS, also be applied here?[361] It would seem difficult to do so because safeguard measures should be applied non-discriminatorily, regardless of the source of imports.[362] The negotiators of the SA were concerned that the authorization of selective applications of a safeguard measure would lead to discrimination against imports from particular countries.[363] This MFN application of safeguards is the core of the current discipline and must be observed, and for this reason, the differentiated

---

[357] Supra note 293. See Lee (2005), supra note 293, Chapter 2.3.

[358] Id.

[359] Terence P. Stewart (ed.), The GATT Uruguay Round: A Negotiating History (1986–1992) (Kluwer Law and Taxation, The Hague, 1993), pp. 1728–1729.

[360] SA, art. 11. WTO, The Results of the Uruguay Round of Multilateral Trade Negotiations, supra note 53, pp. 280–281.

[361] See the relevant discussion in Chapter 3 supra.

[362] SA, art. 2.2. WTO, The Results of the Uruguay Round of Multilateral Trade Negotiations, supra note 53, p. 275.

[363] Lee (2005), supra note 293, Chapter 2.

treatment proposed in the context of the DFT and DFS may not be applied to safeguards.

An alternative treatment in favor of developing countries could be to limit the total duration of a safeguard measure applied by developed countries to the initial four years and not to authorize any extension of the measure where the absolute majority of imports subject to the particular measure (e.g., two-thirds or more) originates in developing countries. This ban on the extension of the safeguard should reduce damage to the trade of developing countries caused by safeguards. The current S&D treatment based on the market share of imports originating in developing countries[364] should also be expanded by raising the current percentage ceilings that seem to be too limiting.[365]

Another area for consideration is compensation. As safeguard measures are applicable regardless of the existence of any unfair trade practice on the part of exporters, safeguards inevitably upset the balance of concessions between the importing and the exporting countries. In an effort to maintain the balance of concessions, the SA requires consultations between the importing and the exporting countries *prior to* the application of a safeguard measure[366] in hopes of finding a mutually satisfactory settlement. The consultations may lead to an agreement on compensation normally in the form of a reduction of tariff rates applicable to exports from the countries to be affected by the proposed safeguard measure.[367] If no agreement is reached, the affected exporting countries are entitled to adopt counter measures against the trade of the importing country.[368]

However, under the current rules of the SA, the affected exporting countries may not do so for the first three years when the measure is in effect, provided that the safeguard measure is applied based on an

---

[364] *Supra* note 353.
[365] *Id.*
[366] SA, art. 12.3. WTO, *The Results of the Uruguay Round of Multilateral Trade Negotiations, supra* note 53, pp. 281–282.
[367] SA, art. 8.1. *Id.*, p. 279.
[368] SA, art. 8.2. *Id.*

absolute increase in imports and the measure conforms to the provisions of the SA.[369] This suspension of retaliation is meant to provide an incentive for the importing countries to comply with the safeguard rules and not to resort to any other illegal import restraints, such as the gray-area measures. This rule, however, needs a revision with respect to safeguard measures applied to exports from developing countries for the following reason: safeguard measures may adversely affect the development interests of developing countries, particularly those countries relying on a limited number of "major" export products as an engine for their development when some of these products are subject to safeguards. If a safeguard measure should nevertheless be applied to these exports from developing countries, compensation should be required to reduce harm to the development interests of developing countries relying on their exports for development.

Compensation should be made as a *prior* condition for the application of a safeguard measure when the measure is applied by a developed country to a product originating in a developing country. The compensation should be discussed between the exporting and importing countries during the consultations before the application of the safeguard measure, but even if there is no agreement on compensation, the importing developed country should nevertheless make compensation at the time of the safeguard application and continue negotiations with the affected country without retracting compensation. Furthermore, the affected developing countries should be allowed to apply a retaliatory measure to the extent that there is a gap between the compensation and the injury. The Committee on Safeguards[370] can assume the role of determining the adequacy of compensation provided by the developed country. The current rule should be revised to this effect to achieve a balance between the need for temporary protection of the domestic industry in the presence of an

---

[369] SA, art. 8.3. *Id.*
[370] The Committee on Safeguards is established under Article 13 of the SA. *Id.*, pp. 282–283.

acute increase in imports and the need for continued access to export markets by developing countries.

Lastly, an important clarification needs to be made to the current disciplines on safeguards. The SA provides the comprehensive rules on the application of a safeguard measure.[371] The SA provisions include both substantive rules and procedural requirements for safeguards and replace the outdated provisions of GATT Article XIX that governed the application of safeguards before the WTO.[372] Nonetheless, the Appellate Body[373] of the WTO determined that a clause in Article XIX, which is not included in the SA, is a legal requirement for the application of a safeguard measure.[374] Paragraph 1 (a) of Article XIX states that

> if, *as a result of unforeseen developments* and of the effect of the obliga-
> tions incurred by a contracting party under this Agreement, including
> tariff concessions, any product is being imported into the territory of
> that contracting party in such increased quantities and under such con-
> ditions as to cause or threaten serious injury to domestic producers in
> that territory of like or directly competitive products, the contracting
> party shall be free, in respect of such product, and to the extent and
> for such time as may be necessary to prevent or remedy such injury, to

[371] Lee (2005), *supra* note 291, Chapter 3.

[372] *Id.*

[373] The Appellate Body is the standing appellate dispute resolution body in the WTO. Members may bring trade disputes before a panel constituted under the rules of the Understanding of Rules and Procedures Governing the Settlement of Disputes (Dispute Settlement Understanding; DSU) and may also appeal panel decisions to the Appellate Body. The text of the DSU is found in the Annex 2 of the WTO Agreement. WTO, *The Results of the Uruguay Round of Multilateral Trade Negotiations, supra* note 53, pp. 354–379. For a discussion of the dispute settlement process in the WTO, see Jackson (1997), *supra* note 43, Chapter 4.

[374] *Korea – Definitive Safeguard Measure on the Imports of Certain Dairy Products* (*Korea – Dairy Products*), Report of the Appellate Body, WTO doc. WT/DS98/AB/R (Dec. 14, 1999), para. 90 and *Argentina – Safeguard Measure on the Imports of Footwear* (*Argentina – Footwear*), Report of the Appellate Body, WTO doc. WT/DS121/AB/R (Dec. 14, 1999), para. 97.

suspend the obligation in whole or in part or to withdraw or modify the concession.[375] (Emphasis is added.)

Although the WTO dispute settlement panels in the first two safeguard disputes determined that this "unforeseen developments" clause in Article XIX:1 (a) is merely a descriptive clause and does not constitute an affirmative condition to be met by the Member proposing to apply a safeguard measure,[376] the Appellate Body disagreed with the panel findings and ruled that the clause constitutes an affirmative legal condition, and Members proposing to apply a safeguard measure are required to demonstrate the existence of unforeseen developments leading to the increase in imports that causes or threatens to cause serious injury to the domestic industry.[377] This "unforeseen developments" clause is not included in the SA.

This Appellate Body decision has faced criticism because it adds ambiguities to the disciplines on safeguards as follows. First, the clause is too ambiguous to be an objective legal requirement, and no clear legal standard to determine the existence of "unforeseen developments" can be derived from this clause.[378] The Appellate Body distinguished "unforeseen" developments as written in the clause in question, from "unforeseeable" developments.[379] The former refers to a factual absence of foresight that is inherently subjective, and therefore, it does not allow an objective review.[380] The latter may allow an objective review, but it is not what the clause states.

---

[375] GATT Article XIX, para. 1 (a). WTO, *The Results of the Uruguay Round of Multilateral Trade Negotiations, supra* note 53, p. 454.

[376] *Korea – Dairy Products*, Report of the Panel, WTO doc. WT/DS98/R (June 21, 1999), paras 7.51 –7.52 and *Argentina – Footwear*, Report of the Panel, WTO doc. WT/DS121/R (June 25, 1999), para. 8.108.

[377] *Supra* note 374.

[378] Lee (2005), *supra* note 291, Chapter 3.2.

[379] *Korea – Dairy Products, supra* note 374, para. 84.

[380] *Supra* note 378.

Second, it is clear from certain provisions in the SA that only those provisions of the SA and not those of Article XIX are meant to govern the application of safeguards. For instance, the reference to the rules on safeguards in Article 8.3, which sets out the condition for the suspension of retaliatory measures, includes only the provisions of the SA and not those of Article XIX. If Article XIX was meant to comprise part of the rules on safeguards, the provisions of Article XIX should have also been mentioned.[381] Next, it has also been pointed out that the negotiation process of the SA and the specific changes in the wording of the draft agreement suggest that the omission of the "unforeseen developments" clause from the SA was rather intentional.[382] Lastly, imposing this ambiguous requirement seems to serve no useful purpose since the availability of safeguards would encourage Members to increase market access.[383]

This new requirement set by the Appellate Body decision was further elaborated by the recent WTO panel and the Appellate Body decisions: they determined that Article XIX:1 (a) requires Members applying a safeguard measure to explain *why* certain developments leading to the injurious increase in imports were unforeseen at the time the relevant obligation was negotiated and *why* the injurious increase occurred as a result of the unforeseen developments.[384] As the Appellate Body decision serves as the authority on the interpretation of the WTO law, a Member proposing to apply a safeguard measure must demonstrate, in conformity with this decision, that certain "unforeseen" developments have led to an increase in imports causing injury to their domestic industry. This is

---

[381] Lee (2005), *supra* note 291, Chapter 3.2.

[382] *Id.*

[383] *Id.*

[384] *United States – Lamb Meat*, Report of the Panel, *infra* note 385, paras. 7.29–7.31, Report of the Appellate Body, *infra* note 385, paras. 72–73; *Argentina – Definitive Safeguard Measure on Imports of Preserved Peaches*, Report of the Panel, WTO doc. WT/DS238/R (Feb. 14, 2003), paras. 7.23–7.28; *United States – Steel Products*, Report of the Panel, *infra* note 385, paras. 10.104, 10.121–10.126, Report of the Appellate Body, *infra* note 385, paras. 316, 326, 329.

an onerous analytical requirement for any Member proposing to apply a safeguard measure, particularly those developing countries with limited analytical resources, to "foresee" and "explain" such developments leading to an injurious increase in imports as a result of their import concessions that may have been made at trade negotiations decades ago.[385]

Safeguard measures may also serve the interests of developing countries in that rapid increases in imports may cause critical damage to their infant industries, and therefore, the availability of safeguards would be imperative to protect the development interests of developing countries in the presence of rapid import increases. In this regard, the Appellate Body decision requiring the demonstration of "unforeseen developments" is a considerable barrier to their resort to safeguards. This requirement, which is created by the Appellate Body rather than the participants of the UR,[386] adds nothing but ambiguities to the disciplines on safeguards. Perhaps the relevant provision of the SA needs to be modified to clarify that the provisions of the SA constitute the sole authority on the application of safeguard measures.[387]

---

[385] Apparently, this requirement is ambiguous enough even for an advanced country such as the United States to fail to demonstrate unforeseen developments repeatedly in previous safeguards disputes: United States – *Definitive Safeguard Measures on Imports of Wheat Gluten From the European Communities* (*United States – Wheat Gluten*), Report of the Panel, WTO doc. WT/DS166/R (July 31, 2000), Report of the Appellate Body, WTO doc. WT/DS166/AB/R (Dec. 22, 2000); *United States – Safeguard Measures on Imports of Fresh, Chilled or Frozen Lamb Meat from New Zealand and Australia* (*United States – Lamb Meat*), Report of the Panel, WTO docs WT/DS177/R, WT/DS178/R (Dec. 21, 2000), Report of the Appellate Body, WTO docs WT/DS177/AB/R, WT/DS178/AB/R (May 1, 2001); *United States – Definitive Safeguard Measures on Imports of Steel Wire Rod and Circular Welded Carbon Quality Line Pipe* (*United States – Line Pipe*), Report of the Panel, WTO doc. WT/DS202/R (October 29, 2001), Report of the Appellate Body, WTO doc WT/202/AB/R (February 15, 2002); *United States – Definitive Safeguard Measures on Imports of Certain Steel Products* (*United States – Steel Products*), Report of the Panel, WTO docs WT/DS248~DS259/R (July 11, 2003), Report of the Appellate Body, WTO docs WT/DS248~DS259/AB/R (November 10, 2003).

[386] *Supra* note 382.

[387] Lee (2005), *supra* note 291, Chapter 3 and Appendix 4.

FIVE

"Expansion" of Trade Disciplines and Development

5.1 Agriculture and Textile

Agriculture products and textiles[388] have a particular importance for the trade of developing countries because these products tend to be the major export products for developing countries in the early stages of economic development.[389] The lower labor costs of developing countries create a competitive advantage in labor-intensive products such as textile and some agricultural products. This advantage makes agricultural products and textiles competitive export items for developing countries and is reflected in the lower prices of these products.[390] Therefore, it will

---

[388] The term, "textile" is understood to include "clothing" unless indicated otherwise.

[389] According to the WTO/World Bank Trade and Development Centre, "Textiles and clothing are important export products for developing countries. They make up about 22% of industrial exports. A third of developing countries have substantial export interest in textiles and clothing (i.e. exports in textiles and clothing make up more than 20% of total exports), and in one out of seven developing countries they account for the majority of exports." <http://www.itd.org/guides/dv_faq13.htm>.

Agricultural products also make up around 10 percent of the total exports from developing countries (2000/01). Prema-Chandra Athukorala, "Agricultural Trade Reforms in the Doha Round: A Developing Country Perspective" (2004) 38 *Journal of World Trade* 880, Table 2.

[390] This advantage will not apply to capital-intensive agricultural products because many developing countries lack capital. This explains that certain developed countries,

be important to promote the export of these products from developing countries to facilitate their development, particularly in the initial development stages where developing countries do not typically have the technology to produce and export more sophisticated manufactured products.

Nonetheless, developed countries showed reluctance in bringing these products into the framework of the international trading system. First, agriculture had long been outside the purview of GATT disciplines.[391] Significant political influence representing the interests of agricultural sectors in many developed countries has made it difficult for these developed countries to increase market access for agricultural imports. The UR went through difficulties due to the controversies over the treatment of agricultural products in the new trading system; a number of countries exporting agricultural products pushed for the full integration of agricultural products into the trading system, demanding market access as well as the elimination of production subsidies for agricultural products.[392] However, countries with a vulnerable agricultural sector, such as Japan, were reluctant to open their agricultural market and resisted this pressure.

including the United States, Canada, Australia, and New Zealand, have a competitive advantage in certain agricultural products, such as meat products, that employ considerable capital. The same analysis can be applied to textile and clothing products, where certain developed countries, including France and Italy, have a competitive advantage in textile and clothing products such as fashion-design products that use high levels of capital and design technique.

[391] In 1955, the United States obtained a broad waiver for its measures restricting imports of agricultural products. This waiver led other members of the GATT, which did not receive such a waiver, to believe that they are also entitled to the same under the notion of reciprocity and subsequently refused to comply with GATT rules with respect to their agricultural trade.

[392] Namely, the "Cairns group," an interest group of seventeen agricultural exporting countries, Argentina, Australia, Bolivia, Brazil, Canada, Chile, Columbia, Costa Rica, Guatemala, Indonesia, Malaysia, New Zealand, Paraguay, the Philippines, South Africa, Thailand, and Uruguay, actively advocated the integration of agricultural products in the trading rule system.

A compromise was finally reached toward the end of the UR in the Agreement on Agriculture. This complex and elaborate agreement did not eliminate special protections for agricultural products altogether; for example, the agreement recognizes various agricultural subsidies. Importantly, the agreement requires Members to convert various non-tariff import limitations on agricultural products into tariffs (i.e., "tariffication"). It also obligates Members to provide minimum market access for agricultural products in their Schedule of Concessions to initiate market liberalization for agricultural products. The agreement seems to be an interim arrangement for the agricultural sector as it maintains special provisions and protections for this sector, and many more negotiations will be needed before the full integration of agricultural products into WTO disciplines.[393]

Textiles and clothing are another area in which exporting developing countries have faced serious import restrictions. Quotas and high tariffs had been prevalent in textiles and clothing trade, as represented by the Multifiber Arrangement (MFA) that allowed extensive import restrictions on these products. Textiles and clothing are labor-intensive products in which developing countries with lower labor costs tend to have a competitive advantage, and therefore, these products have been typically promoted in the early stages of industrialization effort.[394] Although textile and clothing exports are essential for the facilitation of development for many developing countries,[395] developed countries have

---

[393] For further discussions of the Agreement on Agriculture, see GATT, *The Result of the Uruguay Round of Multilateral Trade Negotiations* (GATT, Geneva, 1994) and Joseph F. Francois, Bradley McDonald, and Hakan Norstrom, *Assessing the Uruguay Round* (WTO, Geneva, 1995).

[394] For instance, South Korea focused on the production of these "light" products, including textile and clothing, in the 1960s and began to produce more capital-intensive products, such as chemical and steel products, in the 1970s as development progressed. Before South Korea, the success of the wool and cotton industries in Britain and the capital accumulation from this success made the Industrial Revolution possible in the late eighteenth century.

[395] *Supra* note 389.

systematically limited imports of these products by implementing import restrictions.

The Agreement on Textiles and Clothing (ATC) was settled during the UR to reduce these import restrictions on textiles and clothing and to integrate them fully into the trading system without extensive quantitative restrictions, such as the MFA. The ATC was an interim agreement to carry out the integration process of textiles and clothing products and expired with the completion of the integration by January 2005. As in the case of the Agreement on Agriculture, the ATC also maintained the status quo, authorizing the existing import limitations on textiles and clothing. Yet the ATC required the phase out of the MFA in stages and the full integration of textiles and clothing into WTO disciplines at the end of the process. This type of full integration is not planned for agricultural products in the Agreement on Agriculture, as many participants of the UR were not ready for the political consequences of the full integration of agricultural products.[396] The issue of the integration of agricultural products spurred intense political struggles in many countries.[397]

From the development perspective, it is unfortunate that the two major categories of export products from developing countries did not benefit from the market liberalization effort of the GATT and were subject to systematic import restrictions for over five decades. One may look on this and conclude that the GATT made consistent efforts to reduce both tariff and non-tariff barriers to the manufactured products in which developed countries tend to have a competitive advantage but not those products in which developing countries have this advantage, such as agricultural

---

[396] Regarding the integration of agricultural products, the position was split among developed countries as well as developing countries. For instance, developed countries exporting agricultural products, such as Canada, Australia, and New Zealand, pushed for the integration, whereas some developing countries with a vulnerable agricultural sector, such as South Korea, adamantly opposed it during the UR.

[397] Thousands of farmers in countries such as France and South Korea took to the streets in fierce opposition to the initiative taken to open their markets for agricultural products and to reduce agricultural subsidy.

products and textiles.[398] This is an example of a failure on the part of the international trading regime to provide an adequate regulatory environment for the promotion of export from developing countries, although many developing countries may also have had their own problems failing to carry out effective development policies.[399]

This imbalance and inadequacy have been finally addressed, at least to some extent, by the Agreement on Agriculture and the ATC. The ATC made a significant achievement for the liberalization of textile and clothing trade.[400] Agriculture remains a difficult area, and significant trade barriers,[401] as well as domestic subsidies, including direct export subsidies otherwise prohibited under the SCM Agreement,[402] are still remaining. These barriers to agricultural trade and the subsidies provided by developed countries to their own agricultural producers are serious impediments to agricultural exports from developing countries.[403] Efforts to reduce these barriers and subsidies should be continued to better facilitate the development of developing countries.

The Agreement on Agriculture also authorizes "special safeguard measures" (SSGs) to restrict agricultural imports based on specified

---

[398] *Supra* note 47.

[399] Domestic political instability, corruption, lack of education, and failure to adopt consistent economic policies are just a few of the problems that many of developing countries have faced for decades.

[400] Agreement on Textile and Clothing, art. 9. WTO, *The Results of the Uruguay Round of Multilateral Trade Negotiations, supra* note 53, p. 87. Shoenbaum observes that the invocation of safeguards and other loopholes in the ATC prevent full liberalization even after the 2005 deadline, as already shown by recent actions by the United States. He suggests that the Doha Round should assure that the ATC is fully implemented. Shoenbaum (2004), *supra* note 9.

[401] Market access for agricultural imports is in its initial stages, and tariff-quota arrangements are allowed where higher tariffs are applied to imports above the assigned quota level.

[402] In 2002, the total of 31.5 million USD was granted for export subsidies in the United States. WTO doc. G/AG/N/USA/53 (June 2, 2004). For the European Union, the amount reached 1,997.2 million ECU during 2001/2 marketing year. WTO doc. G/AG/N/EEC/44 (June 11, 2003).

[403] See also, Shoenbaum (2004), *supra* note 9.

reductions of price or specified increases in imports.[404] Developed countries have actively applied SSGs.[405] SSGs are considered relatively easier to apply than the general safeguards authorized under the SA because the former does not require an injury test unlike general safeguards[406] and set substantial barriers to agricultural exports from developing countries.

These trade barriers and agricultural subsidies are not only a serious impediment to agricultural exports from developing countries but also costly to their own economy.[407] Despite political difficulties, developed countries should make consistent efforts to reduce these barriers and subsidies with clear policy objectives to liberalize agricultural trade. In particular, developed countries should have a plan to reduce higher tariff rates applicable to agricultural imports down to the rates similar to those applicable to manufactured products by a set deadline.[408] Agricultural subsidies should be reduced and eventually eliminated except where it is

---

[404] For more discussion of special safeguard measures and the trigger prices and import quantities, see Lee (2005), *supra* note 291, Chapter 11.3.

[405] In 2002, SSGs were being applied in the United States to as many as fifty-two products. WTO doc. G/AG/N/USA/49 (Jan. 23, 2004). For the European Union, SSGs were made operational to thirty-four tariff items (EC schedule) in the 2001–2 marketing year. WTO doc. G/AG/N/EEC/43 (June 5, 2003).

[406] A Member proposing to apply a safeguard measure is required to establish that an increase in imports has caused or threatened to cause serious injury to the domestic industry. Article 4.2 of the SA specifies injury factors for mandatory assessment. WTO, *The Results of the Uruguay Round of Multilateral Trade Negotiations, supra* note 53, pp. 276–277. Such an injury test is not required for the application of an SSG.

[407] The total Aggregated Measurement of Support (AMS) for agricultural sectors amounted to 43,654 million Euro in the 2001–2 marketing years for the European Union. WTO doc. G/AG/N/EEC/49 (April 1, 2004). The AMS amount reached to 16,803 million USD in the United States for the same period. WTO doc. G/AG/N/USA/51 (March 17, 2004).

[408] According to the WTO, the numerical targets for agriculture (1995–2000) included the reduction of tariffs for all agricultural products by 36 percent on average (15 percent minimum cut per product) by developed countries. WTO Web site, <http://www.wto.org/english/thewto_e/whatis_e/tif_e/agrm3_e.htm>.

In 1998, the average tariffs on agricultural products were still almost twice as high as those applied to manufactured products. Athukorala, *supra* note 389, p. 887, Table 5.

justified under the SCM Agreement.[409] In reducing and eliminating agricultural subsidies, the DFS scheme should also be applicable to promoting agricultural production in developing countries.[410]

A question has been raised whether all agricultural subsidies by developed countries should be treated equally; for example, can we really treat small Japanese or Swiss farmers, who may be still rich by international standards but may be at the bottom of the economic ladder of their respective societies, in the same way we treat large American agrobusiness firms? Developed countries may certainly have a legitimate interest in giving financial aid to less privileged members of their society, but this aid should be provided in the context of a general social welfare scheme, not in the form of industry-specific subsidies at the expense of agricultural imports, particularly those from developing countries. The difference between developed countries and developing countries on this issue is that the treasury of the former may afford to help less fortunate members of the society under the general welfare scheme, but the latter may not and may have to resort to external measures such as trade protection.

The suggested liberalization of the agricultural market should not be imposed on developing countries.[411] For instance, SSGs, with some

---

[409] The WTO's numerical targets for agriculture also included the reduction of domestic support. The current WTO arrangement (special ministerial decision) for the LDCs and those depending on food imports should be maintained. This arrangement provides food and aid for agricultural development and also refers to the possibility of assistance from the IMF and the World Bank to finance commercial food imports. WTO, Ministerial Decision on Measures Concerning the Possible Negative Effects of the Reform Programme on Least-Developed and Net Foot-Importing Developing Countries; WTO, *The Results of the Uruguay Round of Multilateral Trade Negotiations, supra* note 53, pp. 392–393. A recent study has analyzed how the trade regime may affect the food security of LDCs and net-food importing countries; see Ruosi Zhang, "Food Security: Food Trade Regime and Food Aid Regime" (2004) 7 *Journal of International Economic Law* 565–584.

[410] For a discussion of the DFS, see Chapter 3.3 *supra.*

[411] Nonetheless, the WTO also imposed the reduction of tariffs on developing countries although the extent of targeted reduction was somewhat less for developing countries.

modification of the rules, might be helpful to address some agricultural problems in developing countries after market liberalization, such as extended periods of low prices.[412] It has already been discussed that reciprocity should not be expected in the trade relations between developed and developing countries in consideration of the development interests of developing countries.[413] Although I subscribe to the premise that import barriers and subsidies do not in general promote economic welfare, I stress that their utilities in the facilitation of an industry may well compensate for this initial welfare loss.[414] Therefore, if developing countries have a legitimate development interest, as well as a solid plan in promoting particular agricultural and/or textile industries, they should be allowed to use import restrictions and subsidies for development. This argument does not necessarily advocate the preservation of the Agreement on Agriculture as it stands now but nonetheless calls for some leeway in favor of developing countries so that they may adopt a more flexible tariff structure and provide subsidies for development purposes in the agricultural and textile areas.

5.2 Trade-Related Investment Measures

Another area that has significant relevance to the economic development and trade of developing countries is foreign investment. Foreign investment may provide developing countries with the resources necessary for the development that these countries typically lack, including financial capital, technological resources, production facilities, and managerial expertise. In accepting foreign investment, the governments of host

---

See the numerical targets for agriculture. WTO Web site, <http://www.wto.org/english/thewto_e/whatis_e/tif_e/agrm3_e.htm>.

[412] For more discussion, see Alberto Valdés and Willam Foster, "Special Safeguards for Developing Country Agriculture: A Proposal for WTO Negotiations" (2003) 2 *World Trade Review* 5–31.

[413] See the relevant discussion in Chapter 4.1 *supra*.

[414] *Id.*

developing countries may be inclined to set a series of conditions to steer foreign investment to maximize their contribution to the development objectives that they may have. For example, to facilitate export industries, these governments may adopt investment measures that require foreign investors to export a certain portion of products that they produce in the host country.

This tendency to adopt investment measures is not unique to current developing countries. A historical study has revealed that today's developed countries also imposed regulations on foreign investment during their development, when they were net recipients of foreign investment, in order to ensure that such investment contributed to their long-term development objectives.[415] These regulations included a simple ban on the entry of foreign investment into particular sectors, as well as conditional entries (e.g., requirements for joint ventures, ceilings on foreign ownership) as also applied by today's developing countries.[416] Bans on entry enabled local producers to establish themselves without competition with potentially more efficient foreign investment, and conditional entries made it possible for the host country to extract greater benefit from permitted investment.[417]

Investment measures may affect trade. For instance, a foreign company may decide to make an investment to build manufacturing plants. If the host country adopts investment measures requiring foreign investment to export a certain portion of its product in order to promote exports and to reduce competition with other domestic producers, this foreign company may be compelled to export more than it would have otherwise. Thus, these investment measures would have clearly affected trade by increasing exports from this country. In addition, investment measures that require foreign investment to purchase domestic products

---

[415] Ha-Joon Chang and Duncan Green, *The Northern WTO Agenda on Investment: Do As We Say, Not As We Did* (South Centre/CAFOD, June 2003), p. 33.
[416] *Id.*
[417] *Id.*

may reduce the importation of these products from other countries that it may have purchased in the absence of such measures.

The participants of the UR were concerned about investment measures that have adverse effects on trade (trade-related investment measures, TRIMs) and set out rules on TRIMs for the first time in the multilateral trading system. The TRIMs Agreement, composed of nine articles and an annex, is rather brief and only includes a few provisions:[418] the agreement prohibits investment measures that are inconsistent with Articles III and XI of the GATT, which require national treatment[419] and the general elimination of quantitative restrictions, respectively.[420] The rationale for this prohibition is that these particular TRIMs distort trade by requiring investors to make certain export or import commitments.

The TRIMs Agreement is not meant to provide a comprehensive multilateral legal framework for investment. It is far more general and limited in scope than other agreements on investment, such as the Multilateral Agreement on Investment (MAI) previously promoted by the Organisation of Economic Co-operation and Development (OECD),[421] or various bilateral investment treaties (BITs). International investment has been governed by bilateral, rather than multilateral arrangements,[422] and

---

[418] WTO, *The Results of the Uruguay Round of Multilateral Trade Negotiations, supra* note 53, pp. 143–146.

[419] Refer to the relevant discussion of the national treatment principle in Chapter 2.2.

[420] GATT arts. III and XI and WTO, *The Results of the Uruguay Round of Multilateral Trade Negotiations, supra* note 53, pp. 427–249, 437, respectively.

[421] The OECD launched negotiations on MAI in 1995 to be a "free standing international treaty, open to all OECD Members and the European Communities, and to accession by non-OECD Member Countries." Its proposed objective was to "provide a broad multilateral framework for international investment with high standards for the liberalization of investment regimes and investment protection and with effective dispute settlement procedures." A series of intense negotiations ceased in 1998 without reaching an agreement on the final version. The background of the MAI and the negotiations are introduced in the official OECD Web site, <http://www1.oecd.org/daf/mai/intro.htm>.

[422] According to the World Bank record, more than 1,100 BITs are known to exist, and 800 of them were concluded after 1987. <http://www.worldbank.org/icsid/treaties/intro.htm>.

the TRIMs Agreement may be viewed as a small step toward a multilateral regulatory framework for investment now that the MAI has failed.[423] Some developed countries believe that a more comprehensive multilateral agreement on investment than the TRIMs Agreement is desirable and have made efforts to begin discussions on this issue at the WTO. This attempt has faced considerable resistance, and this issue is further discussed later in this chapter.

Trade-related investment measures are closely relevant to development policies because many of them are actually intended to facilitate development, that is, to optimize investment to serve development needs. The two examples of TRIMs that I have illustrated can typically be adopted for the development purpose of promoting exports and protecting domestic industries. In addition, the host country may require technology transfer as a condition for allowing foreign investment and may also want the equity of foreign investment to be shared by the local investors to ensure such transfer. The specific terms of TRIMs will affect the decision of foreign investors to invest in a particular host developing country because, while these measures may serve development interests, they also impose limiting conditions on the terms by which investment may operate in the host country. Therefore, BITs, which are designed to facilitate foreign investment, ban many of these TRIMs with respect to investments covered by them.[424]

The TRIMs Agreement also outlaws some of these TRIMs for trade-distorting effects. The Annex of the TRIMs Agreement provides an illustrative list of prohibited TRIMs[425] that include local content requirements (imposing the use of a certain amount of local inputs in production); import controls (requiring imports used in local production to be

---

[423] *Supra* note 421.

[424] For a study of BITs, see Rudolf Dolzer and Margrete Stevens, *Bilateral Investment Treaties* (Martinus Nijhoff Publishers, New York, 1995).

[425] WTO, *The Results of the Uruguay Round of Multilateral Trade Negotiations, supra* note 53, pp. 146.

equivalent to a certain proportion of exports); foreign exchange balancing requirements (requiring the foreign exchange made available for imports to be a certain proportion of the value of foreign exchange brought in by the foreign investment from exports and other sources); and export controls (obligating exports to be equivalent to a certain proportion of local production). The TRIMs Agreement also establishes the Committee on TRIMs to monitor the implementation of the TRIMs Agreement and provides Members with opportunities to consult on any matters relating to the operation and implementation of the agreement.

Trade-related investment measures have been criticized for discouraging investment and distorting international trade. Industrial promotion effects of TRIMs have been doubted and discredited by many.[426] The criticism includes the followng: TRIMs are economically inefficient because the terms of investment are controlled by investment measures rather than market forces; the governments of the host countries may abuse TRIMs politically, for instance, to serve the interests of select producers that are not necessarily relevant to the needs for development; and the restrictive terms of TRIMs may also discourage investors from making investments in developing countries adopting these measures and thereby deprive the host developing countries of the opportunities to benefit from the investment that can provide necessary resources for development.

Nevertheless, TRIMs can also play an important role in industrial promotion because they can help facilitate infant domestic industries by promoting exports and encouraging the use of domestic products. Note that all of today's developed countries also adopted investment measures to meet their development objectives during their own development.[427] Trade-related investment measures can be either effective or counter-effective to the development interest of a particular developing country

---

[426] The criticism about TRIMs is in line with the objections to state industrial promotion. See Chapter 3.1 *supra.*
[427] *Supra* note 415.

depending on the economic conditions and the development stage that the individual developing country is in. For instance, an imposition of a local content requirement may be unnecessary and economically inefficient at a time when the domestic industry can compete with imports. However, this particular investment measure may be useful and facilitate domestic infant industries in the initial stages of development where domestic industries require some protection. This suggests that TRIMs can be a means to facilitate development.

The TRIMs Agreement intends to eliminate certain TRIMs because they are believed to distort trade. However, the TRIMs Agreement recognizes the development needs of developing counties and provides certain special and differential treatment.[428] From the development perspective, TRIMs need to be tolerated when applied by developing countries to facilitate economic development. This tolerance would be justified because a relatively smaller portion of investment flows into developing countries worldwide[429]; therefore, the trade effects of TRIMs adopted by developing countries seem rather limited. This indicates that the same rationale in support of the DFT and DFS, on the basis of their relatively limited effect on international trade and the greater development needs, can be applied here to support TRIMs adopted by developing

[428] The Preamble of the TRIMs Agreement recognizes "the particular trade, development and financial needs of developing country Members, particularly those of the least-developed country Members" *Id.*, p. 163. Article 4 also provides that developing country Members may deviate from the obligations of Article 2 (national treatment and general prohibition of quantitative restrictions) to apply BOP measures and the measures permitted under GATT Article XVIII. *Id.*, p. 164. Developing country Members are also allowed to maintain the prohibited TRIMs for five years from the implementation of the WTO (seven years for LDC Members). *Id.* Because the development needs of these countries may not expire after the end of these periods, a mere suspension of the requirements for a limited period of time would not be sufficient to meet the needs of developing countries.

[429] It is reported that in 2003 developing countries took in foreign direct investment (FDI) amounting to 172 billion USD out of the total FDI of 556 billion USD, less than a third of the FDI worldwide. UNCTAD, *World Investment Report 2004*, Annex Table B1, FDI Inflows, by Host Region and Economy 1992–2003, p. 367.

countries;[430] that is, if we consider economic development of developing
countries a priority, these countries should be allowed to adopt investment measures that could best facilitate their industries and promote
economic development.

Therefore, the multilateral control on TRIMs needs to be lifted in favor
of developing countries.[431] There seems no clear need for such multilateral control on investment. For instance, major investors are often in
a position to negotiate with the corresponding host country about the
terms of their investment. In addition, developed countries that do not
want their own investors to accept certain investment measures adopted
by foreign governments can discourage or even prevent them from doing
so, for instance, by legislating against accepting such measures. In addition, over 1,100 BITs around the world[432] already require national treatment in favor of foreign investors and prohibit a wider range of TRIMs
than those restrained by the TRIMs Agreement. If a developing country is ready to give up certain TRIMs because of a determination that
the benefit from foreign investment outweighs the need to preserve their
ability to adopt TRIMs, it will do so, by accepting terms of these BITs
prohibiting TRIMs, or by simply not adopting them even without any
treaty obligations.

Furthermore, the TRIMs Agreement may have more extensive impact
on the developing country's ability to adopt investment-related industrial
policy than many Members may have initially anticipated since a previous
WTO panel decision determined that the scope of the TRIMs Agreement
includes investment measures adopted with regard to domestic, as well
as foreign, investment.[433] State industrial promotion may be made more

---

[430] See the relevant discussions in Chapter 3 *supra*.

[431] Reflecting this concern, twelve countries proposed to change the text of the TRIMs
Agreement to make commitments under the agreement optional and not mandatory.
WTO doc. WT/GC/W/354 (dated Oct. 11, 1999).

[432] *Supra* note 422.

[433] *Indonesia – Certain Measures Affecting the Automobile Industry*, Report of the Panel,
WT/DS54/R, WT/DS55/R, WT/DS59/R, WT/DS64/R (dated July 2, 1998), para. 14.73.

effective when it is linked with some performance requirement by the recipient of the support, such as a requirement to export,[434] and TRIMs provisions prohibiting such a requirement will impede the execution of domestic industrial policies. It is not clear whether this expanded application of the TRIMs Agreement is what the participants of the UR contemplated; the text of the TRIMs Agreement is written in the context of the GATT, referring to specific GATT articles to be observed. These GATT articles (Articles III and XI) pertain to the treatment of imports rather than domestic transactions.

This suggests, arguably, that the TRIMs Agreement was contemplated with respect to investment measures applied with regard to foreign, rather than domestic, investment to confer national treatment on foreign investment and prohibit measures amounting to quantitative restrictions on foreign investment. Perhaps one may argue that the expanded application of the TRIMs Agreement is justified because investment measures that apply to domestic investment are as equally inefficient and as trade distorting as those applied to foreign investment. An individual developing country proposing to apply TRIMs should be trusted with its best judgment to determine the issue of inefficiency, and there is justification to tolerate the possible trade-distorting effect, if any, for the interest of development.

As to the regulation of foreign investment, it should be noted that some of the government measures that favor and support foreign investment, as well as those limiting and controlling it, can also be subject to the sanctions of WTO disciplines. For instance, the rules of subsidy discussed in Chapter 3.3 apply to government subsidies offered to enterprises owned by foreigners as well as its own nationals. Some provisions of GATS and the TRIPS Agreement make distinctions based on nationalities in order to apply the national treatment standard to covered foreign investment, but WTO disciplines on general trade policies, such as subsidies, do not make such distinctions and are also applied to government measures to

[434] Rodrik (2004), *supra* note 189, p. 11.

foreign affiliates on equal terms. This means that government measures to attract and support foreign investment may not be allowed under WTO disciplines and may be also subject to sanctions when these measures have certain trade effects as stipulated in the relevant provisions (e.g., a specific subsidy causing injury to the domestic industry of another importing country). The proposed DFS should be applicable to foreign investment as well as domestic enterprises where such support for foreign investment would be consistent with the development objective of a given developing country.[435]

Lastly, initiatives have been taken in the WTO to go beyond the TRIMs Agreement and enter into negotiations for a more comprehensive, MAI-type investment agreement. Despite strong opposition from some developing countries, such as India, negotiation for a new investment agreement was adopted as an agendum for the Doha Round.[436] There are still significant objections to the beginning of this negotiation, and it is not altogether clear whether this negotiation will actually take place.[437] Although the importance of an investment agreement for the expansion of international trade has been emphasized,[438] there seems to be no consensus on the need for such an agreement in WTO disciplines. It is not clear that WTO disciplines, which many believe should be limited to the governance of international trade, requires a new agreement on investment.

From the development perspective, a new investment agreement would expand the duties and obligations of the host countries beyond those already stipulated in the TRIMs Agreement and would further limit the ability of developing countries to adopt investment measures to promote domestic industries and facilitate development. Therefore, the

---

[435] For a discussion of the DFS, see Chapter 3.3 *supra*.
[436] WTO Ministerial Declaration, WTO doc. WT/MIN(01)/DEC/1 (Nov. 20, 2001), paras. 20–22.
[437] Members failed to launch negotiations for the new investment treaty at the recent Cancun Ministerial Conference.
[438] *Supra* note 436.

initiative for a new investment agreement does not serve the development interests of developing countries so long as the agreement is to be applied to developing countries. Some argue that the new investment agreement will provide a regulatory safeguard for foreign investors, and thereby help attract foreign investment to developing countries.[439] Individual developing countries can also provide such safeguard by setting their own rules that are consistent with their development interests and that also provide some measure of protection for foreign investors. This approach would be more sensible than imposing the same set of multilateral obligations on developing countries that have different development needs.[440]

5.3 Trade-Related Aspects of Intellectual Property Rights

WTO rules on trade-related aspects of intellectual property rights also raise concern for development. Advanced knowledge, such as new technology and production techniques, is instrumental to facilitating industries. It has been suggested that the ability to copy technologies developed in advanced countries has been historically one of the most essential elements in determining the ability of developing countries to catch up.[441]

---

[439] Richard Eglin, "Trade and Investment in the WTO," paper presented at the seminar, *The Way Forward to Successful Doha Development Agenda Negotiations*, United Nations University, Tokyo, Japan (May 24–25, 2004).

[440] In relation to trade among developed countries, the existing TRIMs Agreement will help reduce the distortion of trade that results from TRIMs, and the application of the Agreement may, therefore, be justified. Any inadequacies and ambiguities with the current provisions can be corrected by modifying the provisions of the TRIMs Agreement, and therefore, it is not clear that a comprehensive investment treaty is needed. It should also be noted that the previous attempt to create a multilateral legal framework on international investment, MAI, was made primarily for the participation of the OECD countries rather than developing countries. Perhaps, the continuation of the negotiations for the MAI in the OECD would seem more proper than trying to undertake negotiations in the WTO where there seems to be no consensus among Members about the need for a new investment agreement.

[441] Richard R. Nelson, "The Changing Institutional Requirements for Technological and Economic Catch Up" (Columbia University, New York, June 2004) *cited in* Rodrik (2004), *supra* note 189, p. 35.

Developed countries today prevent unauthorized use (i.e., copy) of this technology by assigning a propriety right to it (intellectual property right [IPR]). Thus, the enforcement of IPRs affects the ability of developing countries to acquire advanced technology for the purpose of development. Current WTO disciplines include rules on the trade-related aspects of IPRs, namely, the Agreement on Trade-Related Aspects of Intellectual Property Rights (TRIPS Agreement).

The introduction of the TRIPS Agreement was an ambitious undertaking in the UR.[442] The idea of including IPR disciplines in trade rules was new and controversial, and many developing countries protested against this initiative.[443] Critics pointed out that IPRs were not an essential trade issue that concerned most Members but was brought in the multilateral trading system to serve the interests of a relatively few Members, such as the United States. The effectiveness of enforcement using trade remedies was considered to be a motivation to bring this subject into the international trading system.[444] In the course of the UR negotiations, the attitude of developing countries changed, and they eventually accepted the inclusion of the TRIPS Agreement in the WTO regime since developed countries, particularly the United States, continued to pressure for its adoption and conditioned its inclusion in the WTO regime for other concessions to developing countries.[445]

The TRIPS Agreement, composed of seventy-three articles in seven parts, is one of the most extensive provisions in WTO disciplines. It establishes binding standards for the protection of various IPRs, including copyrights, trademarks, geographical indications, industrial designs,

---

[442] Annex 1 C of the WTO Agreement. WTO, *The Results of the Uruguay Round of Multilateral Trade Negotiations, supra* note 53, pp. 320–353.

[443] Jackson (1997), *supra* note 43, p. 310.

[444] Jackson observed that one of the most important reasons why the intellectual property rights (IPR) interests wished to move this subject into the international trading context was the admiration of the GATT dispute settlement mechanism that had been evolving to a point where it appeared to be a reasonably effective procedural mechanism for establishing enforceability of international treaty norms. *Id.*, p. 311.

[445] *Supra* note 443.

patents, and layout designs of integrated circuits, providing substantial minimum terms of their protection (e.g., fifty years for copyright, twenty years for patent and indefinite renewal of trademark with the minimum of seven years for each registration).[446] The TRIPS Agreement requires Members to apply national treatment and the MFN treatment for the protection of foreign IPRs.[447] It also obligates Members to provide effective enforcement procedures under their own law.[448] Rules of the previous IPR conventions are also incorporated by reference in the relevant provisions of the TRIPS Agreement.[449]

The inclusion of the TRIPS Agreement in WTO disciplines raises important concerns. First, the TRIPS Agreement goes much beyond what seems directly relevant to trade issues. It attempts to establish IPR regimes in all WTO Members, including those whose economic and social developments do not yet embrace the concept of IPRs.[450] It is doubtful that a prescription of an economic and legal system such as an IPR regime should be the role of the trade disciplines. In general, WTO rules address the behavior of nations that affects international trade directly and attempts to control such behavior by imposing certain obligations and authorizing trade sanctions.[451] Members are required to bring their laws and regulations in conformity with the WTO disciplines.[452] Yet they

---

[446] WTO, *The Results of the Uruguay Round of Multilateral Trade Negotiations, supra* note 53, pp. 325–339.

[447] TRIPS Agreement, arts. 3 and 4. *Id.*, pp. 323–324.

[448] *Id.*, pp. 339–343.

[449] The Paris Convention (1967), the Berne Convention (1971), the Rome Convention (1961), and the Treaty on Intellectual Property in Respect of Integrated Circuits (1989) are incorporated by reference. *Id.*, pp. 322–339.

[450] A historical study shows that IPRs began to be recognized and protected when considerable economic and social developments had taken place. Chang, *supra* note 41, pp. 83–85.

[451] A reputable economist stated that the purpose of international rules should be not to impose common rules on countries with different regulatory systems but to accept these differences and regulate the interface between them to reduce adverse spillovers. Dani Rodrik, *The Global Governance of Trade as If Development Really Mattered* (UNDP, New York, 2001).

[452] WTO Agreement, art XVI.4. WTO, *The Results of the Uruguay Round of Multilateral Trade Negotiations, supra* note 53, p. 14.

are not required to establish a specific legal regime as they are by the requirements of the TRIPS Agreement.

For instance, WTO AD rules may be used to restrain certain dumping, but these rules do not require Members to create a domestic legal regime against anti-competitive behavior, such as dumping practices.[453] In areas other than TRIPS, the adoption of an appropriate regulatory framework is largely left to individual Members; thus it is difficult to understand why the TRIPS issues should be treated any differently. It is not the role of trade disciplines, such as the WTO, to dictate what IPR regime Members should adopt. The role of the WTO should have been limited to remedying the negative trade effect of IPR violations if any. The adoption of the TRIPS Agreement in the WTO, primarily for the effectiveness of enforcement, is not a desirable precedent[454] where it is doubtful that most Members would need an extensive IPR regime as required by the TRIPS in promoting their trade interests. The implementation of the TRIPS Agreement in the WTO would tempt the advocates of other values or systems to push for their adoption into WTO disciplines, which may not be essentially relevant to trade. The adoption of values or systems with limited relevance to trade will, in turn, cause disagreements and protests by Members not supporting them. This may diminish political support for the international trading system and undermine the effectiveness of the system.

The international trading system and its enforcement mechanism should not be used as a means to impose a system or value favored by certain Members on others. The objective of the international trading system remains promoting and facilitating trade among nations and not imposing particular values and systems, no matter how noble they may be, through the vehicle of the international trading system. An attempt to impose them through the trading system will detract from the issues

---

[453] For instance, Hong Kong, a Member of the WTO and an advanced economy, does not have competition law.
[454] *Supra* note 443.

that demand our attention as being more essential for the promotion of trade.[455] It is necessary to remember that the previous attempt to impose labor standards and environmental conditions in WTO disciplines over serious objections of many Members was an important cause of the failure to launch a new round at the 1999 Seattle Ministerial Conference.[456]

From the development perspective, the TRIPS Agreement raises particular concerns. In the history of development, advanced technologies acquired from more developed countries have played an important role in economic development.[457] Many of today's developed countries, which have strongly advocated the establishment of IPR regimes throughout the world, also made considerable efforts to acquire advanced technologies from other countries during their own development in the nineteenth and the early twentieth centuries.[458] In the process, these countries often ignored IPRs of other countries whose compliance may have impeded their effort to acquire advanced technologies.[459] The majority of today's developed countries did not protect IPRs in any significant way until the early twentieth century, when they achieved developed economic status.[460] Today, these developed countries stand to lose if the dissemination of advanced technologies is not controlled, and therefore, it is not surprising to see that they are inclined to protect their IPRs through effective means, including using the enforcement procedures in trade disciplines.

The imposition of the IPR regime has put a considerable regulatory burden on developing countries in continuing their development efforts

---

[455] In line with this concern, T. N. Srinivasan highlighted "the folly of trying to achieve too many policy objectives with one instrument and suggested that the TRIPS be taken out of GATT and handled by WIPO; the CTE be wound up and environment tackled by UNEP; and labour be excluded from the purview of GATT and handled by the ILO." WTO, *Report on the WTO High- Level Symposium on Trade and Development* (1999), *supra* note 38.

[456] John S. Odell, *supra* note 62.

[457] *Supra* note 441.

[458] Chang, *supra* note 41, pp. 54–58, 81–85.

[459] *Id.*

[460] *Id.*

because such a regime will prematurely set economic and legal barriers in acquiring advanced technologies for their development. This concern is amplified because the current TRIPS provisions require long durations of IPR protections.[461] One may argue that the protection of IPRs will provide an incentive for creations and innovations that can help develop industries, but in today's world, where the technological gap between the developed and developing countries is wider than ever, it would seem unlikely that developing countries can close this gap by relying on their own "creativity" alone.[462] The application of the TRIPS Agreement will leave developing countries today at a considerably larger disadvantage than those in the past when no international IPR regime was imposed on them, certainly not to the extent imposed by the TRIPS Agreement today. Although the trade effect of IPR violations may need to be addressed, the imposition of the IPR regime clearly and unnecessarily impedes the development interests of developing countries.

What then should be done in the area of TRIPS? The application of the TRIPS Agreement has been suspended for developing countries for a specified period (five years after the entry of the WTO for developing country Members; ten years for LDCs),[463] but this type of a temporary preference is not sufficient: the development needs that called for this preference may continue to exist after the expiration of temporary S&D treatment. In addition, concern was raised that the compliance requirement of the TRIPS Agreement will impose a considerable financial burden on developing countries, particularly LDCs.[464] The provisions of the

[461] *Supra* note 446.

[462] If a developing country considers that the extensive protection of IPRs is in their own interest, this country, rather than the WTO, should be trusted to set its own standards for the protection under their own laws and regulations.

[463] TRIPS Agreement, arts. 65 and 66. WTO, *The Results of the Uruguay Round of Multilateral Trade Negotiations, supra* note 53, pp. 349–350.

[464] According to a study, implementing the TRIPS obligations would require "the least developed countries to invest in buildings, equipment, training, and so forth that would cost each of them $150 million – for many of the least-developed countries this represents a full year's development budget." Finger, *supra* note 159, p. 435.

TRIPS Agreement should not be applied to developing countries to the extent that it imposes on these countries the establishment of an IPR regime. I do not suggest that developed countries should give up trade-related IPR interests entirely. They should protect their IPRs without imposing a regulatory system for which developing countries may not be ready. It can be achieved by authorizing trade sanctions where a complainant demonstrates that an IPR violation has caused injury to their trade.

The general exceptions of Article XX already allow trade sanctions to protect IPRs.[465] What seems necessary is to set detailed rules for the substantive and procedural requirements for the application of a trade measure to remedy injury cased by an IPR violation. A Member should be authorized to apply trade measures only where a violation of its IPRs causes injury to its domestic industry through trade. An injury test, such as the one found in Article 4.2(a) of the Safeguards Agreement,[466] should be required to ensure that the measure is applied based on a reasonable assessment of injury caused by IPR violations and not on an arbitrary determination by national authorities. This way, developed countries will be able to protect their own IPR interests by applying their own laws as well as the rules of relevant international IPR conventions,[467] without imposing regulatory burden on developing countries such as the one currently imposed by the TRIPS Agreement.

The Doha Round proposes continuing negotiations on TRIPS. The Doha Ministerial Declaration sets out a negotiation agenda on TRIPS that is relevant to development issues.[468] First, the declaration emphasizes the

---

[465] GATT Article XX provides in relevant part, "nothing in this Agreement shall be construed to prevent the adoption or enforcement by any contracting party of measures:... (d) necessary to secure compliance with laws or regulations which are not inconsistent with the provisions of this Agreement, including those relating to ... the protection of patents, trade marks and copy rights... " *Id.,* p. 519.

[466] *Id.,* pp. 276–277.

[467] *Supra* note 449.

[468] WTO Ministerial Declaration, WTO doc. WT/MIN(01)/DEC/1 (Nov. 20, 2001), para. 17–19.

importance of the implementation of the TRIPS Agreement in a manner supportive of public health by promoting both access to existing medicine and R&D into new medicines.[469] There has been significant controversy over the limitations imposed by the IPR protection of pharmaceutical products on the ability of people in developing countries to access necessary medicines. A great sense of urgency has been added to the debate as a number of developing countries face the AIDS epidemic that has already claimed tens of millions of lives in developing countries and will claim many more in the decades to come.[470]

This question of the promotion of health and IPR protection is not only an essential moral issue but also an important problem from the perspective of economic development because development would be significantly hampered where public health is not protected. It is not adequately protected where the public cannot access necessary medicines. The rigidity of the IPR protection of pharmaceutical products that drives up the price of medicines can significantly reduce this access. A flexible approach needs to be taken regarding IPR issues in the area of public health. Methods such as compulsory licensing have been authorized to promote access to medicines in developing countries. Compulsory licensing is authorized under Article 31 of the TRIPS Agreement, but it has been pointed out that the use of this provision has been limited for several requirements included therein.[471] A separate ministerial

---

[469] *Id.*, para. 17.

[470] Haochen Sun, "Reshaping the TRIPs Agreement Concerning Public Health: Two Critical Issues" (2003) 37 *Journal of World Trade* 163–197; Lee Petherbridge, "Intelligent TRIPS Implementation: A Strategy for Countries on the Cusp of Development" (2001) 22, *University of Pennsylvania Journal of International Economic Law* 1029–1066; James Thuo Gathii, "Rights, Patents, Markets, and the Global AIDS Pandemic" (2002) 14 *Florida Journal of International Law* 261–352; James Thuo Gathii, "Construing Intellectual Property Rights and Competition Policy Consistently with Facilitating Access to Affordable AIDS Drugs to Low-end Consumers" (2001) 53 *Florida Law Review* 727–788.

[471] For a more detailed discussion, see Sun (2003), *supra* note 470.

declaration has been adopted to address this health issue at the beginning of the Doha Round.[472]

The Doha Ministerial Declaration also provides a mandate for negotiation to establish a multilateral system of notification and registration of geographical indications for wines and spirits and for examination of the protection of traditional knowledge and folklore.[473] Currently, many top-quality wines and spirits are produced in developed countries, but some developing countries, including Chile, also produce excellent products that have been well received in export markets. It is possible that more developing countries will develop their own traditional wines and spirits into valuable export products. The protection of geographical indication can benefit the producers of wines and spirits in developing countries by ensuring the geographic authenticity, which can secure the value and protect the reputation of these products.

The protection of traditional knowledge and folklore is also relevant to development interests. Export of cultural contents, such as traditional music, has been increasing, thanks to the advent of the Internet.[474] Many developing countries with rich cultural heritages may have traditional cultural contents that are exportable to the rest of the world, which can bring significant revenue. The IPR protection of those cultural contents would contribute to the development of these developing countries by enabling them to secure earnings from the sale of these contents.[475] Traditional IPR protections, such as copyrights and trademarks, may

---

[472] WTO Ministerial Declaration, WTO doc. WT/MIN(01)/DEC/2 (Nov. 20, 2001).

[473] WTO Ministerial Declaration, WTO doc. WT/MIN(01)/DEC/1 (Nov. 20, 2001), paras. 18–19.

[474] The ability of the Internet to transfer information at unprecedented speeds has significant effects on the development of new industries that involve cultural contents.

[475] India has been a pioneer in legislation for the registration of traditional knowledge. Arvind Subramanian, "Proprietary Protection of Genetic Resources and Traditional Knowledge" *in* Bernard Hoekman, Aaditya Mattoo, and Philip English (eds.), *Development, Trade, and the WTO: A Handbook* (World Bank, Washington D.C., 2002), p. 388.

be inadequate for the protection of these traditional cultural contents because, among other things, the original inventors and contributors entitled to the propriety rights of these contents would be difficult to identify and, consequently, be susceptible to disputes and false claims. Other adequate ways to recognize and protect IPRs in these contents should be further studied.[476]

The TRIPS Agreement has opened a new chapter for the international protection of IPRs. It has also left us a legacy that the enforceability mechanism of the trade regime can be used to promote a set of values or systems whose relevance to international trade and necessity to be part of trade disciplines may be controversial. A significant risk associated with this type of "expanded" use of the trading system has been mentioned earlier in this chapter. The protection of IPR should be sought in the context of international trade to address clear injuries caused by IPR violations but not to inhibit the development of developing countries by placing undue barriers to acquiring new technologies and knowledge with substantial compliance costs.[477] The proposed modification of the current IPR rules could be considered an alternative approach to the protection of IPRs in the context of trade.

5.4 Trade in Services

The UR brought a new area of trade into multilateral disciplines: trade in services.[478] The importance of services in both domestic economies,

---

[476] A recent study provides a discussion of the feasibility of devising a new form of IPR protection for traditional knowledge in the context of international trade and domestic legal regimes. Thomas Cottier and Marion Panizzon, "Legal Perspectives on Traditional Knowledge: The Case for Intellectual Property Protection" (2004) 7 *Journal of International Economic Law* 371–399.

[477] *Supra* note 464.

[478] The service sector is extraordinarily diverse: more than 120 specific service sectors have been identified. GATT doc. MTN.GNS/W/120 (dated July 1991). Unlike trade in goods, trade in services takes place in multiple modes. The General Agreement on Trade in Services (GATS) prescribes four modes of supply of a service in international trade:

particularly those of developed countries[479] and international trade,[480] has grown significantly over the past few decades. Developed countries with a competitive advantage in service industries have sought ways to export services and to overcome measures of foreign governments designed to preserve business for domestic service providers.[481] This effort led to the settlement of the GATS in the UR, which seeks GATT-type multilateral disciplines on trade in services.[482] GATS rules are in their infancy, and much remains to be negotiated and developed[483] for decades to come before we may see reasonably complete disciplines on service trade. Nevertheless, the GATS is an important beginning for the liberalization of trade in services as the GATT was for trade in goods five decades ago.

(a) from the territory of one Member into the territory of any other Member; (b) in the territory of one Member into the territory of any other Member; (c) by a service supplier of one Member, through commercial presence in the territory of another Member; (d) by a service supplier of one Member, through presence of natural persons of a Member in the territory of any other Member. GATS, art. I.2. WTO, *The Results of the Uruguay Round of Multilateral Trade Negotiations, supra* note 53, pp. 286–286.

[479] For instance, when the Uruguay Round was completed in 1994, approximately 70 percent of American jobs were tied to the service sector. U.S. Trade Representative, *1994 Annual Report*, p. 29.

[480] The export of commercial services has increased from 364,300 million USD in 1980 to 1,762,600 million USD in 2003 worldwide and the import from 397,900 million USD to 1,742,700 million USD in the same period. WTO, Commercial Services Trade by Region and Selected Economies, 1980–2003, available online at the WTO Web site, <http://www.wto.org/english/res_e/statis_e/statis_e.htm/>.

[481] Jackson (1997), *supra* note 43, p. 306.

[482] Annex 1 B of the WTO Agreement. WTO, *The Results of the Uruguay Round of Multilateral Trade Negotiations, supra* note 53, pp. 286–319. The GATS consists of twenty-nine articles in six parts. The GATS sets out a series of underlying principles similar to those in the GATT applying to the trade in goods, such as specific commitments for concessions, national treatment, and MFN treatment. Nonetheless, the application of these principles in the GATS are rather relaxed; i.e., the requirement of MFN treatment can be exempted under certain conditions as provided in the Annex on Article II (*Id.*, p. 352) and the national treatment requirement can also be modified in the Schedule of Commitments (Article XVII, *id.*, pp. 342–343).

[483] For instance, the rules on ESGs and subsidies are not yet provided in the GATS and are being negotiated for trade in services.

From the perspective of economic development, trade in services presents unique problems. First, a wide competitive gap exists in service industries between developed and developing countries, particularly in those industries that require advanced technology and expertise, as well as substantial capital, such as financial services and telecommunication services. Because of this considerable gap, the opening of domestic service markets primarily for these services may result in one-directional trade between developed and developing countries: export of services from developed countries into the markets of developing countries but not *vice versa*. Therefore, a balance should be sought in market access negotiations in a way to ensure export opportunities for developing countries as well as developed countries.[484]

Export of services can help facilitate the development of developing countries the same way that export of goods can.[485] To promote exports of services from developing countries, market access needs to be provided for the kinds of services in which developing countries have a competitive advantage. As in the goods area, developing countries would have a competitive advantage in services that do not require high-level technology or substantial capital. Many developing countries would have a competitive advantage in low-technology labor services that can be provided by movement of people into countries that have demands for them.[486]

---

[484] This effort would be consistent with the development objective enumerated in the GATS Preamble, which seeks "to facilitate the increasing participation of the developing countries in trade in services and the expansion of their service exports including, *inter alia*, through the strengthening of their domestic services capacity and its efficiency and competitiveness." WTO, *The Results of the Uruguay Round of Multilateral Trade Negotiations, supra* note 53, p. 286.

[485] See the relevant discussions in Chapter 1.2 *supra*.

[486] In the 1960s, thousands of Korean coal miners and nurses were sent to Germany to aid the shortage of German labor at that time. Construction workers were also sent to the Middle East in the 1970s. Shoenbaum lists the following service items potentially exportable by developing countries: (1) consulting services for enterprises (information, management, professional and hiring services); (2) construction and engineering; (3) education; (4) ecological; (5) tourism; (6) leisure, cultural and sport; and (7) transportation. Shoenbaum (2004), *supra* note 9.

Export of this type of labor services can be important, particularly for the development of developing countries that do not have exportable natural resources. In these developing countries, the income earned by those workers abroad subsequently sent to their home countries can form capital resources that can be used for development projects.[487] Yet most developed countries today are reluctant to accept unskilled foreign labor because, among other things, they are afraid that foreign workers may take away employment opportunities for their own population.[488]

In line with this concern, the "Annex on Movement of Natural Persons Supplying Services under the Agreement" of the GATS exempts foreign labor supply from the multilateral control of the GATS. It provides in relevant part, "This Agreement shall not apply to measures affecting natural persons seeking access to the employment market of a Member."[489] In addition to this exemption, the Annex authorizes Members to negotiate *specific commitments* applying to the movements of all categories of natural persons supplying services separately from the other modes of supply.[490] These GATS provisions give complete discretion to developed countries in accepting foreign labor, free of any obligations under the GATS. This sort of blanket exemption and discretion is hardly found in other areas of service trade, and its fairness and justification need to be questioned.

Perhaps some discretion should be allowed for governments to control the movement of persons into Members' territories because it raises not only economic issues but also social, political, and security issues

---

[487] For instance, South Korea had limited exportable natural resources. The income earned by the Korean coal miners and nurses in Germany during the 1960s and by the Korean construction workers in the Middle East during the 1970s became Korea's important financial source for development.

[488] However, critics argue that the kinds of jobs typically taken by the foreign workers are not those favored by the domestic people, and therefore, these foreign workers do not necessarily threaten the employment of domestic population.

[489] WTO, *The Results of the Uruguay Round of Multilateral Trade Negotiations, supra* note 53, p. 309.

[490] Paragraph 4. *Id.*

that the movement of goods do not typically present.[491] Nonetheless, the complete exemption of foreign labor supply from the control of the GATS seems hardly justifiable, and the provisions in paragraph 2 of the Annex should be replaced with a set of provisions that ensure reasonable market access for foreign labor. The concerns associated with accepting foreign labor require adequate solutions and should not be used as a convenient excuse to shield domestic labor markets from foreign workers.[492] Failure to provide adequate market access to foreign labor would be inequitable because it would mean a denial of trade opportunities in the area of services where developing countries have a competitive advantage, while developed countries actively seek and begin to acquire market access in the service areas where they have a competitive advantage.

In recent years, developed countries have promoted the opening of service markets of developing countries, and the settlement of GATS marks the acceptance of this initiative by developing countries. This acceptance has expanded multilateral trade disciplines into service areas for the first time. In light of this acceptance by developing countries, reciprocal effort should also be made on the part of developed countries by increasing market access for services in which developing countries have a competitive advantage, such as labor. Nonetheless, a recent study suggested that the facilitation of service trade through the movement of people should exclude unskilled workers to remain politically feasible. It also observes that greater progress may be made on the movement of the unskilled through bilateral agreements to which the WTO could acquiesce.[493]

---

[491] Concern about domestic unemployment is the primary economic reason to oppose the admission of foreign labor. In addition to the unemployment issues, problems associated with accepting foreign workers and their families may include housing, health care, education, potential cultural conflicts, possible crime issues, and security issues.

[492] *Supra* note 491. Welfare networks of the host countries, either public or private, can play an important role in solving these concerns.

[493] Sumanta Chaudhauri, Aaditya Mattoo, and Richard Self, "Moving People to Deliver Services: How Can the WTO Help?" (2004) 38 *Journal of World Trade* 364.

Nonetheless, it is doubtful that the bilateral treatment of this issue will be sufficient. For many developing countries with underdeveloped technology and limited educational opportunity, unskilled labor may be the only service available to export. The bilateral treatment of this issue will only help a limited number of developing countries participating in the bilateral arrangements to send labor to a limited number of markets of the participating developed countries. That a developing country Member has to be engaged in potentially lengthy negotiations with every Member that it wants to send workers to would be an extraordinary burden. Furthermore, a developed country that is not willing to open its labor market on a multilateral basis may not show much enthusiasm in bilateral negotiations, either. These problems with the bilateral treatment indicate that a multilateral, rather than bilateral, effort is necessary. The liberalization of trade in services should not induce one-directional trade: developing countries, as well as developed countries, should also be allowed adequate opportunities to supply services in which they have advantage.

Political feasibility is an issue in accepting unskilled labor, and consideration should be given to find a way to ease political concern about a large inflow of unskilled workers that may result from opening the market, which is believed to threaten domestic employment.[494] A solution may be found in emergency safeguard measures (ESGs) now being discussed in the WTO.[495] Article X of the GATS requires multilateral negotiation on the question of ESGs, which have continued since 1995.[496] Members have not yet agreed on a text agreement on ESGs,[497] and there still seems to be doubt among some Members about the necessity and

---

[494] But cf. supra note 488.

[495] For a discussion of ESGs, see Y. S. Lee, "Emergency Safeguard Measures Under Article X in GATS – Applicability of the Concepts in the WTO Agreement on Safeguards" (1999) 33(4) Journal of World Trade 47–59, and Lee (2005), supra note 291, Chapter 10.

[496] GATS, art. X. WTO, The Results of the Uruguay Round of Multilateral Trade Negotiations, supra note 53, p. 294.

[497] A proposed text of the agreement on ESGs can be found in Lee (2005), supra note 291, Appendix 5.

feasibility of ESGs.[498] Nonetheless, the implementation of the emergency safeguard mechanism will provide safeguard against a rapid increase in the unskilled labor supply that seriously hurts or threatens domestic employment just as the existing safeguard under the SA does for the trade in goods.[499] Perhaps developed country Members opposing the introduction of ESGs with the belief that these measures would primarily be applied to their supply of services should consider that the safety net that these measures provide may actually enable developed countries to increase market access for unskilled labor, thereby balancing trade between developed and developing countries in the area of services.

It should also be noted that just as high trade barriers against competitive foreign products have often caused illegal smuggling of foreign products and created black markets for imports, excessively restrictive terms of the acceptance of foreign labor have already caused millions of people to move illegally across borders, take up residence, and offer services.[500] For instance, it is well known that many labor-intensive industries of developed countries, such as construction and agriculture, have depended on millions of these "unauthorized" foreign workers.[501] It is time that developed countries acknowledged this reality of market forces in labor movements and made realistic and reasonable provisions to allow entry of foreign workers for employment. To this aim, the GATS can provide multilateral disciplines that facilitate the supply of labor

---

[498] *Id.*, p. 58.

[499] See *supra* Chapter 4.3 for a discussion of safeguard measures applicable to trade in goods.

[500] In the United States alone, it has been estimated that there were more than 7 million illegal residents as of January 2000. U.S. Citizenship and Immigration Services, *Estimates of Unauthorized Immigrant Population Residing in the United States: 1990 to 2000* (January 2003). Recently, the Bush administration considered offering a temporary working authorization for these "illegal" immigrants.

[501] A Canadian media outlet recently observed that there are thousands of undocumented workers at construction sites and concluded that the deportation of those workers will lead to the huge loss of industrial productivity. *Toronto Star*, Nov. 8, 2003. Also in the United States, construction and agricultural sectors have been known to depend largely on the "illegal" foreign workers.

by developing countries with terms reasonable to both developing and developed countries.[502]

Finally, the earlier discussions of various trade issues, including binding commitments (import concessions), subsidies, and safeguards, provided in the goods context are also applied to trade in services.[503] GATS disciplines are analogous to those of the GATT/WTO rules for trade in goods, but there are also significant differences. For instance, the GATS has rules that govern specific commitments that are similar to those in the goods area.[504] It does not, however, provide rules on subsidies and safeguards but requires Members to enter into negotiations in these areas.[505] The GATS neither includes any rule to authorize AD measures nor requires negotiation to establish any such rule in the service area.[506] The absence of an AD mechanism in the service trade is satisfactory in light of the feeble economic justification and the significant problems of abuse.[507] In developing other rules on trade in services in coming decades, Members should be mindful of the development needs of developing countries.[508] Members should carefully consider any possible

---

[502] Developing countries should take an initiative and make concerted efforts to bring this issue on the negotiation Table. C. Fred Bergsten enumerated the liberalization of the movement of natural persons among possible priority interests the developing countries could pursue. WTO, *Report on the WTO High-Level Symposium on Trade and Development* (1999), *supra* note 38.

[503] See the relevant discussions in Chapters 3 and 4 *supra*.

[504] GATS, arts. XVI–XXI. WTO, *The Results of the Uruguay Round of Multilateral Trade Negotiations*, *supra* note 53, pp. 298–302.

[505] GATS, arts. X and XV. *Id.*, pp. 294, 341. For the negotiation on the safeguard measures in service trade, see Y. S. Lee, "Emergency Safeguard Measures Under Article X in GATS – Applicability of the Concepts in the WTO Agreement on Safeguards" *supra* note 495.

[506] The earlier Chapter concludes in favor of the elimination of AD measures in international trade because of the ambiguities and inadequacies of AD disciplines. The absence of an AD mechanism in the GATS seems to be another indication of the inherent ambiguities and inadequacies in the current AD disciplines. See Chapter 4 *supra* for the relevant discussions.

[507] See Chapter 4.2 *supra*.

[508] With respect to further negotiations on trade in services, the Doha Ministerial Declaration affirmed the importance of development interests. It stated in relevant part:

ramifications on development of proposed rules and refrain from adopting those rules that have restrictive effects on development. If there should be a compelling reason to adopt rules with restrictive effects on development, ways should be sought to minimize such effects.

"The negotiations on trade in services shall be conducted with a view to promoting the economic growth of all trading partners and the development of developing and least-developed countries." WTO Ministerial Declaration, WTO doc. WT/MIN(01)/DEC/1 (Nov. 20, 2001), para. 15.

SIX

Foreign Direct Investment and Regional Trade Liberalization

6.1 Regionalism in International Trade and Investment

While the global multilateral trading system represented by the WTO provides a regulatory framework for international trade today,[509] more than 130 regional trade arrangements (RTAs) also exist.[510] Regional Trade Agreements are authorized by the WTO[511] and include important economic entities, such as the EU, and they have significant effects on international trade because about 90 percent of WTO Members, including a number of developing country Members, have signed at least one or more RTAs. The trade of many developing country Members is thus affected by the terms of RTAs as well as WTO disciplines. Therefore, RTAs create significant implications for the economic development of developing countries just as WTO rules affect the ability of these countries to adopt development policies. The trade of developing countries not participating

---

[509] *Supra* note 55. Chapter 2.2 *supra* also provides a discussion of key principles of WTO disciplines.

[510] References to regional trade agreements in this book include both bilateral trade arrangements with two participating countries and other regional agreements that include more.

[511] Article XXIV of the GATT authorizes a formation of customs union and free trade area. WTO, *The Results of the Uruguay Round of Multilateral Trade Negotiations, supra* note 53, pp. 457–460.

in particular RTAs may also be affected by the terms of these RTAs because the competitive position of their exports in the markets of RTA members ("members") may be relatively weakened by trade preferences offered to the members but not to the non-member developing countries.

Most of these RTAs are free trade agreements (FTAs). An FTA is an agreement between two or more countries to eliminate both tariff and non-tariff trade barriers and thereby create a free trade area among the participating countries (e.g., the North American Free Trade Agreement [NAFTA], the Jordan–U.S. Free Trade Agreement). The WTO approves the formation of an FTA where it eliminates trade barriers with respect to substantially all the trade among its members *and* where it does not raise trade barriers to non-members after formation of the FTA.[512] The latter requirement is to ensure that these FTAs do not develop into exclusive trade blocs, which worsened the worldwide depression and also led to major conflicts in the 1930s. The rationale for the authorization of an FTA is that a free trade zone created by an FTA would eventually expand to include more countries to benefit from free trade.

In recent years, FTAs have proliferated as multilateral negotiations in the WTO framework have become more difficult because these negotiations have come to deal with more and more sensitive areas, such as trade and investment, trade and competition policy, IPRs, and epidemics.[513] As an alternative to multilateral negotiations on a global scale that could take years to come to any consensus, nations have begun to resort to trade negotiations among a more limited number of countries sharing common interests in trade and investment, closer economic and cultural ties, and geographic proximities. This trend has led to the formation of a number of FTAs around the world. Concerns have been expressed against

---

[512] *Id.*

[513] Mitsuo Matsushita, "Legal Aspects of Free Trade Agreements in the Context of Article XXIV of the GATT 1994," paper presented at the seminar, *The Way Forward to Successful Doha Development Agenda Negotiation*, United Nations University, Tokyo, Japan (May 24–25, 2004).

this proliferation of FTAs because it may erode WTO disciplines and distract Members from important multilateral negotiations. Yet FTAs, which liberalize trade among the participating countries, have been promoted as a way to enhance regional economic development.[514]

How does this trade liberalization by FTAs affect economic development? In the preceding chapters, I have made proposals for changes in the current multilateral trade provisions on the premise that the promotion of infant industries, by way of export facilitation and trade protection, can be an essential strategy for the economic development of developing countries. I have also discussed that today's developed countries used infant industry promotion policies during their own development process, although these countries may not currently advocate and recommend their own policies in the past to developing countries today. My proposals may seem contrary to the promotion of free trade through FTAs at least in the context of development; while FTAs seek to remove trade barriers, my proposals, such as the DFT scheme, advocate temporary increases in tariffs as a vehicle of strategic development.[515]

In advocating state industrial support and trade measures for the development purpose, I do not refute the general economic efficiency of free trade and the market economy. My proposals advocate *limited modifications* of the open trading system to better facilitate the development of developing countries and do not suggest a change of this system otherwise. The argument highlighting the economic inefficiency of state industrial promotion is sensible from the perspective of a *static* economic model at a given point in time where state interventions (other than those to correct market failures), such as trade protections, may only cause welfare loss.[516] This initial welfare loss resulting from state industrial facilitation is only justified when government industrial facilitation leads to economic development that would produce greater economic welfare

---

[514] *Id.*
[515] See Chapter 3.2 *supra* for the relevant discussions of DFT.
[516] See Salvatore (2003), *supra* note 173, Chapters 8 and 9 for the general economic effects of trade measures.

in the future.[517] There are some well-known objections to infant industry promotion, and I have already concluded that infant industry promotion *can facilitate* development but does not necessarily *guarantee* it.[518] The pro-development provisions in the GATT, such as Article XVIII, are nevertheless based on infant industry promotion arguments.[519]

One may ask whether there is an alternative way to economic development that does not involve even short-term welfare losses associated with trade measures and state industrial support that may involve problems such as inefficient bureaucracy and possible corruption. Free trade agreements have been promoted as a means for development because they remove economically inefficient trade barriers vis-à-vis other participating countries. The promotion of FDI[520] also has been considered to be an alternative way because FDI may bring resources to facilitate development without incurring the inefficiencies involved in state interventions. Advocates of FTAs and FDI argue that the "old" ways of industrial promotion, such as infant industry facilitation, should give way and that efforts should instead be made to promote FTAs and FDI (which were not readily available in the past) since they can now be used as a vehicle of development. The remainder of this chapter considers the effects of FDI and FTAs on development.[521]

It needs to be noted there are no comprehensive multilateral disciplines on investment. The TRIMs Agreement is limited in scope and extent.[522] A previous OECD attempt to create a MAI was not successful,[523] and FDI is governed primarily by the terms of bilateral arrangements called BITs. An initiative to create a set of multilateral investment rules as part of the

---

[517] See the relevant discussions in Chapter 3.1 *supra*.

[518] *Id.*

[519] *Id.*

[520] FDI refers to foreign investment made directly in productive assets (e.g., building production facilities), as opposed to investment in shares of local companies.

[521] See also Y.S. Lee, "Foreign Direct Investment and Regional Trade Liberliazation: A Viable Answer for Economic Development?" (2004) 39 *Journal of World Trade* 707–717.

[522] See Chapter 5.2 *supra* for the discussion of TRIMs Agreement.

[523] *Id.*

WTO disciplines has begun, but the likelihood of such an agreement is unclear because of serious objections among Members.[524]

6.2 Proliferation of Foreign Direct Investment and Free Trade Areas

6.2.1 Foreign Direct Investment and Development

Rapid development of transportation and communication and the increasing availability of information across national borders have resulted in great increases in FDI around the world in recent decades.[525] The growing number of multinational businesses and the reduction of regulatory restrictions against foreign investors also have contributed to the proliferation of FDI. Nearly all countries, regardless of whether they are in a developed or developing economic status, welcome FDI today because FDI provides employment opportunities for the local population and also brings to the host countries essential economic resources, such as capital, technology, information, managerial expertise, and sales and marketing networks. Thus, many countries have tried to attract FDI by offering favorable incentives to foreign investors, including tax and other financial incentives, infrastructure built for or made available to foreign investors, assistance with complying with domestic regulatory requirements, and one-stop services for the needs of foreign investors, trade protections, as well as privileged legal status.

In our concern for development, how can FDI contribute to development? At the outset, FDI seems to replace the role of the state to mobilize economic resources for infant industries[526] because FDI may bring those resources to the host developing country. In addition, using FDI for development also has an advantage in that FDI is driven by

---

[524] *Id.*

[525] FDI outflows increased from 28 billion USD in 1982 to 612 billion USD in 2003 (valued at current prices). UNCTAD, *World Investment Report 2004*, Table 1.3 Selected Indicators of FDI and International Production, 1982–2003, p. 9.

[526] *Supra* note 189.

market forces, and therefore, it is less susceptible to domestic political considerations that often diminish the effect of state industrial support. Bureaucratic inefficiencies and possible corruption, which are landmark problems with state industrial support, may not apply to FDI run by private enterprises. Foreign direct investment is considered to be a positive stimulus for any economy, including that of developing countries, and is believed to be a major engine for the rapid economic growth in China since the 1980s.[527]

Will FDI be a viable answer for economic development and, therefore, replace the need for state industrial support altogether? The following considerations suggest that it is not necessarily the case. The vast majority of FDI has been available only to developed countries[528] and a handful of developing countries[529] and not to the majority of developing countries in any significant amount to facilitate economic development.[530] As suggested by many, developing countries may make efforts to create favorable conditions to attract more FDI (e.g., better infrastructure and more transparent regulatory system). However, it is not likely to be feasible for many of these developing countries to create such conditions that can compete and match up with those of developed countries or a handful

---

[527] See Kevin H. Zhang, "How Does FDI Affect Economic Growth in China?" (2001) 9(3) *Economics of Transition* 679–693.

[528] In 2003, developed countries received FDI amounting to 366.6 billion USD out of the total FDI of 559.6 USD billion worldwide. UNCTAD, *World Investment Report 2004*, Annex Table B.1, FDI Inflows, by Region and Economy, 1992–2003, p. 367.

[529] In 2003, more than 50 percent of all FDI made in developing countries were directed to China (53.5 billion USD), Hong Kong (13.6 billion USD), Brazil (10.1 billion USD), and Mexico (10.8 billion USD). *Id.* Note that some of the countries widely considered to be developed countries, such as South Korea and Singapore, are classified as developing countries in these statistics, and therefore, considerable amounts of FDI that these countries received have been also included in total amount of FDI made in developing countries.

[530] For instance, the amount of FDI that all African countries received in 2003 was 15.0 billion USD in total, consisting of only 2.7 percent of FDI inflows worldwide. More than 50 percent of the FDI in Africa was concentrated in only five African countries: Morocco, Sudan, Angola, Equatorial Guinea, and Nigeria. *Id.*

of developing countries with significant market potential. So, FDI is not an option for most developing countries, whose economic endowments do not allow them to provide attractive incentives for investment.[531]

Second, FDI, unlike state industrial promotion polices, does not necessarily serve the long-term economic interests of the host developing countries: FDI does not necessarily draw "patient capital" that can wait for long-term economic potential to materialize.[532] The stability and consistency of FDI inflows are also questionable. Although FDI is considered more of a long-term investment than short-term financial investments, such as stock purchases, divestments are nonetheless always possible. Major divestments may leave the economy of the host developing country that depends on foreign investment with considerable difficulties and may also disrupt their development plans. In addition to divestment, foreign investors can also easily take the money out of the developing country by borrowing from the local banks, using their fixed assets (e.g., factories, machinery) as collateral, and changing the money into foreign exchange in an open capital market. A recent study has revealed that FDI is also affected by the economic cycle of the investor's home countries, which brings elements of instability and increases the vulnerability of the developing countries depending on FDI for economic development.[533]

---

[531] Unlike developed countries or a handful of developing countries, the majority of developing countries do not have the social and physical infrastructure to attract foreign investment, such as efficient communication and transportation systems, ample supply of utilities (e.g., electricity and water), sufficient markets, financial systems, an educated workforce, a reliable legal system, security, and a stable political environment.

[532] FDI may set a target time frame for the investment return (i.e., may prefer short-term returns) that may not be consistent with the host country's long-term development interests. Multinational companies may not necessarily contribute FDI in a way to maximize the economic potential of the host country but to serve the best interest of their worldwide operation.

[533] Eduardo Levy-Yeyati, Ugo Panizza, and Ernesto Stein, "The Cyclical Nature of North-South FDI Flows," paper presented at the Joint Conference of the Inter-America Development Band and World Bank, *The FDI Race, Who Gets the Prize? Is It Worth the Effort?* (October 2002).

In addition, political considerations, as well as economic rationale, can affect FDI. FDI may be less susceptible to domestic political considerations in the sense that it is less affected by domestic constituencies of the host country. Yet other political elements may affect FDI. For instance, an emergence of hostile public sentiment in the host country against foreign investment may raise concern for the foreign investors and affect their investment decisions although this sort of problem would not necessarily affect domestic investors. Foreign investors may also be affected by changes in foreign policies of their own government in making investment decisions. Even if foreign investors try to maintain political neutrality in making investment decisions, a serious dispute between the host country and the investor's, such as ones that may lead to an economic embargo, may disrupt investment and make partial or total divestment inevitable. This susceptibility to political elements diminishes the reliability of FDI as an engine for development.

In assessing the role of FDI on development, the terms of regional investment treaties that govern foreign investment today also raise concern. As discussed earlier, there is not yet a multilateral legal framework for investment, and more than 1,000 BITs around the world provide bilateral legal disciplines for investment relations.[534] Although specific terms of a BIT are to be negotiated between the participating nations, a typical BIT tends to prohibit a wider range of government measures on foreign investment than the TRIMs Agreement does.[535] Developed countries should not use BITs as a device to unduly restrain the ability of developing countries to adopt investment measures for the purpose of development. The objective of BITs should be limited to protecting foreign investment by prohibiting arbitrary discrimination against foreign investment, and accommodations should be made for measures to facilitate development. The terms of BITs should allow some flexibility for

---

[534] *Supra* note 422.
[535] Chapter 5.2 *supra*.

developing countries to adopt necessary investment measures to facilitate development.

6.2.2 Regional Free Trade and Development

From the development perspective, the promotion of free trade through FTAs is in conflict with trade protection for infant industry promotion. Trade measures, regardless of their purpose, will inevitably cause some welfare loss. The implementation of FTAs, however, will prevent this welfare loss because it eliminates trade barriers that cause such loss. Around 130 FTAs are known to exist, the four largest free trade areas (the EU, the NAFTA, the MERSOSUR, and the AFTA) accounted for 64.5 percent of world exports and 69.5 percent of world imports in 2002.[536] More FTAs are being negotiated between developing and developed countries,[537] and regional trade liberalization by these FTAs is considered to promote development.[538] Can regional trade liberalization facilitate economic development by preventing trade protection vis-à-vis the other participating countries, the protection that may be needed for infant industry promotion?

According to the classical trade theories, the elimination of trade barriers would allow specialization in the production of products in which a country has a relative advantage, and this specialization would eventually improve economic efficiency.[539] This rationale presents the case of promoting free trade for economic development. Nonetheless, a conclusion has already been drawn from the historical study that *this specialization alone* did not bring about economic development, and virtually all developed countries today had applied industrial promotion policies to establish some manufacturing basis with the extensive use of subsidies

---

[536] Matsushita, *supra* note 513.

[537] For instance, Chile-Korea FTA and Mexico-Japan FTA have been recently agreed.

[538] Matsushita, *supra* note 513.

[539] *Supra* note 81.

and trade protections.[540] A recent study has also concluded that developing economies tend to diversify, rather than concentrate, production patterns in a large cross section, and this suggests that the driving force of economic development cannot be the forces of comparative advantage.[541]

Free trade between developing and developed countries may actually hamper the facilitation of manufacturing industries in developing countries since the elimination of trade barriers by the terms of the applicable FTA will remove the ability of developing countries to offer trade protection for their infant industries. Then, are there any circumstances where free trade can actually facilitate development? An optimal combination of FDI and free trade might create such a circumstance. Free trade might promote development where there is a substantial and constant inflow of FDI. Again, if FDI can replace the role of the state in mobilizing resources to facilitate development by supplying these needed resources, trade barriers that cause welfare loss to the economy might not be necessary. In this scenario, FDI and free trade can promote economic development in conjunction with each other, provided that FDI seeks to materialize the long-term economic potential of the host country.[542] However, we have already seen that FDI is not available to the majority of developing countries in any significant amount and that the inflow of FDI may not be consistent because of the various political and economic factors.[543]

Problems are compounded as a new breed of FTAs, promoted by certain developed countries such as the United States, does not only seek to eliminate tariff barriers but also attempts to instill certain regulatory elements in developing countries. These elements include enforcement of

---

[540] See the relevant discussions in Chapter 3.1 *supra*.

[541] Jean Imbs and Romain Wacziarg, "Stages of Diversification" (March 2003) 93(1) *American Economic Review* 63–86. The conclusion of this study is also supported by the fact that the number of export products tends to increase, rather than decrease, in the process of economic development. Klinger, Bailey, and Lederman, "Discovery and Development: An Empirical Exploration of 'New' Products," World Bank, August 2004.

[542] *Supra* note 532.

[543] Refer to the relevant discussion in Chapter 6.2 *supra*.

IPRs, requirement of environment and labor standards, and authorization of uninhibited capital transfers.[544] This new type of FTAs will have more ramifications on the development of developing countries than the traditional FTAs focused primarily on the elimination of tariff barriers because these additional requirements in the new FTAs may affect wider aspects of the economic and regulatory systems of the developing country under which development policies are adopted and implemented. For instance, the preceding chapter has examined how the imposition of IPR regimes may affect the economic development of developing countries.[545]

These new requirements go beyond the facilitation of international trade just as the introduction of TRIPS Agreement did. Developed countries that promote these additional requirements may have their own economic and political agendas and interests to include them in trade disciplines. Nonetheless, it creates certain risks for the trading system. The danger of imposing a set of values and regulatory frameworks not essential to the facilitation of international trade has already been discussed in the context of the TRIPS Agreement.[546] The same concerns and conclusions can also be applied here: those new requirements in FTAs would burden the economy of participating developing countries and would be counter-effective to their development interests.

6.3 Foreign Direct Investment and Free Trade: The Answer for Economic Development?

The preceding discussions allow us to conclude whether FDI and free trade will be a viable answer for economic development and can replace the need for state industrial support and trade measures; free trade alone cannot facilitate economic development as long as FDI does not

---

[544] Alvin Hilaire and Yongzheng Yang, "The United States and the New Regionalism/Bilateralism" (2004) 38 *Journal of World Trade* 609. See *also* Rodrik (2004), *supra* note 189, p. 33.

[545] See Chapter 5.3 *supra*.

[546] *Id.*

replace state industrial support altogether. There is a particular concern when an FTA is used to get around the terms of multilateral trade disciplines, attempting to penetrate the markets of developing countries and to impose various other requirements on developing countries, which these developing countries may not have been ready to agree on during multilateral negotiations. Of course, a developing country is not required to join any FTA, but in reality, the country may not afford to stay outside where strong initiatives for an FTA are made by powerful economies bilaterally or regionally where the developing country has essential economic interests.

An FTA should not be used as a device for developed countries to circumvent the rights of developing countries agreed upon during previous multilateral trade negotiations and protected under the terms of the multilateral trading system. To prevent this circumvention, the current WTO rules must prohibit Members from compromising the rights of developing countries protected under the WTO provisions by regional agreements or any other means. There is a case where a WTO provision stipulates a similar requirement: a provision of the SA prohibits Members from entering into *any* arrangement to allow gray-area measures by which trading countries agree to restrain trade between them to protect the interest of domestic producers of the importing country.[547]

Free trade and FDI can facilitate economic development of developing countries under certain optimized conditions.[548] However, this does not mean that they can always replace state industrial support for every developing country.[549] Developing countries may try to use FDI for the facilitation of their development objectives, but this would not seem feasible for many small developing countries with limited economic incentives and conditions to attract foreign investors. Only a few developing

---

[547] Article 11.1 of the SA provides such a prohibition. See Chapter 4.3 *supra* for a discussion of gray-area measure.

[548] Refer to the relevant discussion in Chapter 6.2 *supra*.

[549] *Id.*

countries with substantial market potential, such as China, and those possessing essential natural resources (e.g., oil), seem to have a real negotiating power vis-à-vis foreign investors. As to free trade, the implementation of FTAs among countries in similar development stages with a complementary industrial make-up may improve economic welfare and efficiency for the participating countries without undermining their development potential.[550]

I do not rule out the possibility of successful economic development based on FDI and free trade, but I see that the economic conditions required for this success do not seem present in most developing countries; that is, FDI is simply not available for most developing countries in any significant amount to facilitate development, and there is no indication that it would be available in the foreseeable future.[551] The success of development based on free trade will depend on the development status of a particular developing country vis-à-vis the other countries participating in the FTA as well as the specific terms of the FTA. An FTA may work to promote the existing export industries in the participating developing country by reducing tariff barriers in their export markets. In addition, the implementation of FDI and FTAs may not necessarily preclude an implementation of infant industry promotion policies, and some industrial support may still be possible, subject to the specific terms of the applicable agreements. At any rate, it is important that a developing country should not be deprived of the ability to adopt effective development policies with the emergence of regionalism in trade and investment.

---

[550] Friedrich List, who advocated infant industry promotion, believed that free trade is beneficial among countries at similar levels of industrial development. List, *supra* note 198. Many FTAs, such as MERCOSUR and AFTA, include countries in similar economic status.

[551] Some argue that regulatory reforms to create favorable investment conditions in developing countries would help in attracting FDI, but it is doubtful that this reform effort alone would be sufficient to bring in investment in amounts anywhere close to what is needed for development unless the developing country can provide significant market potential, essential economic resources, or any other significant economic incentives.

Caution must be taken against the recent proliferation of FTAs around the world. I have already discussed the potential adverse effect on development for developing countries that join FTAs, particularly those with developed countries as members. In addition, it should be reiterated that the trade of non-participating developing countries can be adversely affected by the proliferation of FTAs because FTAs offer trade preference to their member countries, which may not be available to non-member countries. Although all non-member countries may be equally subject to the same disadvantage vis-à-vis the member countries,[552] the adverse trade effect can be harsher to non-member developing countries whose export industries may not be strong enough to compete with those of the member countries that benefit from the FTAs or those of non-member developed countries.

Therefore, the proliferation of FTAs is likely to create a more difficult trade environment for developing countries: they will be under pressure to join FTAs not to be left out of these preferential trade clubs, or they would have to suffer more harshly from the disadvantage of not belonging. However, joining an FTA may subject the developing country to terms that are adverse to their development interests. This can present a double dilemma for developing countries. The late Professor Robert Hudec, an eminent trade scholar, was critical of trade preference regimes, perceiving the vulnerability of developing countries facing them, and believed that an MFN-based regime is the only genuine protection available to developing countries as "a legal substitute for economic power on behalf of smaller countries."[553]

In recent years, developing countries have been facing an ever-increasing number of RTAs. How can the dilemma be resolved? One possibility is a gradual elimination of trade barriers within regional trade areas at more or less the same rate and on the same timetable as the lowering of barriers towards non-members. Renato Ruggiero, former

---

[552] The MFN treatment under GATT Article I is still applied in trade relations with countries outside the FTA.

[553] Hudec, *Developing Countries in the GATT Legal System, supra* note 90, pp. 216–217.

general-director of the WTO, observed this possibility in certain regional trade areas such as APEC and MERCOSUR.[554] Yet others may not necessarily follow this approach.[555] Nonetheless, in this scenario, the danger of creating trade blocs and the threat to the trade of the non-member developing countries would be minimized.

Another possibility has been suggested by a Yale economist, T. N. Srinivasan, who stated in the 1999 WTO high-level symposium on trade and development that a "sunset clause" should be introduced to the issue of regional agreements whereby preferences available to the members of the regional agreement would be extended to all WTO members in five years.[556] The members of the existing FTAs may not be willing to make their exclusive trade preferences available to all Members of the WTO. Nonetheless, the proposed sunset clause is consistent with the development interests of developing countries because it would allow the non-member developing countries to receive the trade preferences provided under an FTA whose terms may not be consistent with their development interests, without having to join it.

[554] WTO News Release (April 26, 1996).
[555] Id.
[556] WTO, *Report on the WTO High-Level Symposium on Trade and Development* (1999), *supra* note 38.

SEVEN

Conclusion: Putting Back the Ladder

I wrote this book on the premise that the economic development of developing countries should be considered a priority for moral, economic, human rights, and security reasons and that the international trading system should provide an adequate regulatory framework that allows developing countries to adopt effective development policies. These policies include a state promotion of infant industries through export facilitations and trade protections. A careful examination of the WTO provisions leads to the conclusion that the current WTO disciplines are not sufficient to facilitate development, and some of these provisions in fact prohibit developing countries from adopting effective development policies.[557] With this conclusion, I have explored the ways in which we may better promote economic development, while preserving the current basis of multilateral trade disciplines.

We can provide a more development-friendly regulatory environment for trade by carefully calibrating preferential treatment to developing countries without altering the current regulatory framework for open trade in a fundamental way. To facilitate development, I have introduced the concept of the "sliding scale" in the DFT and DFS that would allow differentiated treatment to developing countries according to their

---

[557] *Supra* note 18.

respective development stages gauged by income levels. I also suggest the exemption of imports from developing countries from AD measures. The current AD disciplines are dubious and ambiguous in nature and have become a major impediment to trade of both developed and developing countries. As more developing countries have begun to apply AD measures, the trade-restrictive effect of AD measures will continue to increase for years to come. I have also proposed modifications of the rules on safeguards, the TRIMs Agreement, the TRIPS Agreement, the GATS, as well as the rules on agricultural and textile trades, all to provide better assistance with economic development.

My proposals suggest that differentiated preferences should be granted to developing countries in accordance with their development stages and that more discretion should be allowed to developing countries in adopting and implementing development policies by providing "policy space" for them.[558] Much of the current special and differential (S&D) treatments for developing countries have expired after a stipulated time period. This type of temporary S&D treatment does not serve the development interests of developing countries adequately: the need for S&D treatment to facilitate development may not expire after the end of these time periods but may continue to exist until the country has attained a desired level of economic development. This suggests that preferential treatment should not be removed after a certain passage of time and should continue to be applied to an individual developing country until it attains a developed economic status. A passage of time should not be a cut off standard for the preference; development should be. The proposed preferences in the DFT and DFS are gradually reduced as its economy develops even before a developing country achieves the developed status.

I note that the concept of a "level playing field" has been emphasized as essential to achieve "fair" trade. Many seem to believe that fair trade means applying the same set of rules to every nation with respect to trade.

---

[558] Bernard Hoekman, "Operationalizing the Concept of Policy Space in the WTO: Beyond Special and Differential Treatment," World Bank, 2004.

Would my suggestion for the differentiated regulatory treatments then create an "unfair" playing field? What makes things truly "fair" is not necessarily applying exactly same rules and conditions to everyone. We can see this by making a simple analogy. Many nations, including the vast majority of developed countries today, apply differential income tax rates according to individual income levels. This differential tax treatment is not necessarily "unfair" because the preferential treatment for the poor and disadvantaged is recognized as a reasonable accommodation rather than unjustifiable discrimination. The same rationale can be applied in trade relations, and the preferential treatment for developing countries in consideration of their development needs is justified just as the aforementioned differential treatment to domestic constituencies.

I do not assume that a more development-friendly international trading system would be sufficient to achieve successful economic development, nor do I expect that the change in the trading system would automatically bring about an immediate economic improvement for the majority of developing countries. Nonetheless, to facilitate development in many developing countries with only limited domestic markets and insufficient resources, the role of international trade remains essentially important because it can augment the limited economic endowments of many developing countries. Many of today's developed countries, notably the East Asian countries, have achieved economic development through successful exports. Export facilitation is crucially important in promoting economic development, particularly for developing countries with small domestic markets. The regulatory framework for international trade should support and not inhibit exports from developing countries.

Economists disagree among themselves about the effectiveness of state-led development policies such as infant industry promotion.[559] The

---

[559] Many economists tend to discredit the effectiveness of infant industry promotion. A commentator has stated, in the context of S&D treatment, that "it is little more than a variant on the seductive, but much discredited, argument in favour of protecting infant industries, which continues to appeal to politicians and humanitarians, despite

classical economic models originated by Adam Smith and developed by his successors tend to discount the role of the state in facilitating development through policy interventions. The classical theory emphasizes economic inefficiencies caused by state interventions. However, a group of other economists, including Friedrich List and many others, have advocated state industrial promotion. History has shown that virtually all of today's developed countries have adopted state industrial promotion policies and achieved economic development. More and more economists today seem to accept that state interventions are necessary to initiate structural changes in an economy to bring poor countries out of poverty.[560] The GATT also allows, albeit under limiting conditions, Members to adopt infant industry promotion policies. Despite the controversies about the effectiveness of state-led industry promotion, it is only fair that developing countries should be allowed to decide for themselves the best development policy, just as today's developed countries were during their own development.

The current WTO system has expanded on GATT provisions in many areas of trade, resulting in elaborate agreements. What I would like to see is a similar expansion on the GATT's development-facilitation provisions of Article XXVIII and Part IV so that the principles and objectives embodied in these GATT provisions can be turned into specifically enforceable provisions. Some WTO provisions, such as subsidy rules, inhibit development efforts. To promote economic development, developing countries

its failure both in practice and in gaining theoretical support. The benefits of an open economy, and the cost of a closed economy, are now among the most widely shared canons of economic orthodoxy." Michael Hart and Bill Dymond (2003), *supra* note 157, p. 395. This statement represents the prevalent belief that infant industry promotion is not compatible with an open economy that pursues outward-looking development based on the facilitation of trade. Nonetheless, we have seen from historical cases that today's developed countries in fact adopted infant industry promotion policies including tariff protections and subsidies while actively pursuing exports. *Supra* note 21. Other economists believe that state interventions are necessary to initiate changes needed for economic development. *Supra* note 180.

[560] *Supra* note 180.

should be able to adopt effective development policies, including trade measures. Significant gaps that exist between this objective of facilitating development and the actual provisions should be bridged with necessary modifications. In doing so, I do not suggest that we should replace the current multilateral trading system pursuing open trade with any other. What I propose is a set of provisions in the current regulatory framework that allows (as an exception rather than a principle) developing countries to adopt development policies, including industrial subsidization and trade protections, in conjunction with organized development plans.

It will take more than a development-friendly trading system to lift poor nations above the poverty lines. A good education system, consistent and coherent economic policies, access to capital, an efficient, reliable, and non-corrupt government, social peace, political stability, entrepreneurship, and sound work ethics are examples of many essential ingredients for successful development.[561] Not all of these conditions can be readily made available but are rather developed over time to varying degrees in the relevant political, historical, and cultural contexts of individual developing countries. Noting this complexity, the International Bank for Reconstruction and Development (World Bank) conceded in its 1993 report that it did not fully discover "why governments of these [the East Asian] economies have been more willing and better able than others to experiment and adopt; answers go beyond economics to include the study of institutions and the related fields of politics, history, and culture." (Explanation added.) Therefore, a comprehensive approach to development, which is beyond the scope of this book,[562] should necessarily

---

[561] The representative of the United Kingdom noted in the 1999 WTO high-level symposium on trade and development the need for integration of trade policies into a wider set of development policies. WTO, *Report of the WTO High-Level Symposium on Trade and Development* (1999), *supra* note 38.

[562] The scope of this book is to identify the problems with the current regulatory system for international trade (the "roadblocks") and suggest alternative regulatory treatment to better facilitate trade.

include not only the assessment and determination of specific economic policies to adopt but also the examination of political, institutional, historical, and cultural elements relevant to development that tend to create the essential conditions as previously described.

Some have suggested that no change in the external regulatory environment would be likely to have any significant effect on development without internal reforms and improvements of the conditions in the individual developing countries that have hampered development. Although this has certain truth, it is nevertheless not an excuse to avoid the necessary reform of the international regulatory system. I stress that when the government and people of a developing country are ready for undertaking development; that is, when they have achieved all or many of necessary conditions, a development-friendly international trading system should be in place to assist with their development, rather than inhibiting it by imposing obligations that are not consistent with their development interests. The current WTO provisions, stipulating rigid tariff bindings and restraining trade-related subsidies, have substantially reduced the ability of developing countries to adopt effective trade-related development policies.[563]

Free trade areas and foreign direct investment have been rapidly increasing in the recent decades. While FDI and free trade can contribute to economic development under certain conditions, we have seen that they cannot completely replace the need for state industrial promotion. FDI has been available only to a handful of developing countries in any significant amount, and an FTA may actually inhibit, rather than promote, the facilitation of industries in developing countries, particularly where the FTA seeks to instill a set of "new values and regulatory systems" in participating developing countries that may not be consistent with their development interests. The danger of undermining the rights of developing countries protected under the current WTO disciplines by regionalism should also be remembered.

---

[563] *Supra* note 18.

In line with this concern, caution has to be taken against the introduction of "new agenda," such as the environment, labor standards, and competition law (i.e., "the Singapore issues")[564] into trade disciplines. The effectiveness of enforcement in trade disciplines has led to the introduction of an elaborate IPR regime in the WTO. This precedent has led some developed countries to consider yet another set of new values and systems to be placed in WTO disciplines. Although the enforcement mechanism of the WTO may certainly be helpful in bringing these new interests to be enforced as it was for IPR issues, it must also be remembered that the primary objective of the international trading system is to facilitate trade, not to serve as a vehicle to advance values and systems that the majority of Members do not consider to be essentially relevant to international trade.[565]

While the relevance of these new issues to the facilitation of trade may need to be studied further, their premature introduction into the multilateral trade disciplines would only cause divisions and disagreements among Members and would also distract them from focusing on issues that are truly essential for the facilitation of trade. It would eventually diminish the effectiveness of the international trading system. In addition, even if Members reached a consensus about bringing these new issues into trade disciplines, a balance between promoting such agenda and preserving the ability of developing countries to adopt development policies should carefully be sought. This balance is not found in the result

---

[564] These new issues were raised in the first WTO Ministerial Conference held in Singapore, 1996. WTO, Singapore Ministerial Declaration, Doc. WT/MIN(96)/DEC (Dec. 18, 1996).

[565] *Supra* note 455. A recent study cautioned that an agreement on competition in WTO disciplines "will create compliance costs for developing countries while not addressing the anti-competitive behavior of firms located in foreign jurisdictions." It also made a case that traditional liberalization commitments using existing WTO forums will be the most effective, and perhaps feasible, means of lowering prices and increasing access to an expanded variety of goods and services. Bernard Hoekman and Petros C. Mavroidis, "Economic Development, Competition Policy and the World Trade Organization" (2003) 37 *Journal of World Trade* 1–27.

of past negotiations with respect to some major trade issues, such as the treatment of trade-related government subsidies.

The WTO should seek to balance the interests of developing countries and those of developed countries. There is widespread skepticism that the issues promoted by developed countries, such as IPRs and services, have resulted in regulatory requirements in trade disciplines; investment and competition policy resulted in the creation of working groups within the WTO and the environment issues resulted in the creation of the Committee on Trade and Environment (CTE).[566] Yet developing country concerns such as technology transfer, financial mechanisms, capacity-building, debt relief, and supply-side constraints, only began to be discussed in the recent Doha Round.[567] Although the lack of participation in relevant negotiations by developing countries may have contributed to their own marginalization in the process,[568] it is also true that adequate attention has not been given to the concerns of developing countries.[569] It has been observed that WTO rules have not been interpreted with development objectives and concerns in mind[570] and that the participation of developing countries in the WTO has been made difficult, although it may have not been deliberate.[571] Efforts must be made to integrate developing countries in the organization better and to reflect their concerns in the interpretation and application of WTO disciplines.[572]

---

[566] Per India, WTO, *Report of the WTO High-Level Symposium on Trade and Development* (1999), *supra* note 38.

[567] *Id.*

[568] *Per Srinivasan, id.*

[569] Some of these issues are now being discussed in WTO working groups under the DDA. *Supra* note 165.

[570] For more discussion of this issue, see Asif H. Qureshi, "Interpreting World Trade Organization Agreements for the Development Objective" (2003) 37 *Journal of World Trade* 847–882.

[571] *Supra* note 171.

[572] To assist developing countries, the WTO provides technical support for Members under the guidelines of the CTD: the WTO offers regular training sessions and holds seminars and workshops in various countries, and it initiated WTO Reference Centre Programme in 1997 with the objective of creating a network of computerized

A separate agreement on trade and development should be considered, which would encompass the existing preferential provisions for developing countries, and elaborate on GATT Article XVIII and Part IV, as well as the proposals to facilitate development made in this book, including the DFT and DFS. The results of negotiations in the WTO working groups on trade and development can also be incorporated into this agreement, provisionally titled the "Agreement on Development Facilitation (ADF)."[573] As discussed in Chapter 2, a separate agreement would provide a cohesive, permanent regulatory structure to facilitate development in WTO disciplines, while elevating regulatory attention to development issues. This structure of preferential treatment to developing countries would not necessarily be an unjustifiable dual standard or a harmful fragmentation of the system, but rather a reasonable and rational accommodation of their need for economic development.

A note should be made with regard to LDCs whose economic circumstances are the direst among developing countries. The role of international trade in facilitating economic development would be all the more important to these LDCs, and special regard should be made to their treatment in the international trading system. Preferential treatment to LDCs offered by some developed countries should be implemented on the WTO level and be offered by all developed country Members, as well as developing country Members that can afford to provide such treatment to LDCs. Consideration should also be given to the criticism that the effect of this type of preferential treatment on the trade of LDCs would be rather insignificant: the key to facilitating exports of LDCs is not so

---

information centers in least-developed and developing countries. This effort must be maintained, and additional institutional support should be provided to developing countries to build their negotiation capacities and to increase their participation in WTO processes. The current WTO budget of 1.36 million Swiss francs for technical cooperation and of 4.29 million Swiss francs for training seems inadequately low to meet the ever-increasing need of developing countries with their participation in the WTO.

[573] Refer to the relevant discussion in Chapter 2.3.2 *supra*.

much in increasing market access for LDCs, but in diversifying their export products.[574] Restrictive rules of origin are known to have created difficulties for LDCs in efforts to diversify their exports and, therefore, need to be addressed.

Developed countries should realize that their long-term security and prosperity are, in large part, linked to the successful economic development of developing countries. As noted at the beginning of this book, poverty tends to breed the resentment and violence that undermine the security interests of developed countries. One may have a different view of the importance of economic prosperity in securing peace, but few would disagree that a world consisting of economically stable nations and peoples with their basic economic needs met will be more likely to succeed in preserving peace than one filled with hunger and economic struggles. In addition, the successful economic development of developing countries will provide today's developed countries with new, rich markets tomorrow, as this has been the result of economic development of East Asian countries in the past few decades. Herein lies the wisdom and the need to support the economic development of developing countries by "putting back the ladder" through necessary reforms of the international trading system.

[574] *Supra* note 147.

Epilogue

By the time I was finishing this book, the *Journal of World Trade*, a premier journal in the field of international trade law and policy with which I have the privilege of association, decided to run a special issue on trade and development. Wishing for the success of the special issue, I shared my small thoughts on an interesting aspect of development with my colleagues, which I would also like to share with my readers of this book.

Many consider development primarily in terms of economic improvement. The approach is not incorrect, but there are other, perhaps more important, human sides to development. Development brings more than an increase in the income figure; it brings the people a sense of confidence, pride, joy, and responsibility. If readers would bear with me for a few more pages, I would like to talk about these "other sides" by telling you the tales of my birth country, Korea, and of my own family, who lived through the ages of the Korean development.

When the late President Park Jung Hee started development initiatives in 1962, South Korea was not only among the poorest nations in the world by any economic standard, but also torn up from inside. The physical and psychological horrors of the Korean War were still vivid in the memories of Korean people. The remnants of brutal foreign rule, which enslaved millions of Koreans, were still lingering in the minds of many Koreans. The military coup of Park had just shattered the dream of democracy.

Poverty that seemed never to end dried up all hope from people. All of this caused widespread defeatism and despair. Tomorrow did not mean much in Korea just as in so many developing countries today.

And it started. Through the success of a series of development initiatives, Korea started to achieve the "economic miracle" that brought it from the economic bottom of the world to OECD status in the 1990s. Its modern industries and trade literally made a quantum leap from virtual non-existence to the top ten of the world within one generation. According to a recent media report, Samsung, a Korean electronics company, has recorded higher profits than those of the ten largest Japanese electronics companies combined. I remember that this company used to sell the cheapest stuff in Wal-Mart stores not long ago. I could not believe this news, and in some sense, it does not still feel like truth. Some economists say that there is no economic miracle, but to those who breathed this change, it surely felt like one.

Successful economic development put more cash in the pockets of Koreans, but it also brought the even more important gifts of confidence, pride, joy, and self-respect. These gifts did not only stem from increased wealth but from a sense of achievement; through the 1960s and 1970s, many Koreans escaped from the hopeless defeatism and despair that haunted them for ages. They found hope in their lives. They finally found the meaning of tomorrow, understanding that they can achieve success despite what seemed to be insurmountable barriers. Immense joy and a sense of liberation and achievement were felt upon escaping from generations of hopeless poverty and becoming citizens of the developed world.

My own family changed from one that could barely afford one pack of rice per month in the 1960s to a family that sent all three children, including me, to North America and Europe for college and postgraduate school, all within a single generation. My family did not win a lottery. They benefited from enormously successful development just like so many other families in Korea at that time. Many people (including the World Bank, it seems) say that South Korea was special and so was my family (which obviously benefited from my mother, who had a better sense of the economy than anyone else in the family). But those who have read this small book know that I have strong reservations about this and believe that there is hope for every developing country.

I do not intend to discuss my own thoughts about the mechanisms and policies of development again in this epilogue, but I hope that my small suggestions are understood and discussed, and I would like to see others making many more suggestions in coming years that could actually help developing countries. I once asked my mother whether she had any regrets for all those years of hard work. She said that she really did not have one, in that she started from nothing, worked hard, and was able to provide far more for families than she could possibly imagine when she started her family. She was proud, grateful, and happy. That is what successful development can do for a human being. I only hope to see many more Koreas and would like to see more families like mine around the developing world finally find hope in their lives and live with joy and a great sense of achievement as so many Koreans have felt.

Bibliography

Athukorala, Prema-Chandra, "Agricultural Trade Reforms in the Doha Round: A Developing Country Perspective" (2004) 38 *Journal of World Trade* 877–897.

Bardhan, Pranab, "Economics of Development and the Development of Economics" (1993) 7(2) *Journal of Economic Perspectives* 129–142.

Bartels, Lorand, "The WTO Enabling Clause and Positive Conditionality in the European Community's GSP Program" (2003) 6 *Journal of International Economic Law* 507–532.

Bovard, James, *The Myth of Fair Trade*, Cato Institute, Policy Analysis No. 264 (Nov. 1. 1991).

Bovard, James, *The Fair Trade Fraud* (St. Martin's Press, 1991).

Brenton, Paul, "Integrating the Least Developed Countries into the World Trading System: The Current Impact of European Union Preferences Under 'Everything But Arms'" (2003) 37 *Journal of World Trade* 623–646.

Brohman, John, "Postwar Development in the Asian NICs: Does the Neoliberal Model Fit Reality?" (1996) 72(2) *Economic Geography* 107–130.

Brons, Martijn R. E., Henri L. F. DeGroot, Peter Nijkamp, "Growth Effects of Governmental Policies: A Comparative Analysis in a Multi-Country Context" (2000) 31(4) *Growth & Change* 547–572.

Bruton, H., "Import Substitution," *in* H. B. Chenery and T. N. Srinivasan (eds.), *Handbook of Development Economics*, Vol. 2 (North-Holland, Amsterdam, 1989), pp. 1601–1644.

Bruton, H. "A Reconsideration of Import Substitution" (1998) 12 *Journal of Economic Perspective* 903–936.

Chang, Ha-Joon, *Kicking Away the Ladder: Development Strategy in Historical Perspective* (Anthem Press, London, 2002).

Chang, Ha-Joon, and Duncan Green, *The Northern WTO Agenda on Investment: Do As We Say, Not As We Did* (South Centre/CAFOD, June 2003).

Chaudhauri, Sumanta, Aaditya Mattoo, and Richard Self, "Moving People to Deliver Services: How Can the WTO Help?" (2004) 38 *Journal of World Trade* 363–393.

Cho, Sungjoon, "A Bridge Too Far: The Fall of the Fifth WTO Ministerial Conference in Cancun and the Future of Trade Constitution" (2004) 7 *Journal of International Economic Law* 219–244.

Conkin, P., *Prophets of Prosperity: America's First Political Economists* (Indiana University Press, Bloomington, 1980).

Cottier, Thomas and Marion Panizzon, "Legal Perspectives on Traditional Knowledge: The Case for Intellectual Property Protection" (2004) 7 *Journal of International Economic Law* 371–399.

Crozier, Andrew J., *The Causes of the Second World War* (Blackwell Publishers, Oxford, 1997).

Dolzer, Rudolf and Margrete Stevens, Bilateral Investment Treaties (Martinus Nijhoff Publishers, New York, 1995).

Dorfman, J., and R. Tugwell, *Early American Policy – Six Columbia Contributors* (Columbia University Press, New York, 1960), pp. 31–32.

Eglin, Richard, "Trade and Investment in the WTO," paper presented at the seminar, *The Way Forward to Successful Doha Development Agenda Negotiations*, United Nations University, Tokyo, Japan (May 24–25, 2004).

Findlay, R., "Growth and Development in Trade Models," *in* R. W. Jones and P. B. Kenen (eds.), *Handbook of International Economics*, Vol. 1 (North-Holland, New York, 1984), pp. 185–236.

Finger, J. Michael, and A. Alan Winters, "Reciprocity in the WTO" *in* Bernard Hoekman, Aaditya Mattoo, and Philip English (eds.), *Development, Trade, and the WTO: A Handbook* (World Bank, Washington D.C., 2002), pp. 50–60.

Finger, J. Michael, "The WTO's Special Burden on Less Developed Countries" (2000) 19(3) *Cato Journal* 435.

Francois, Joseph F., Bradley McDonald, and Hakan Norstrom, *Assessing the Uruguay Round* (WTO, Geneva, 1995).

Gathii, James Thuo, "Rights, Patents, Markets, and the Global AIDS Pandemic" (2002) 14 *Florida Journal of International Law* 261–352.

Gathii, James Thuo, "Construing Intellectual Property Rights and Competition Policy Consistently with Facilitating Access to Affordable AIDS Drugs to Low-end Consumers" (2001) 53 *Florida Law Review* 727–788.

GATT, *The Result of the Uruguay Round of Multilateral Trade Negotiations* (GATT, Geneva, 1994).

GATT, Decision of November 28, 1979, on Differential and More Favourable Treatment, Reciprocity and Fuller Participation on Developing Countries, GATT B.I.S.D. (26th Supp.), p. 203 (1980).

Handerson, W, *Friedrich List – Economist and Visionary, 1789–1846* (Frank Cass, London, 1983).

Hart, Michael, and Bill Dymond, "Special and Differential Treatment and the Doha 'Development' Round" (2003) 37 *Journal of World Trade* 395–415.

Heiskanen, Veijo, "The Regulatory Philosophy of International Trade Law" (2004) 38 *Journal of World Trade* 1–36.

Helleiner, G. K. (ed.), *Trade Policy, Industrialization, and Development* (Oxford University Press, Oxford, 1992).

Heston, Alan, Robert Summers, and Bettina Aten, Penn World Table Version 6.1, Center for International Comparisons at the University of Pennsylvania (CICUP) (October 2002).

Hilaire, Alvin, and Yongzheng Yang, "The United States and the New Regionalism/Bilateralism" (2004) 38 *Journal of World Trade* 603–625.

Hoekman, Bernard, and Petros C. Mavroidis, "Economic Development, Competition Policy and the World Trade Organization" (2003) 37 *Journal of World Trade* 1–27.

Hoekman, Bernard, "Strengthening the Global Trade Architecture for Development" (2002) 1 *World Trade Review* 23–46.

Hoekman, Bernard, "Operationalizing the Concept of Policy Space in the WTO: Beyond Special and Differential Treatment," World Bank, 2004.

Hudec, Robert E., *Developing Countries in the GATT Legal System*, Thames Essays (Trade Policy Research Centre, London, 1987).

Imbs, Jean, and Romain Wacziarg, "Stages of Diversification" (March 2003) 93 (1) *American Economic Review* 63–86.

Inama, Stefano, "Market Access for LDCs: Issues to Be Addressed" (2002) 36 *Journal of World Trade* 85–116.

International Trade Centre UNCTAD/WTO and Commonwealth Secretariat, *Business Guide to the Uruguay Round* (ITC/CS, Geneva, 1995), p. 181.

Jackson, John H., *The World Trading System* (2nd ed., MIT Press, Cambridge, Mass. 1997), pp. 31–78, 247–277.

Kerr, William A., and Laura J. Loppacher, "Anti-Dumping in the Doha Negotiation: Fairy Tales at the World Trade Organization" (2004) 38 *Journal of World Trade* 211–244.

Khan, Hider A., *Global Markets and Financial Crises in Asia* (Palgrave Macmillan, New York, 2004).

Kim, Kwang-suk, and Joon-kyung Park, *Sources of Economic Growth in Korea: 1963–1981* (Korea Development Institute, Seoul, 1985).

Klinger, Bailey, and Daniel Lederman, "Discovery and Development: An Empirical Exploration of 'New' Products," World Bank, August 2004.

Krueger, Anne O. "Alternative Strategies and Employment in LDCs" (1978) 68(2) *American Economic Review* 270–274.

Krueger, Anne O., and Baran Tuncer, "An Empirical Test of the Infant Industry Argument" (1982) 72(5) *American Economic Review* 1142–1152.

Krueger, Anne O., "Trade Policies in Developing Countries," *in* R. W. Jones and P. B. Kenen (eds.), *Handbook of International Economics*, Vol. 1 (North-Holland, New York, 1984), pp. 519–569.

Krueger, Anne O., "The Developing Countries and the Next Round of Multilateral Trade Negotiations" (1999) 22(9) *The World Economy* 909–932.

Lankes, Hans Peter, "Market Access for Developing Countries" (2002) 39(3) *Finance and Development* 8–12.

Lee, Y. S., "Foreign Direct Investment and Regional Trade Liberliazation: A Viable Answer for Economic Development?," (2004) 39 *Journal of World Trade* 707–717.

Lee, Y. S., *Safeguard Measures in World Trade: The Legal Analysis* (1st ed. Kluwer Law International, The Hague, 2003; 2nd ed., 2005).

Lee, Y. S., "Facilitating Development in the World Trading System – A Proposal for Development Facilitation Tariff and Development Facilitating Subsidy" (2004) 38 *Journal of World Trade* 935–954.

Lee, Y. S., "Emergency Safeguard Measures under Article X in GATS – Applicability of the Concepts in the WTO Agreement on Safeguards" (1999) 33(4) *Journal of World Trade* 47–59.

Leontief, Wassily W., *The Structure of American Economy, 1919–1929: An Empirical Application of Equilibrium Analysis* (Harvard University Press, Cambridge, Mass., 1941).

Levy-Yeyati, Eduardo, Ugo Panizza, and Ernesto Stein, "The Cyclical Nature of North-South FDI Flows," paper presented at the Joint Conference of the Inter-America Development Band and World Bank, *The FDI Race, Who Gets the Prize? Is It Worth the Effort?* (Oct. 2002).

Lindsey, Brink, and Dan Ikenson, "Reforming the Antidumping Agreement: A Road Map for WTO Negotiations," Cato Institute Trade Policy Analysis No. 21 (December 11, 2002).

Lindsey, Brink, and Daniel J. Ikenson, "Coming Home to Roost: Proliferating Antidumping Laws and the Growing Threat to U.S. Exports," Cato Institute Trade Policy Analysis No. 14 (July 30, 2001), pp. 1–2.

Lindsey, Brink, "The U.S. Antidumping Law: Rhetoric versus Reality," Cato Institute Trade Policy Analysis No. 7 (August 16, 1999).

List, Friedrich, *The National System of Political Economy* (1841).

Little, I. et al., *Industries and Trade in Some Developing Countries* (Oxford University Press, London, 1970).

Mah, Jai S., "Injury and Causation in the Agreement on Safeguards" (2001) 4 *Journal of World Intellectual Property* 380–382.

Mason, Edward S., "The Role of Government in Economic Development" (1960) 50(2) *American Economic Review* 636–641.

Mastel, Greg, "The U.S. Steel Industry and Antidumping Law" (1999) 42(3) *Challenge* 84–94.

Matsushita, Mitsuo, "Legal Aspects of Free Trade Agreements in the Context of Article XXIV of the GATT 1994", paper presented at the seminar, *The Way Forward to Successful Doha Development Agenda Negotiation*, United Nations University, Tokyo, Japan (May 24–25, 2004).

Michalopoulos, Constantine, "WTO Accession" *in* Bernard Hoekman, Aaditya Mattoo, and Philip English (eds.), *Development, Trade, and the WTO: A Handbook* (World Bank, Washington D.C., 2002), p. 69.

Ministry of Foreign Affairs and Trade of the Republic of Korea, *The Import and Export Status per Major Regional Categories* (2004), available online at <www.mofat.go.Kr>.

Ndhlovu, Ashella Tshedza, *Mobilization of Capital Funds by Urban Local Authorities: Zimbabwe* (South African Development Community [SADC] Information Centre on Local Governance, 2001).

Odell, John S., "The Seattle Impasse and Its Implications for the World Trade Organization," *in* Daniel L. M. Kennedy and James D. Southwick (eds.), *The Political Economy of International Trade Law: Essays in Honor of Robert E. Hudec* (Cambridge University Press, Cambridge, 2002).

Ohlin, Bertil, *Interregional and International Trade* (1933).

Pangestu, Mari, "Industrial Policy and Developing Countries," *in* Bernard Hoekman, Aaditya Mattoo, and Philip English (eds.), *Development, Trade, and the WTO: A Handbook* (World Bank, Washington D.C., 2002), pp. 149–159.

Petherbridge, Lee, "Intelligent TRIPS Implementation: A Strategy for Countries on the Cusp of Development" (2001) 22, *University of Pennsylvania Journal of International Economic Law* 1029–1066.

Petrone, A. F. (ed.), *Causes and Alleviation of Poverty* (Nova Science Publishers, Inc., 2002).

Poot, Jacques, "A Synthesis of Empirical Research of the Impact on Long-Run Growth" (2000) 31 (4) *Growth & Change* 516–546.

Porter, Michael, *Can Japan Compete?* (Macmillan, Basingstoke, U.K., 2000).

Posner, Richard, *The Robinson-Patman Act: Federal Regulation of Price Differences* (American Enterprise Institute, Washington, D.C., 1976).

Qureshi, Asif H., "Interpreting World Trade Organization Agreements for the Development Objective" (2003) 37 *Journal of World Trade* 847–882.

Reinert, E., "Diminishing Returns and Economic Sustainability: The Dilemma of Resource-based Economies under a Free Trade Regime," *in* H. Stein et al. (eds.), *International Trade Regulation, National Development Strategies and the Environment – Towards Sustainable Development?* (Centre for Development and the Environment, University of Oslo, 1996), p. 5.

Ricardo, David, *Principles of Political Economy and Taxation* (1817).

Rodrik, Dani, "King Kong Meets Godzilla: The World Bank and the East Asian Miracle," CEPR Discussion Paper No. 944 (Centre for Economic Policy Research, London, 1994), available online at <http://www.cepr.org/pubs/dps/DP944.asp>.

Rodrik, Dani, *The Global Governance of Trade as If Development Really Mattered* (UNDP, New York, 2001).

Rodrik, Dani, *Industrial Policy for the Twenty-First Century* (prepared for UNIDO, September 2004), available at <http://ksghome.harvard.edu/~drodrik/UNIDOSep.pdf>.

Ross, Thomas W., "Winners and Losers under the Robinson-Patman Act" (1984) 27 *Journal of Law and Economics* 243.

Salvatore, Dominick, *International Economics* (8th ed., John Wiley and Sons, New Jersey, 2003), pp. 233–320.

Sen, Amartya, "Culture and Development," World Bank Paper (Dec. 13, 2000).

Shoenbaum, Thomas J., "The WTO and Developing Countries," paper prepared for the University of Tokyo International Law Study Group (Sep. 24, 2004).

Singer, Peter, "Famine, Affluence, and Morality" (1972) 1 *Philosophy & Public Affairs* 229–243.

Smith, Adam, *An Inquiry into the Nature and Causes of the Wealth of Nations* (1776).

Srinivasan, T. N., "Trade, Development, and Growth," *Princeton Essays in International Economics No. 225* (December 2001).

Stewart, Terence P. (ed.), *The GATT Uruguay Round: A Negotiating History (1986–1992)* (Kluwer Law and Taxation, The Hague, 1993), pp. 1728–1729.

Subramanian, Arvind, "Proprietary Protection of Genetic Resources and Traditional Knowledge" *in* Bernard Hoekman, Aaditya Mattoo, and Philip English (eds.), *Development, Trade, and the WTO: A Handbook* (World Bank, Washington D.C., 2002), pp. 382–389.

Sun, Haochen, "Reshaping the TRIPs Agreement Concerning Public Health: Two Critical Issues" (2003) 37 *Journal of World Trade* 163–197

Suranovic, Steven M., "A Positive Analysis of Fairness with Applications to International Trade" (2000) 23(3) *World Economy* 283–307.

United Nations Commission on Trade and Development, *World Investment Report 2004.*

United States Citizenship and Immigration Services, *Estimates of Unauthorized Immigrant Population Residing in the United States: 1990 to 2000* (January 2003).

United States Trade Representative, *1994 Annual Report,* p. 29.

Viner, Jacob, *Dumping: A Problem in International Trade* (Kelly, New York, 1966), p. 120.

Weiler, Joseph (ed.), *The EU, the WTO and the NAFTA: Towards a Common Law of International Trade* (Oxford University Press, Oxford, 2000).

Westphal, Larry E., "Industrial Policy in an Export Propelled Economy: Lessons from South Korea's Experience" (in Symposia: The State and Economic Development) (1990) 4(3) *Journal of Economic Perspectives* 41–59.

World Bank, *World Bank Development Report 1997.*

World Bank, *The East Asian Miracle* (Oxford University Press, New York, 1993).

World Bank, *The East Asian Miracle: Economic Growth and Public Policy* (Oxford University Press, New York, 1992).

World Bank Statistics: Korea, Rep. at a Glance (Sep. 16, 2004); World Development Indicator Database (September 2004); World Development Indicators (2001).

World Trade Organization Annual Reports: 2003, p. 24; 2004, pp. 43, 45–46.

World Trade Organization, International Trade Statistics 2003, 2004.

World Trade Organization, *The Results of the Uruguay Round of Multilateral Trade Negotiations: The Legal Texts* (Cambridge University Press, reprint 2003).

World Trade Organization, *Report on the WTO High-Level Symposium on Trade and Development* (1999).

World Trade Organization, WTO, *Implementation of Special and Differential Treatment Provisions in WTO Agreements and Decisions – Note by Secretariat*, WTO doc. WT/COMTD/W/77 (October 25, 2000).

World Trade Organization Ministerial Declarations, WTO docs WT/MIN(96)/ DEC (December 18, 1996); WT/MIN(01)/DEC/1 (November 20, 2001); WT/ MIN(01)/DEC/2 (November 20, 2001).

World Trade Organization Panel Case Reports, *Korea – Definitive Safeguard Measure on the Imports of Certain Dairy Products* (*Korea – Dairy Products*), Report of the Panel, WTO doc. WT/DS98/R (June 21, 1999), Report of the Appellate Body, WTO doc. WT/DS98/AB/R (December 14, 1999); *Argentina – Safeguard Measure on the Imports of Footwear* (*Argentina – Footwear*), Report of the Panel, WTO doc. WT/DS121/R (June 25, 1999), Report of the Appellate Body, WTO doc. WT/DS121/AB/R (December 14, 1999); *United States – Definitive Safeguard Measures on Imports of Wheat Gluten From the European Communities* (*United States – Wheat Gluten*), Report of the Panel, WTO doc. WT/DS166/R (July 31, 2000), Report of the Appellate Body, WTO doc. WT/DS166/AB/R (December 22, 2000); *United States – Safeguard Measures on Imports of Fresh, Chilled or Frozen Lamb Meat from New Zealand and Australia* (*United States – Lamb Meat*), Report of the Panel, WTO docs WT/DS177/R, WT/DS178/R (December 21, 2000), Report of the Appellate Body, WTO docs WT/DS177/AB/R, WT/DS178/AB/R (May 1, 2001); *United States – Definitive Safeguard Measures on Imports of Steel Wire Rod and Circular Welded Carbon Quality Line Pipe* (*United States – Line Pipe*), Report of the Panel, WTO doc. WT/DS202/R (October 29, 2001), Report of the Appellate Body, WTO doc. WT/202/AB/R (February 15, 2002); *United States – Definitive Safeguard Measures on Imports of Certain Steel Products* (*United States – Steel Products*), Report of the Panel, WTO docs. WT/DS248-DS259/R (July 11, 2003), Report of the Appellate Body, WTO docs. WT/DS248-DS259/AB/R (November 10, 2003).

Zhang, Kevin H., "How Does FDI Affect Economic Growth in China?" (2001) 9(3) *Economics of Transition* 679–693.

Zhang, Ruosi, "Food Security: Food Trade Regime and Food Aid Regime" (2004) 7 *Journal of International Economic Law* 565–584.

Index

AD. *See* Anti-dumping (AD)
ADF. *See* Agreement on Development Facilitation (ADF)
Administered protection
  examples, 82
  government allowance, 82
  WTO, 82–87
Administered protection measures, 87
ADP Agreement. *See* Anti-dumping Practices Agreement (ADP Agreement)
Afghanistan
  and terrorist, 2
Africa Growth and Opportunity Act, 38
African countries. *See also* specific countries
  FDI, 146
Aggregate Measurement of Support (AMS), 112
Agreement on Agriculture
  AMS, 112
  imbalance and inadequacy, 111
  preservation, 114
  special safeguard measures, 111
  Uruguay Round, 109

Agreement on Development Facilitation (ADF), 47, 48, 164
Agreement on Safeguards (SA), 67, 86, 98, 103, 129, 138, 152
  agricultural problems, 113
  Article 2, 96
  Article 2.2, 91
  Article 4.2, 112
  Article 9, 99
  Article 9.1, 40
  Article 9.2, 40, 99
  balance of concessions, 101
  domestic agricultural producers, 112
  gray-area measure, 152
  import quotas, 91
  measures, 90
  minimum quota level, 96–98
  negotiators, 100
  S&D treatment, 86
Agreement on Subsidy and Countervailing Measures (SCM), 42, 62, 74, 75, 77, 111
  Article 6, 75
  developing countries, 79
  export subsidies prohibition, 42
  LDC status, 77

Agreement on Textile and Clothing
(ATC)
imbalance and inadequacy, 111
safeguards, 111
Uruguay Round, 110
Agricultural imports
market access, 111
Agricultural market
liberalization, 113
Agricultural production
tariff, 112
reduction, 112
Agricultural products, 107
integration, 110
restricting imports, 108
tariffs, 109
Agricultural subsidies equality,
113
Agricultural trade
barriers, 111
Agriculture
and textile, 107–114
Al-Qaeda
and terrorist, 2
American System, 55
AMS. *See* Aggregate Measurement of
Support (AMS)
Angola
FDI, 146
Annex on Movement of Natural Persons
Supplying Services, 135
Anti-competitive behavior, 94, 126
Anti-dumping (AD), 87–96
actions, 23, 88
abuse, 93
exports, 89
disciplines, 94
dumping margins, 87
measures, 16, 82
abuse reduction, 93
complete removal, 95
international trading system, 94
level playing field, 94

problem for developing countries, 94
statistics, 88
yearly application, 93
practices
authorizing, 126
safeguards, 82–106
trade policy, 94
Anti-dumping Practices Agreement
(ADP Agreement), 87
Article 2.1, 88
Article 2.2, 88
Appellate Body
safeguard disciplines, 104
unforeseen developments, 105
Argentina
agricultural exporting countries, 108
Asia. *See also* specific countries
export success, 58
ATC. *See* Agreement on Textile and
Clothing (ATC)
Australia
agricultural exporting countries,
108
Uruguay Round, 110

Balance of concessions
safeguards, 101
Balance-of-payment (BOP), 19
GATT, 27, 30
measures, 119
understanding provisions, 30
Belgium
infant industry promotion, 57
Bergsten, Fred C., 139
Bilateral investment treaties (BITs), 116,
144
existence, 116
foreign investment, 117
government measures, 148
Bolivia
agricultural exporting countries,
108
BOP. *See* Balance-of-payment (BOP)

Brazil
    agricultural exporting countries, 108
    FDI, 146
    import-substitution policies, 7
Bretton Woods Conference, 14
Britain
    developed countries, 60
    infant industry protection, 57
    wool and cotton industries, 109
British System, 55

Cairns group
    agricultural exporting countries, 108
Canada
    AD measures, 88
    agricultural exporting countries, 108
    Uruguay Round, 110
Center for International Comparisons at
    the University of Pennsylvania
    (CICUP), 7
Chang, H-J, 57
Chile
    agricultural exporting countries, 108
    export markets, 131
China
    FDI, 146
    market potential, 153
    socialist market economy, 92
    WTO, 17
CICUP. See Center for International
    Comparisons at the University of
    Pennsylvania (CICUP)
Classical economics market theory, 52
Clay, Henry, 55
Clothing
    ATC
        imbalance and inadequacy, 111
        safeguards, 111
        Uruguay Round, 110
    developing countries, 109
    integrating WTO disciplines, 110
    production, 109
        labor-intensive products, 109

Commercial services
    export, 133
Committee on Balance-of-Payment
    Restrictions, 30
Committee on Safeguards, 67, 97, 102
Committee on Trade and Development
    (CTD), 43, 45, 163
Compensation
    safeguard measures, 102
Contracting parties, 27, 29
Costa Rica
    agricultural exporting countries, 108
Council for Trade and Development and
    Agreement on Development
    Facilitation, 43–48
Countervailing duties (CVD), 76
    actions, 79, 82
        subsidies imposed, 79
    limitations, 87
CTD. See Committee on Trade and
    Development (CTD)

DDA. See Doha Development Agenda
    (DDA)
Decision on Measures in Favour of
    Least-Developed Countries, 73
Democratic institutions
    and economic development, 4
Developed countries, 13
    definition, 3
    manufacturing industries, 60
    subsidies, 76
Developing countries
    binding concessions, 65
    confidence in government, 5–6
    cultural content, 131
    definition, 3
    development policies, 71
    DFT, 68
    difficulties, 77
    domestic industry subsidies, 81
    economic and political factors, 81
    economic development, 11–12

Developing countries (*cont.*)
  effective policy adoption, 49
  GDP, 61
  and government corruption, 5
  import shares, 70
  income per capita, 3
  industrial policies, 60, 79
  infant industry promotion, 66
  open market adaptation, 72
  problems, 111
  S&D treatment, 80
  service industries, 61
  state-led industrial policy, 58
  textiles and clothing, 109
Developing economies
  diversification, 58
Development, 6–9
  changes associated with, 9
  definition, 3
  economics, 56
  effect of culture, 3
  strategy of East Asia, 9
  trade-related policies, 10
  working proposal for, 12
Development-Facilitation Subsidy (DFS)
  administration, 80
  application, 98
  application schedule, 80
  developed countries, 79
  foreign investment, 122
  procedural safeguards, 80
  proposed preferences, 157
  scheme
    agricultural product promotion, 113
  sliding scale, 156
Development-Facilitation Tariff (DFT), 66
  abuse prevention, 66
  administrations and implementations,
    67
  application, 79, 98
  application waiting period, 66
  developing countries, 68
  impact on international trade, 70

infant industry promotion, 66
  proposed preferences, 157
  rates, 69
  scheme, 143
  sliding scale, 156
Development-friendly international
    environment, 2
Development-friendly international
    trading system, 5, 158, 161
Development policies
  implementation, 157
DFS. *See* Development-Facilitation
    Subsidy (DFS)
DFT. *See* Development-Facilitation Tariff
    (DFT)
Differential tax treatment, 158
Dispute Settlement Body
  WTO, 75
Dispute Settlement Understanding
    (DSU), 103
Divestment, 147
Doha Development Agenda (DDA), 45
  issues addressed, 45
Doha Ministerial Declaration, 131, 139
Doha Round, 15, 111, 122, 163
  agenda, 93
Domestic employment, 137
Domestic industry
  material injury, 78
  safeguards, 91
    measure protection, 83
Domestic products, 75
Domestic unemployment
  opposition, 136
DSU. *See* Dispute Settlement
    Understanding (DSU)
Dumping, 90. *See also* specific types
  causing import injury, 91
  concept, 92

East Asian countries, 7–9, 158. *See also*
    specific countries
  developing countries, 100

development, 60
  successful, 9
economics, 160
  development, 165
  export industries, 98
  infant industry promotion, 60
  success, 5, 6–9
  government role, 9
  industry subsidies, 75
  infant industry protection, 57
  outward-oriented policies, 59
EBA. *See* Everything But Arms (EBA)
Economic development
  definition, 3
  and democratic institutions, 4
  of developing countries, 10–12
  facilitation, 5
  factors affecting, 4
  government role, 9
  regional trade liberalization, 149
  successful factors, 3
Economies of poor countries. *See also*
    specific countries
  characteristics, 51
Emergency safeguard measures, 137
Emergency safeguard mechanisms, 138
Enabling Clause, 36, 37
  effective sanctions, 38
Equatorial Guinea
  FDI, 146
European Communities
  AD measures, 88
Everything But Arms (EBA), 38
  evaluation, 38
Export-driven development, 8–9
Export facilitation, 158
Export-oriented, 7
  development policies, 8
Export price
  determining, 92
Export products
  development perspective, 110
  economic development, 150

Export services, 134
Export subsidies
  prohibition, 41
External regulatory environment, 161

Fair trade, 157
  concept, 83
  disciplines, 36
  domestic producers, 84
  trade relations, 85
Foreign direct investment (FDI), 57, 119,
    144
  availability, 153
  China, 146
  definition, 144
  and development, 145–149
  employment opportunities, 145
  Equatorial Guinea, 146
  free trade, 151–155, 161
  FTA, 145–151
  Hong Kong, 146
  long-term economic interests, 147
  Mexico, 146
  Morocco, 146
  Nigeria, 146
  private enterprises, 146
  regional investment treaties, 148
  regional trade liberalization, 43, 141–155
  reliability, 148
  Singapore, 146
  South Korea, 146
  state industrial support, 146
  Sudan, 146
  target time frame, 147
Foreign investment
  attraction, 147
  economic development, 114
  national treatment standard, 121
  regulation, 121
Foreign investment measures
  history, 115
  investment measures, 115
Foreign investor protection, 123

Foreign labor
    opposition, 136
Foreign products
    illegal smuggling, 138
Foreign workers
    domestic labor markets, 136
    entry provisions, 138
France
    agriculture subsidy, 110
    industry subsidies, 75
    infant industry promotion, 57
Freer trade. *See* Free trade
Free trade, 23
    disciplines, 36
    manufacturing industries, 150
    promotion, 149
Free trade agreements (FTA), 43
    definition, 142
    economic burden, 151
    export industries, 153
    multilateral negotiations, 142
    new values and systems, 161
    problems, 150
    proliferation, 154
    regional trade liberalization, 149
    trade barriers, 144
    trade liberalization, 143
    trade relation risks, 151
    WTO Members, 155

GATS. *See* General Agreement on Trade in
        Services (GATS)
GDP. *See* Gross domestic product (GDP)
General Agreement on Tariffs and Trade
        (GATT), 15
    Article I
        MFN treatment, 154
    Article II, 63
        binding import concessions, 70
        import concessions, 71
        Schedule of Concessions, 63
    Article III, 21, 116
    Article VI, 24
        dumping threat, 95

Article XI, 116
Article XIX, 103
    safeguard measure, 105
    safeguard measure application, 96,
        103
    safeguards, 19
    unforeseen development, 103
    WTO, 96
Article XVIII, 26, 42, 119, 144, 164
    BOP, 27, 30
    DFT, 67
    import restrictions, 30, 31
    infant industry promotion, 42, 67
    infant industry promotion policy, 27
    multilateral control, 67
    preferential treatment, 28
    Schedule of Concessions, 29, 67
    tariff reduction, 29
    tariff structure, 31
    WTO, 65
Article XX, 129
    IPR protection, 129
Article XXIV, 21, 141
Article XXVIII
    BOP measures, 27
Article XXXVI, 32–36, 85
    economic diversification structure, 33
    Enabling Clause, 47
    export earnings, 32
    WTO membership, 71
Article XXXVII, 32–36
    Enabling Clause, 47
    import barriers, 33
Article XXXVIII, 32–36
    aiding developing country Members,
        34
    collaboration with other
        organizations, 35
    Enabling Clause, 47
    WTO involvement, 34
conduct of international trade, 19
disciplines, 25
    agriculture, 108
dispute settlement mechanism, 124

LDC, 32
multilateral trade negotiations, 15, 64
notes and supplementary provisions, 28
Protocol of Provisional Application, 17
rules, 139
rules and regulations, 16
state-led industry promotion, 159
tariff and non-tariff barriers, 15
tariff reductions, 15
General Agreement on Tariffs and Trade Decision, 36
General Agreement on Trade in Services (GATS), 22, 132–140
AD measure, 94
anti-dumping measures, 139
article X, 137
economic development, 133
foreign labor supply exemption, 136
liberalization, 133, 137
multilateral control, 135
supply modes, 132
Generalized System of Preferences (GSP), 36
scheme, 37
WTO, 21
Germany, 2
industry subsidies, 74
infant industry promotion, 57, 60
labor shortage, 134
Globalization, 23
Global multilateral trading system, 141
GNI. *See* Gross National Income (GNI)
Government Assistance to Economic Development, 26
Government corruption
and developing countries, 5
Government subsidies, 74
Gray-area measures, 100, 102
Great Britain
trade protection, 54
Gross domestic product (GDP), 7
developing countries, 61

Gross National Income (GNI), 65, 68
per capita, 6
South Korea, 68
World Bank, 68
GSP. *See* Generalized System of Preferences (GSP)
Guatemala
agricultural exporting countries, 108

Ha-Joon Chang, 10
Hamilton, Alexander, 55, 56
Hecksher-Ohlin model, 23
Hong Kong
economic success, 5, 6–9
export success, 58
FDI, 146
GDP increase, 7
Hostile public sentiment, 148
Hudec, Robert, 71, 154

IMF. *See* International Monetary Fund (IMF)
Import(s)
tolerance and trade accommodation, 86
Import concessions, 72
balance of concessions, 70
Import restraint legislation, 33
Import-substitution policies, 7, 58, 59
Import-substitution subsidies, 75
Income per capita, 4
India
AD measures, 89
import-substitution policies, 7
import substitution policy, 59
MAI-type investment agreement, 122
traditional knowledge registration, 131
Uruguay Round, 64
Indonesia
agricultural exporting countries, 108
Industrialized countries, 4
Industrial policies, 6, 49
definition of, 49
implementation of, 54
promotion of, 49–62, 66

Industrial Policy for the Twenty-First Century, 12
Industrial promotion
  definition, 49
  developing countries, 60
  TRIMS, 117
Infant industries
  developing countries, 66
  DFT, 66, 67
  government support, 76
  opponents, 57
  policies
    GATT/WTO disciplines, 62
  promotions, 27, 56, 61, 143, 153
    debate, 59–62
    effectiveness, 158
    manufactured products, 60
    objections, 144
    policies, 54, 143
    service industries, 61
  protection, 57
  trade protection, 150
Input-output analysis, 56
Intellectual property rights (IPR), 163
  enforcement, 124
  foreign investment, 125
  historical study, 125
  international trading, 124
  protection, 128, 132
    cultural content, 131
    GATT, 129
    pharmaceutical products, 130
    public health promotion, 130
  regime, 127, 162
    imposition, 127
  trade-related aspects, 123–132
  trade sanctions, 129
International environment
  development-friendly, 2
International investment
  bilateral government, 116
  liberalization, 116
International Monetary Fund (IMF), 52

International regulatory environment, 12
International trade, 6–9, 126, 165
  and development, 6–9
  DFT impact, 70
  facilitation, 151
  government intervention, 22, 23
  importance of, 4
  and investment
    regionalism, 141–145
  IPR, 124
  legal framework for, 4, 42
  objective, 162
  purpose, 9
  role, 164
  rules, 125
International Trade Centre, 44
International trading system
  AD measures, 94
International treaty norms, 124
Internet
  international industries, 131
Investment agreement
  importance, 122
Investment measures, 115
Investment relations
  bilateral legal framework, 148
  multilateral legal framework, 148
Invisible hand, 57
  infant industry promotion, 50–59
IPR. *See* Intellectual property rights (IPR)
Israel, 2

Japan
  export success, 58
  gray-area measures, 84
  industry subsidies, 75
  infant industry promotion, 57, 60
Jefferson, Thomas, 55

Kicking Away the Ladder, 10
Korea, 8, 166
  economic growth indicators, 8
  economic miracle, 167

and Germany labor shortage,
    134
growth, 8
value of imports, 11
Korean War, 166

Labor intensive products, 107
Labor services
    export of, 135
Least developed country (LDC)
    exclusion policies, 47
    export limits, 39
    food security, 113
    members subsidy rules, 77
    merchandise export shares,
        99
    multilateral trading system, 44
    preferential treatment, 73
    safeguard application, 99
    S&D treatment, 39, 77
    Subcommittee, 44
    subsidies, 99
    UN, 26
    WTO membership, 73
Level playing field, 85, 157
Liberal trade, 22. *See* Free trade
Limited modifications, 143
Lincoln, Abraham, 55
List, Friedrich, 27, 56, 153, 159

Magariños, Carlos, 72
MAI. *See* Multilateral Agreement on
    Investment (MAI)
Malaysia
    agricultural exporting countries,
        108
Manufacturing process
    separation, 51
Market
    government intervention, 50
Market economy
    efficiency, 53
Marrakesh Agreement, 14–16, 18

Marrakesh Agreement Establishing the
    World Trade Organization, 17, 25
Marxism, 52
Mass production techniques, 51
Material injury, 75
    domestic industry, 78
MDG. *See* Millennium Development
    Goals (MDG)
Mercado Comun der Sur, 155
Merchandise trade volume, 15
Mexico
    FDI, 146
MFA. *See* Multifiber Arrangement (MFA)
MFN. *See* Most favored nation (MFN)
    treatment
Middle East
    potential exports, 134
Millennium Development Goals (MDG),
    2
Ministerial Declaration, 130
Monopsony
    definition, 50
Morocco
    FDI, 146
Most favored nation (MFN) treatment, 19,
    22, 133
    application, 100
    based regime, 154
    imports, 20
    principle, 20
    DFT, 67
    exception, 21
    tariff rate, 37
Movement of Natural Persons Supplying
    Services, 135
Multifiber Arrangement (MFA), 109
Multilateral Agreement on Investment
    (MAI), 116, 123
    investment agreement type, 122
Multilateral Agreements on Trade in
    Goods, 48
Multilateral system
    wine and spirits, 131

Multilateral trade disciplines, 152
  expansion, 136
Multilateral trade negotiations
  tariff bindings, 65

Nakagawa, Junji
National industry policies
  trade measures and subsidies, 50
National treatment, 21
NAZI party, 2
Neoclassical economic stance, 52
  definition, 52
Neoliberal economics, 52
Netherlands
  industry subsidies, 75
  infant industry promotion, 57
Newly industrializing countries (NIC), 6,
  7–9
  developing industries, 78
  development strategies, 7
  economic development factors, 8
  exports, 83
  fair-trade argument, 83
  industry subsidies, 75
  unfair trade practices, 84
New Zealand
  agricultural exporting countries, 108
  Uruguay Round, 110
NIC. See Newly industrializing countries
  (NIC)
Nigeria
  FDI, 146
Nontraditional production activities, 57
Normal price, 94
  market economy, 93
Normal value
  determination, 92

OECD. See Organization of Economic
  Cooperation and Development
  (OECD)
Official development assistance (ODA), 11
Open trade, 22. See also Free trade

Orderly market arrangements (OMA), 84,
  100
Organization of Economic Cooperation
  and Development (OECD), 123
Outward-development scheme
  infant industry promotion, 61
Outward development strategy, 7
Outward-oriented development policy, 58

Palestine
  and terrorist, 2
Paraguay
  agricultural exporting countries, 108
Patient capital, 147
Persistent dumping, 89
Persistent poverty, 1
  perspective, 2
Philippines
  agricultural exporting countries, 108
Policy space, 157
Poverty, 1–6
  causes, 3
  definition, 1
  1999 estimates, 6
  governmental action, 3
  lines, 1
  population statistics, 1
  solution, 2
  undermine security, 165
  World Bank definition, 1
PPP. See Purchasing Power Parity (PPP)
Predatory dumping, 90
  safeguard measures, 95
Preferential treatment, 40
  least developed countries (LDC), 38
Price discrimination, 90
Private sectors
  government, 54
  infant establishment and promotion, 74
  nontraditional production activities, 51
Producers' fixed cost, 89
Productive sector
  industrial policy, 50

Profit-maximizing mechanism, 51
Protectionists, 94
Protocol of Provisional Application, 17
Public goods
    provisions, 50
Purchasing Power Parity (PPP), 1

Raymond, Daniel, 56
Reasonable profit, 93
Reclaiming development, 49–81
Regional economic development, 143
Regional free trade
    development, 149–151
Regional Trade Agreement (RTA),
    141
    elimination, 154
Regional trade liberalization
    economic development, 149
    FTA, 149
Relative advantage, 22
Ricardo, David, 22, 51
Rodrik, Dany, 4, 6, 12, 53
RTA. *See* Regional Trade Agreement
    (RTA)
Ruggiero, Renato, 21, 24, 47, 154
Russia
    WTO, 17

SA. *See* Agreement on Safeguards (SA)
Safeguard(s), 82–106
    domestic industry, 91
Safeguard disputes
Safeguard measures
    alternative treatment, 101
    application, 112
    developed countries, 101
        exports, 102
    differentiated treatment, 101
    existence, 97
    hampering exports, 98
    infant industries, 106
Safeguard rule
    imports, 99

Safeguards Agreement, 129. *See also*
    Agreement on Safeguards (SA)
Safety net, 97
Samsung, 167
Schedule of Commitments
    Article II, 133
Schedule of Concessions, 20, 31, 67
    agricultural products, 109
SCM. *See* Agreement on Subsidy and
    Countervailing Measures (SCM)
S&D. *See* Special and different (S&D)
    treatment
Seattle and Cancun Ministerial
    Conference, 18
Seattle Ministerial Conference (1999), 127
Second World War, 2
Sensitive products, 37
    trade barrier removal, 39
Service sector
    diverse, 132
Service trade facilitation, 136
Shoenbaum, Thomas J., 3
Singapore
    economic success, 5, 6–9
    export success, 58
    FDI, 146
    GDP increase, 7
    issues, 162
Sliding scale
    DFT and DFS, 156
Smith, Adam, 51, 53, 54, 55, 57, 61, 159
South Africa
    AD measures, 89
    agricultural exporting countries, 108
South African Development Community
    (SADC), 54
South Korea, 11, 167
    agriculture subsidy, 110
    economic development factors, 8
    economic status, 68
    economic success, 5, 6–9
    exportable natural resources, 135
    export-driven development, 7

South Korea (*cont.*)
  export success, 58
  FDI, 146
  GDP increase, 7
  GNI, 68
  GNP, 7
  manufacturing sectors, 51
  tariff protection, 7
  United Nations Conference on Trade
      and Development, 68
  Uruguay Round, 110
Special and different (S&D) treatment,
      39–43
  and developed countries, 41
  developing countries, 80
  LDC, 39
  temporary subsidy rules, 48
  transition period, 40
Special safeguard (SSG). *See also*
      Agreement on Safeguards (SA)
  agricultural problems, 113
  domestic agricultural producers,
      112
Sporadic dumping, 89
Srinivasan, T.N., 127, 155
SSG. *See* Special safeguard (SSG)
State industrial promotion, 120
  economic viability, 52
  TRIMS criticism, 118
State industrial support and trade
      measures, 143
State-led development policies, 158
State subsidization, 13
Subramanian, Arvind, 131
Subsidies, 74–81
  calculations, 80
  developed countries, 76
  role of, 77
Subsidy and Countervailing Measures. *See*
      Agreement on Subsidy and
      Countervailing Measures (SCM)
Sudan
  FDI, 146

Sunset clause, 155
Sweden
  industry subsidies, 75
  infant industry promotion, 57
Systematic import restrictions, 110

Taiwan
  economic success, 5, 6–9
  GDP increase, 7
  tariff protection, 7
Tariffs
  bindings, 20, 62–74
      multilateral trade negotiations, 65
  escalation, 35
  peaks, 35
  protection, 7, 9, 55
      developing countries, 65
      infant industry promotion, 69
  quotas, 91
  rates, 15
      bound, 62
      industrial countries, 64
      United States, 55
  reduction
      binding concessions, 64
      trade expansion, 64
  structure
      subsidies, 114
      trade restrictive effects, 71
Terrorism
  causes, 2
Textile, 107–114
  and clothing integration
      developing countries, 109
      WTO disciplines, 110
  and clothing production, 109
      labor intensive products, 109
  definition, 107
Thailand
  agricultural exporting countries, 108
The Charter for the International Trade
      Organization, 15
Threshold import concessions, 72

Trade
  development-friendly regulatory
    environment, 156
Trade and Development, 32
Trade barriers
  agricultural subsidies, 112
  elimination, 149
Trade concessions, 37
Trade discipline
  poverty and development, 4
Trade disciplines and development,
    107–140
Trade in services, 132–140. *See also* General
    Agreement on Trade in Services
    (GATS)
  economic development, 133
  liberalization, 133, 137
Trade liberalization, 39
Trade measures
  examples, 82
Trade protection, 13, 113
  American system *vs.* British system, 55
  developing countries, 71
  effectiveness, 66
Trade-related aspects of intellectual
    property rights (TRIPS), 42, 43, 45,
    124
  Article 31, 130
  Article IV, 45
  development perspective, 127
  Doha Ministerial Declaration, 129
  effects, 124
  international protection, 132
  LDCs, 129
  public health, 130
  Uruguay Round, 124
Trade-related development policies, 10
Trade-related government subsidies, 24
Trade-related investment measures
    (TRIMs), 43, 114–122, 123, 144, 149
  development policies, 117
  investment related industrial policy,
    120

multilateral control, 120
  special and differential treatment, 128
  trade distortion, 123
Trade rules, 6
Trading system
  development-friendly, 5
Training and Technical Cooperation
    Institute
  WTO, 44
Transportation and communication
    development, 145
TRIMs. *See* Trade-related investment
    measures (TRIMs)
TRIPS. *See* Trade-related aspects of
    intellectual property rights
    (TRIPS)
Turkey
  development economics, 56

Umbrella waiver, 73
Unauthorized foreign workers, 138
UNCTAD. *See* United Nations Conference
    on Trade and Development
    (UNCTAD)
Understanding Rules and Procedures
    Governing the Settlement of
    Dispute, 103
Unemployment
  domestic
    opposition, 136
UNIDO. *See* United Nations Industrial
    Development Organisation
    (UNIDO)
United Kingdom
  export subsidies, 74
  trade policies, 160
United Nations (UN)
  LDC, 26
United Nations Conference on Trade and
    Development (UNCTAD), 5, 32,
    44, 119
United Nations Industrial Development
    Organisation (UNIDO), 5

United Nations Millennium Declaration,
        12
United States
    AD practices, 93
    developed countries, 60
    GSP scheme, 37
    high tariff barriers, 55
    illegal residents, 138
    infant industry protection, 57
    railway company subsidies, 74
    safeguard disputes
    SSGs, 112
    tariff rate, 55
    trade protection, 54
    unfair practices, 85
Unskilled labor, 136
    market access, 138
    political feasibility, 137
Uruguay
    agricultural exporting countries, 108
Uruguay Round, 16, 47
    Agreement on Textiles and Clothing,
        110
    agriculture product, 108
    benefits of, 64
    free trade disciplines, 36
    GATS, 133
    India, 64
    LDC
        imports, 99
    multilateral disciplines, 132
    service sector, 133
    special and differential treatment, 39, 41
    tariff escalation, 35
    tariff peaks, 35
    trade and development, 14
    TRIMs, 116

Voluntary export restraints (VERs), 84
Voluntary restraint agreements (VRAs),
        84, 100
Voluntary trade restriction agreements,
        100

Washington Consensus, 52
Wealth of Nations, 51
World Bank, 52
    and GNI, 68
World Trade Organization (WTO), 10, 42.
        See also Agreement on Safeguards
        (SA); General Agreement on
        Tariffs and Trade (GATT)
    accession process, 73
    administered protection, 82–87
    Advisory Center, 44, 46
    agreement, 17, 22, 25, 70
        AD, 87
    beginning, 77
    agricultural targets, 112
    aiding developing country Members, 34
    Appellate Body, 103
    barrier rules, 43
    budget, 46, 164
    developed country Members, 34
    developing countries interest balancing,
        163
    development assisting provisions, 39
    disciplines, 25, 47, 141
        agricultural products, 109
        sufficiency, 156
        textile and clothing integration, 110
    Dispute Settlement Body, 18, 75
    Doha Development Agenda, 163
    enforcement mechanisms, 162
    FTA, 142
    GATT, 17
        provision, 159
    GSP, 21
    high-level symposium, 64
    historical development, 14
    import concession negotiations, 62
    international trade regulatory
        framework, 14–48
    International Trade Statistics, 89
    mandatory implementation
        requirements, 19
    Members, 17, 18

membership, 73
Ministerial Conference, 26
  location and date, 162
  numerical targets, 113
  provisions, 17
    development facilitation, 25–39
    regulation, 82
    single undertaking, 17
    subsidy rules, 159
    tariff bindings, 161
Reference Centre program, 44
requirements, 41
rule effectiveness, 18
rules, 139
  FTA, 152
  infant industry policy, 59
  major principles, 19–25

safeguard measures, 86
subsidy
  provisions, 76
  rules, 24, 78
system or rules, 17
tariff reduction, 113
trade and development, 43, 72, 73
  symposium, 41
trade facilitation, 26
Training and Technical Cooperation
  Institute, 44
working groups, 45
World War II, 2
Worldwide terrorism
  causes, 2
WTO. See World Trade Organization
  (WTO)